Cold War Negritude
Form and Alignment
in French Caribbean Writing

Contemporary French and Francophone Cultures, 93

Contemporary French and Francophone Cultures

Series Editor

CHARLES FORSDICK
University of Liverpool

Editorial Board

TOM CONLEY
Harvard University

JACQUELINE DUTTON
University of Melbourne

LYNN A. HIGGINS
Dartmouth College

MIREILLE ROSELLO
University of Amsterdam

DEREK SCHILLING
Johns Hopkins University

This series aims to provide a forum for new research on modern and contemporary French and francophone cultures and writing. The books published in *Contemporary French and Francophone Cultures* reflect a wide variety of critical practices and theoretical approaches, in harmony with the intellectual, cultural and social developments which have taken place over the past few decades. All manifestations of contemporary French and francophone culture and expression are considered, including literature, cinema, popular culture, theory. The volumes in the series will participate in the wider debate on key aspects of contemporary culture.

Recent titles in the series:

80 Antonia Wimbush, *Autofiction: A Female Francophone Aesthetic of Exile*

81 Jacqueline Couti, *Sex, Sea, and Self: Sexuality and Nationalism in French Caribbean Discourses, 1924–1948*

82 Debra Kelly, *Fishes with Funny French Names: The French Restaurant in London from the Nineteenth to the Twenty-First Century*

83 Nikolaj Lübecker, *Twenty-First-Century Symbolism: Verlaine, Baudelaire, Mallarmé*

84 Ari J. Blatt, *The Topographic Imaginary: Attending to Place in Contemporary French Photography*

85 Martin Munro and Eliana Văgălău, *Jean-Claude Charles: A Reader's Guide*

86 Jiewon Baek, *Fictional Labor: Ethics and Cultural Production in the Digital Economy*

87 Oana Panaïté, *Necrofiction and The Politics of Literary Memory*

88 Sonja Stojanovic, *Mind the Ghost: Thinking Memory and the Untimely through Contemporary Fiction in French*

89 Lucy Swanson, *The Zombie in Contemporary French Caribbean Fiction*

90 Lucille Cairns, *Eating Disorders in Contemporary French Women's Writing*

91 Sophie Fuggle, *France's Memorial Landscape: Views from Camp des Milles*

92 Clíona Hensey, *Reconstructive Memory Work: Trauma, Witnessing and the Imagination in Writing by Female Descendants of Harkis*

CHRISTOPHER T. BONNER

Cold War Negritude

Form and Alignment in French Caribbean Writing

LIVERPOOL UNIVERSITY PRESS

First published 2023 by
Liverpool University Press
4 Cambridge Street
Liverpool
L69 7ZU

This paperback edition published 2025

Copyright © 2025 Christopher T. Bonner

Christopher T. Bonner has asserted the right to be identified as the author of this book in accordance with the Copyright, Designs and Patents Act 1988.

All rights reserved. No part of this book may be reproduced, stored in a retrieval system, or transmitted, in any form or by any means, electronic, mechanical, photocopying, recording, or otherwise, without the prior written permission of the publisher.

British Library Cataloguing-in-Publication data
A British Library CIP record is available

ISBN 978-1-83764-471-1 (hardback)
ISBN 978-1-83624-554-4 (paperback)

Cover image: Wrocław, 1948-08-28. Hala Ludowa. Wiec ludnooeci Ziem Odzyskanych na rzecz pokoju, w którym uczestniczyli delegaci OEwiatowego Kongresu Intelektualistów. Nz. przemawia delegat z Martyniki, pisarz i polityk Aime Cesaire. ka PAP Wroclaw, Aug. 28, 1948. The People's Hall. A rally for peace staged by residents of the Regained Territories that was attended by delegates of the World Congressof Intellectuals for Peace. Pictured: delegate from Martinica writer and politician Aime Cesaire speaking. ka PAP
Courtesy of Alamy

Typeset by Carnegie Book Production, Lancaster

Contents

Acknowledgments   vii

Introduction   1

1. Black Bloc: Reading the First Congress Through a Cold War Lens   25

2. Comrade Depestre: The National Poetry Debate and René Depestre's Cold War Aesthetic Solidarities   59

3. Poetry of the Césaire–Soviet Split: The Melancholy Geopolitical Vision of Aimé Césaire's Cold War Poems   105

4. Engineer of the Haitian Soul: Jacques Stephen Alexis' Experiments in Socialist Realism   145

Epilogue   189

Bibliography   193

Index   207

Acknowledgments

This book has been a long time in the making. I would first like to acknowledge the outstanding educators who have encouraged and guided me. A special thanks is due to Kaiama L. Glover, who first sparked my fascination with French Caribbean literature when I was a student in her Haitian novel course—longer ago than I wish to discuss here—and encouraged me to pursue further study. I have benefitted from her guidance and her scholarship ever since. Nick Nesbitt gave crucial guidance at an early stage in the process, and I am grateful to him both for his insights and for the example of his writing. I cannot adequately express my indebtedness to the late and sorely missed J. Michael Dash, my teacher, advisor, and mentor. I wish badly that Michael could have read this book, as he has shaped it in so many ways that he will never know. He remains a source of inspiration and a gold standard. This book is dedicated to his memory.

I also thank the many exceptional scholars and educators at NYU to whom I owe my formation in literary criticism and theory, especially Emily Apter, Claudie Bernard, Cécile Bishop, the late Anne Deneys-Tunney, Denis Hollier, Sarah Kay, Judith Miller, Eugène Nicole, Lucien Nouis, and Phillip Usher. I also had the privilege to study with and learn from many gifted friends at NYU, including Daniel Benson, Downing Bray, Suzy Cater, Andrew Dubrov, Manoah Finston, Laura Hughes, Youna Kwak, Michelle Lanchart, Kathrina Laporta, Virginie Lauret, Amanda Perry, and Chelsea Steiber.

My colleagues at Texas A&M have shown extraordinary warmth as I became an adopted Texan, and they provided crucial encouragement and insight as I brought this book to completion. My warm thanks in particular to Nathan Bracher, David Brenner, Rob Carley, Jocelyn Frelier, Carmela Garritano, Joe Golsan, Stefanie Harris, Melanie Hawthorne, Christopher Hemmig, James Howell, Jun Lei, and Adam Rosenthal.

Colleagues at UConn such as Anne Berthelot, Roger Celestin, Eleni Coundouriotis, Jacqueline Loss, Florence Marsal, the late Osvaldo Pardo, Arnab Roy, Valerie Saugera, Bhakti Shringarpure, Jennifer Terni, and Sarah Wood made it a (figuratively) warm place to exist in for the time I was there, and I send them my thanks.

Cold War Negritude is much richer for the many conversations I've had with colleagues at conferences and workshops. These include (but are not limited to) Anthony Alessandrini, Jacqueline Couti, Rachel Douglas, Anna Bjork Einarsdottir, Gul Bilge Han, Cae Joseph-Masséna, Peter Kalliney, Valerie Kaussen, Lanie Millar, Martin Munro, Monica Popescu, James Robertson, Jocelyn Sutton Franklin, Chelsea Steiber, Julie-Françoise Tolliver, Jini Kim Watson, and Duncan Yoon. I thank the organizers of the Centenaire Jacques Stephen Alexis for allowing me to participate in such an invigorating celebration of Alexis' memory. I reserve a special thanks for my comrade and friend Marla Zubel, whose company I always find intellectually enlivening. Andrew Sobanet gave crucial support at an early step in the publication process, and he has my gratitude. Lucy Swanson has been a stalwart writing buddy and a nourishing source of insightful, constructive feedback and cute dog photos.

This project has benefitted from generous funding from the Glasscock Center for the Humanities at Texas A&M. My thanks go out to the Glasscock leadership and staff, and to the talented scholars in my Glasscock Fellows cohort for their engaging questions and helpful comments.

I am delighted that this book is being published with Liverpool University Press. Chloe Johnson, in particular, has helped me at every step, and I thank her for her kind professionalism, reliability, and encouragement. The three anonymous readers were extraordinarily generous in their rigorous and constructive feedback, which helped me clarify my own thoughts and improved the final product immensely. I am immensely grateful to Katelyn Knox and Allison Van Deventer for their elegant program. Both are also exceptionally generous correspondents, and helped me at every step on the path to publication, from proposal to final revisions.

I counted many times—all the time—on the support of dear friends throughout this process. I send my love and thanks to Sahar Ghazanfar, Chris Hemmig, Erika Hendrix, Louise Hogan, James Howell, Karin Isaacson, Adithi Kasturirangan, Bridget O'Brien, Brendan O'Kane, Varuni Prabhakar, Delia Raab-Snyder, Abby Rubinstein, Katy Sosnak, Ariel Tinney, and Lina Wells.

I am fortunate to have a family that I both like and love. My father, Tom Bonner, is among the kindest people I have ever met, and has always encouraged my interest in literature. My in-laws, Dee Aldrich and the late Nelson Aldrich, have provided constant support, kindness, good company, and sage advice. My aunt, Ann Bonner, has been a blessing in my life, and I do not know where I would be if she had not constantly nourished me with unconditional love, in an unbroken thread from late-night Talking Heads dance parties at age four to the present day. My uncle Rick, uncle Roger, and aunt Maggie have shown unwavering love and support. My late mother, Beth, would have been tremendously proud to know her son had written a book. I wish that I could tell her about it. My dogs Laika and Autumn have been the most loving companions I could hope for, although they are incorrigibly bad girls. My husband, Tom Martin, has been a source of strength, insight, laughter, and inspiration since I've known him. I am grateful to share my life with him.

Both images included in Chapter 1 of this book are reproduced with the permission of Présence Africaine. My thanks to Mme Chantal Wintrebert of Présence Africaine for helping me secure the rights.

Portions of Chapter 1 were first published in the article "Alioune Diop and the Cultural Politics of Negritude: Reading the First Congress." *Research in African Literatures*, Vol. 50, No. 2 (2019), pp. 1–19.

Portions of Chapter 3 were first published in the article "The 'Ferrements' of Poetry: The Geopolitical Vision of Aimé Césaire's Cold War Poems." *International Journal of Francophone Studies*, Vol. 19, Nos 3–4 (Dec. 2016), pp. 275–300.

Introduction

"*L'heure est venue d'abandonner toutes les vieilles routes.*"

(Aimé Césaire)

"*Without an ideology a writer can neither narrate nor construct a comprehensive, well-organized and multifaceted composition.*"

(Gyorgy Lukács)[1]

In "Orphée noir," Jean-Paul Sartre claims that Negritude poetry is the single great revolutionary poetic movement of the postwar era. Metropolitan French poetry, he suggests, had degraded into petit bourgeois, onanistic wordplay, whereas the political situation in Europe demanded "pragmatic" prose that would mobilize the proletariat: "it is efficacy alone that counts."[2] But colonial domination and racial oppression placed colonized black subjects in a different situation from that of the European proletariat, one that poetry was better suited to address: "the black person [*nègre*] who revindicates his negritude in a revolutionary movement places himself straightaway upon the terrain of Reflection [...] Thus subjectivity reappears, relation of the self to

---

1 Lukács, Gyorgy. "Narrate or Describe?" *Writer and Critic and Other Essays*. Edited and translated by Arthur D. Kahn. New York: Grosset and Dunlap, 1971, p. 143.
2 Sartre, Jean-Paul. "Orphée noir." *Anthologie de la nouvelle poésie nègre et malgache* [1948]. Edited by Léopold Sédar Senghor. Paris: PUF, 2011, p. xii. All translations mine unless otherwise indicated.

itself, the source of all poetry that the worker has had to cut himself off from."[3] The lyrical reflexivity that Sartre calls "treason" when practiced by contemporary white European poets is, when practiced by black poets, a necessary and appropriate revolutionary practice of self-disalienation. For Sartre, then, the negative work of poetry that leads in other contexts to political impasse performs, in the case of what came to be known as Negritude poetry, a radical undoing of colonial racist ideology that moves everyone closer to the horizon of a "society without races" through its "antiracist racism."[4]

Though Sartre's theory of Negritude has received considerable criticism, many francophone black intellectual contemporaries expressed similar views about the alignment of literary forms with emancipatory politics. Throughout the 1930s and well into the 1940s, radical French Caribbean intellectuals had indeed invested revolutionary political hope in avant-garde poetry, especially surrealism; this is evident in journals such as *Legitime Defense* (1932) and *L'Étudiant Noir* (1935), published by Antillean students in Paris who drew inspiration from the surrealists' union of Marx and Freud;[5] and *Tropiques* (1941–45), published in Martinique, whose editors (including Aimé and Suzanne Césaire) used poetry as a tool of critique against the racist, authoritarian regime of Vichy Admiral Henri Robert. Suzanne Césaire calls surrealism "the tightrope of our hope" in its pages.[6] Martinican critic René Ménil, a communist who had no fondness for Sartrean existentialism or for Negritude as a concept, seems nonetheless to anticipate Sartre's postwar argument about black poetry by several years, writing the following in 1944:

> The problem has turned out to be […] that of the conquest of man by himself. And so much the better for us. For our task, we who want to

---

3 Sartre, "Orphée noir," p. xv.
4 Sartre, "Orphée noir," p. xli.
5 See Introduction. Richardson, Michael and Fijalkowski, Krzysztof. *Refusal of the Shadow: Surrealism and the Caribbean*. New York: Verso, 1996, pp. 1–37. On the journal *L'Étudiant noir* and the early "marxisant" politics of Negritude, see Miller, Christopher L. "The (Revised) Birth of Negritude: Communist Revolution and 'the Immanent Negro' in 1935." *PMLA*, Vol. 125, No. 3 (May 2010), pp. 743–749.
6 Césaire, Suzanne. "1943: Surrealism and Us." *The Great Camouflage: Writings of Dissent (1941–1945)*. Edited by Daniel Maximin. Translated by Keith L. Walker. Middletown, CT: Wesleyan University Press, 2012, p. 38. See also "Tropiques." *Aimé Césaire: Poésie, théâtre, essais, discours*. Edited by A. James Arnold. Paris: CNRS, Planète Libre, 2013, pp. 1311–1314.

reclassify ourselves within humanity, is it not [...] to direct all our effort towards the discovery within us of a novelty likely to bring into our life a content worthy of being universally taken into consideration?[7]

For Ménil, as for Sartre, modernist, Surrealist-inspired poetry was the literary vehicle through which black consciousness would liberate and regenerate itself.[8]

The Second World War and its immediate aftermath saw Surrealist ideas about poetry and revolution spread extensively throughout the French Caribbean.[9] Aimé Césaire invests emancipatory hope in avant-garde poetry in his 1945 essay "Poésie et Connaissance." He sets up a sharp antinomy between poetry and prose—before Sartre's *Qu'est-ce que la littérature?* (1948), it is worth noting—and explicitly associates prose with the Western positivist scientific tradition that emerged alongside imperial conquest, racial oppression, and capitalist exploitation, and that had just culminated in fascist slaughter. In a famous line, Césaire says that "scientific knowledge numbers, measures, classes, and kills."[10] Césaire rejects this positivistic tradition, which he names "la France prose," in favor of the emancipatory tradition of "la France poésie." Sharing with the Surrealists a Hegelian understanding of poetry as a form of thought complete in itself,[11] Césaire celebrates avant-garde poetry as a Dionysian affirmation of life in all its immanent contradiction, a form of knowledge that "through word, image, myth, love and humor installs me at the living heart of myself and of the world," and through which "man bespatters the object with all his mobilized riches."[12] In Haiti, the student militants who founded the

---

7 Ménil, René. "Situation de la poésie aux Antilles." *Antilles déjà jadis, précédé de Tracées*. Paris: Jean Michel Place, 1999, p. 120.

8 One notable exception to this alignment with Surrealism was Jacques Roumain, who dismissed it as "an 'infernal machine,' which is anti-bourgeois but negative and anarchistic." Quoted in Dash, J. Michael. *Literature and Ideology in Haiti 1915–1961*. London: Macmillan, 1981, p. 158.

9 André Breton fled Vichy France to Martinique in 1941; though he stayed only briefly, he met Aimé and Suzanne Césaire, beginning a long-lasting and consequential friendship. See Véron, Kora. *Aimé Césaire*. Paris: Seuil, 2021, pp. 185–194.

10 Césaire, Aimé. "Poésie et connaissance." Arnold ed., *Césaire*, p. 1377.

11 Hegel, G.W.F. *Aesthetics*. Vol. III, Part 3. Marxists Internet Archive.

12 Césaire, "Poésie et connaissance," Arnold ed., *Césaire*, p. 1389. By identifying poetic writing's privileged connection to totality as its main political purchase, Césaire is fully in line with the left-libertarian politics of the Surrealist movement.

journal *La Ruche* in 1944 were also convinced that surrealist poetry held a special radical potential. André Breton's 1945 visit to Port-au-Prince, where he lectured on Surrealism and freedom, was a significant inspiration to these student radicals—led by Jacques Stephen Alexis, René Depestre, Gérald Bloncourt, and Paul Laraque—to form a revolutionary political movement that would go on to successfully overthrow President Elie Lescot in 1946.[13]

From Senghor to Sartre to the Césaires, from existentialists to communists, and from Port-au-Prince to Fort-de-France to Paris, it was thus a widely shared belief that avant-garde poetry held a special political purchase when black writers wrote it: surrealism and anticolonial black liberation were in alignment. From the 1930s through to the years immediately following the Second World War, radical Antillean authors would pursue the liberation and regeneration of black subjectivity through the miraculous weapon of Orphic, lyrical introspection.

On or around the year 1956, however, French Caribbean literature changed. *Cold War Negritude: Form and Alignment in French Caribbean Literature* explores how French Caribbean authors' understanding of the relationship between literary aesthetics and emancipatory political commitment was transformed by their participation in the global Cold War. Over the course of the 1950s, French Caribbean authors reevaluated the modernist literary aesthetics of Negritude that had developed over the course of the 1930s and 1940s, and sought to produce alternatives that would be adequate to a radically different conjuncture wherein the urgent political problem was the need to take the measure of the bipolar world system of the Cold War, realigning themselves and their writing within it. This book traces the 1950s ideological trajectories of three radical French Caribbean authors—René Depestre, Aimé Césaire, and Jacques

---

He explicitly acknowledges this affiliation by quoting Breton's formulation that poetry must seek the "certain point d'esprit" where contradictions are no longer perceived as such. For Césaire, "[j]amais au cours des siècles, ambition plus haute n'a été exprimée plus tranquillement." Arnold ed., *Césaire*, p. 1381.

13 Smith, Matthew J. *Red and Black in Haiti: Radicalism, Conflict, and Political Change, 1934–1957*. Chapel Hill, NC: University of North Carolina Press, 2009, pp. 75–77. See also Bloncourt, Gérald and Michael Löwy ed. *Messagers de la tempête. André Breton et le surréalisme en Haiti*. Pantin, Le Temps des Cerises, 2007.

Stephen Alexis—and offers a comparative analysis of the aesthetic responses to the Cold War that these authors produced.

The Geopolitical Turn of 1956: French Caribbean Literature Between Suez and Budapest

The end of the Second World War saw the defeat of fascism and the exhaustion of European colonialism. With Europe reduced to its own size, a decolonized world order was suddenly not only possible, but imminent. Decolonization became something more than a poetic act of self-disalienation in the 1950s: it became a concrete political horizon, a project that needed urgently to be thought through, planned, and realized. If anticolonial Antillean intellectuals active in the interwar period and during the Second World War contested the alienated, racialized subjectivity imposed upon them by European colonialism and white supremacy through poetic catabasis, the global wave of decolonization called writers outward towards the world—the entire world—rather than inward.

However, although it is a crucially important context, decolonization is only part of the story of postwar French Caribbean literature. *Cold War Negritude* departs from other studies of twentieth-century French Caribbean authors by focusing upon the impact of what Odd Arne Westad calls the "global Cold War" upon their political and aesthetic imaginaries. As Westad explains, the ideological struggle between the United States and the Soviet Union—which had arguably begun with the Russian Revolution in 1917—consolidated in the long postwar decade into an "international system based on two opposing versions of European modernist thought."[14] These postwar empires—Westad refers to the United States and the Soviet Union as "the empire of liberty" and the "empire of equality," respectively—vied with one another to propound their respective views of modernity and progress abroad via diplomatic influence, economic incentive and pressure, covert intelligence operations, and direct military intervention. As Cold War dividing lines quickly solidified in Europe, it was largely the non-European world that was (once again) on the receiving end of evangelization from these two competing empires.

---

14 Westad, Odd Arne. *The Global Cold War*. New York: Cambridge University Press, 2012, p. 4.

The bipolar logic of the global Cold War was imposed in nearly every region of the world, and the Caribbean was no exception. As befits an archipelago in a system of transcontinental blocs, however, the Caribbean was a creolized anomaly in this Cold War/decolonial conjuncture. The region contained some of the last vestiges of the old European colonial empires, now incorporated as overseas departments or Commonwealth territories; decolonizing Third World nation-states; US territories and military outposts, as well as US-backed dictatorships; a short-lived multinational West Indian federation; and, after the Cuban Revolution, the only Soviet-aligned communist state in the Western Hemisphere.

The Cold War's impact in the francophone Caribbean was determined to a significant extent by these islands' particular post/colonial histories.[15] In Haiti, the hopes of 1946 proved short-lived, as the relatively progressive presidency of Dumarsis Estimé was overthrown by a coup and replaced by authoritarian military officer Paul Magloire, a vituperative anticommunist whose suppression of the Haitian Left was noted with appreciation in the US State Department.[16] Right-wing *noiriste* dictator François Duvalier, who took power in 1957, became adept at turning the anticommunist hypervigilance of the US national security apparatus to his political advantage.[17] Though US intervention in Haiti was hardly an invention of the Cold War—Haiti had endured a two-decade US occupation beginning in 1915—US support for right-wing Haitian autocrats was now both solicited and justified in terms of the struggle to contain communism in the Western Hemisphere.[18] Both Depestre and Alexis would be expelled from Haiti and thrust into the broader world of the Cold War, circulating in international communist networks and imbibing the intellectual life of the global postwar Left. Depestre would be tossed around all three Cold War worlds from exile

---

15 For a systematic discussion of the early Cold War geopolitical situation in the Caribbean, see Halliday, Fred, "Cold War in the Caribbean," *New Left Review*, Vol. 141 (Sept.–Oct. 1983), pp. 5–22.

16 Smith, Matthew J. *Red and Black in Haiti*, p. 154.

17 Duvalier frequently appealed to the United States for support against a largely non-existent threat from student Marxist groups; in his 1960 "Cri de Jacmel" speech, he appealed for increased US financial support, lest Haiti be forced to turn to the Soviet bloc for aid. Von Tunzelman, Alex. *Red Heat: Conspiracy, Murder, and the Cold War in the Caribbean*. New York: Henry Holt, 2011, p. 174.

18 See Dubois, Laurent. *Haiti: The Aftershocks of History*. New York: Picador, 2012, pp. 333–342.

to exile, while Alexis' failed (and possibly Soviet-funded) attempt to reinfiltrate Haiti and build a Left resistance to Duvalier would ultimately result in his murder in 1961 at the age of 39.

The French Antilles would also be profoundly transformed during the first decade of the Cold War, starting with their fraught integration into the French Fourth Republic through the departmentalization law of March 19, 1946. This was a period of intense political and social unrest in Martinique especially, as an organized Left struggled against a recalcitrant *béké* ruling class and an especially repressive police apparatus for improved social conditions.[19] While hegemony over Haiti had long since been transferred to the US, with French influence largely reduced to a mostly cultural identification among the ruling elites, Martinique, Guadeloupe and Guyane were linked into the global Cold War political context via their incorporation into the French political system. Though there had been organized workers' movements and active communist parties for decades in the region, the postwar decade saw Communist—local Communist federations affiliated with the French Communist Party (PCF)—rise to political prominence in Guadeloupe and Martinique.[20] Communists Rosan Girard and the intrepid Gerty Archimède became the first elected representatives of Guadeloupe, while Césaire, along with Léopold Bissol, became the Communist representatives of Martinique. Césaire would spend the postwar decade as a French communist statesman as well as a black Antillean poet.

The global Cold War thus exerted a powerful centripetal force upon Haiti and the French Antilles, as it did upon the authors central to this book. As their political communities were integrated into the bipolar order, Depestre, Césaire, and Alexis were carried across the world (and across all three imagined Cold War "worlds") by its currents. Thanks to Kaiama L. Glover and Alex Gil's digital humanities project *In the Same Boats*, it is now easy to visually map the remarkable Cold War trajectories of Depestre and Césaire. A search of their travels around the globe between mid-1945 and late 1961 yields the following results for Depestre: Paris, Prague, East Berlin, Milan, Genoa, Havana, Vienna, Rome, Santiago (Chile), Buenos Aires, Sao Paulo, Port-au-Prince, Moscow, Beijing, Shanghai,

---

19 See Childers, Kristen Stromberg. *Seeking Imperialism's Embrace: National Identity, Decolonization, and Assimilation in the French Caribbean*. Oxford: Oxford University Press, 2016, Ch. 2. See also Dumont, Jacques. *L'Amère patrie: Histoire des Antilles françaises au XXe siècle*. Paris: Fayard, 2010, Ch. 5.
20 Childers, *Seeking Imperialism's Embrace*, p. 53.

Hanoi. For Césaire: Paris, Fort-de-France, Wroclaw, Bucharest, Vienna, Moscow, Rome, Dakar.[21] The site does not provide information about Alexis as of this book's publication, but based on a number of sources we may stipulate (at least) the following itinerary: Paris, Port-au-Prince, Siena (Italy), Bucharest, Mexico, Guatemala, Prague, Moscow, Irkutsk, Beijing, Havana, and (tragically) Mole St Nicholas, the site of his murder. These trajectories tell three different but significantly intertwined stories of Antillean intellectual life within the bipolar world order: where they go and do not go, when, in what sequence, and for how long are all determined significantly by Cold War geopolitical networks and currents as well as neocolonial relationships. Several things become clear when we look at these three itineraries together. First, the major nodal points at which they intersect (though not always at the same time) are Paris, the Caribbean (Fort-de-France, Port-au-Prince, Havana), and the Eastern bloc. Paris is the principal hub of activity for all three authors, a location where all three reside for significant periods of time, where they build literary and political networks, and which connects them to multiple other locations across Cold War dividing lines. The Caribbean is a place of departure and periodic return: though Césaire, an official of a European Communist party, circulates mostly around Europe and returns frequently to Fort-de-France, Depestre and Alexis' trajectories register their status as exiles, largely barred from return to Haiti and forced to relocate frequently. The trajectories also show that the Eastern bloc exerts a significant gravitational pull for all three authors: for Depestre and Alexis, the Moscow connection offers an additional link to Communist China, while Césaire and Depestre's networks extend significantly into Eastern Europe. *Cold War Negritude* is a study of the politico-aesthetic projects that emerge over the course of these authors' astonishing trajectories.

The year 1956 was indeed, as Césaire noted in his "Discours à la Maison du sport" that November, "a long year loaded with grave events"; it is the fulcrum for the story this book is telling.[22] 1956 marked at once the crystallization of the bipolar order and the emergence of worldwide resistance to it. In *Les damnés de la terre* (1961), Frantz Fanon analyzes the overdetermination of worldwide local independence

---

21 Gil and Glover, *In the Same Boats*. http://sameboats.org. These lists do not indicate the authors' exact point-to-point trajectories. I list each location only once for brevity's sake.
22 Césaire, Aimé. "Discours à la maison du sport." In Arnold ed., *Césaire*, p. 1510.

struggles by the bipolar order in a passage that offers theoretical insight into the decolonization/Cold War conjuncture:

> the framework of cutthroat competition between capitalism and socialism [...] *gives an almost universal dimension to even the most localized demands. [...] Each* jacquerie, *each act of sedition in the Third World makes up part of a picture framed by the Cold War*. Two men are beaten up in Salisbury, and at once the whole of a bloc goes into action [...] when Khrushchev threatens to come to Castro's aid with rockets, when Kennedy decides upon some desperate solution for the Laos question, the colonized person or the newly independent native has the impression that whether he wills it or not he is being carried away in a kind of frantic cavalcade. [...] *all the* jacqueries *and desperate deeds, all those bands armed with cutlasses or axes find their nationality in the implacable struggle which opposes socialism and capitalism*. [...] Already the Korean and Indo-Chinese wars had begun a new phase. But it is above all Budapest and Suez which constitute the decisive moments of this confrontation.[23]

Fanon's main argument here is that the entire emergent decolonizing world was always-already and inextricably circumscribed by the Cold War world system. Shifting abruptly between the local and the geopolitical scale, Fanon emphasizes both the extreme disparity in destructive force between the superpowers and the decolonizing world (the former armed with nuclear weapons, the latter with cutlasses and axes) and the great chasm separating the ground-level subject position of the world's "jacqueries" from the geopolitical perspective of the "competition between capitalism and socialism." Local struggles were no longer understood as just anticolonial; they instead became legible to the distant superpowers through a Cold War episteme, and the specific content of each struggle was overdetermined by the master code of the bipolar order. Soviet ideologue Andrei Zhdanov tellingly frames this bifurcation in chiasmus form, as a choice between symmetrically opposed "camps": the "imperialist and anti-democratic" NATO countries and the "anti-imperialist and democratic" Soviet-led bloc.[24] As Fanon understood, to claim a place in

---

23 Fanon, Frantz. *The Wretched of the Earth*. Preface by Jean-Paul Sartre. Translated by Constance Farrington. New York: Grove Press, 2005, pp. 75–79. Emphasis mine.
24 Zhdanov, Andrei. "Report on the International Situation to the Cominform." Sep. 22, 1947. *Seventeen Moments in Soviet History*. https://soviethistory.msu.edu.

this world inevitably involved the question of *alignment*, an unchosen choice between one bloc or the other—or, more commonly, the near certainty of being ascribed one of the two possible alignments from outside.

Fanon's synecdoche of "Budapest and Suez" captures the decolonial/Cold War conjuncture that crystallized around the year 1956.[25] Nasser's nationalization of the Suez Canal was just one event in in a worldwide decolonial sequence in the 1950s, including: socialist Cheddi Jagan's electoral victory in Guyana, overturned by British authorities (1953); the election of Jacopo Arbenz in Guatemala, overthrown in a CIA-backed coup (1954); Vietnam's victory against the French at Dien Bien Phu (1954); the Bandung Conference (1955); Tunisian and Moroccan independence (1956); the escalation of the Algerian liberation struggle (1956); Guinea's vote against joining the Union Française (1958); and the Cuban Revolution (1959). Similarly, "Budapest" stands for a worldwide anti-Stalinist sequence, centered on the Soviet repression of the Hungarian Revolution and Khrushchev's "secret speech" against the Stalin personality cult, both in 1956. These events, which threatened to decenter the Soviet Union, include the Tito–Stalin split (1948); the emergence of the People's Republic of China (1949); workers' revolts in East Germany (1953) and Poznan, Poland (1956); Wladyslaw Gomulka's "Polish road to socialism" (1956); Césaire's "Lettre à Maurice Thorez" and co-founding of the Parti Populaire Martiniquais (1956); and the "polycentric" communism of Italian Communist Party leader Palmiro Togliatti (1961).[26]

Between Budapest and Suez—that is, between a bipolar order settling into hegemony and a residual colonial order—French Caribbean intellectuals sought out alternative paradigms of worldmaking based on cooperation and solidarity rather than domination. In the French-speaking world, an intellectual hub of such anticolonial worldmaking was the publishing house *Présence Africaine*, an international black

---

25 Fanon explicitly counts the United States as an "imperialist" power, grouping it with the Western European colonial nations as a single superpower representing "capitalism" in competition with Soviet and Chinese communism. *Les damnés de la terre*, pp. 73–81.

26 Césaire explicitly declares his solidarity with Togliatti, Gomulka, Tito, the Poznan revolts, and the revolution in Budapest in his "Discours à la Maison du Sport," delivered in Martinique only weeks after the publication of his resignation letter to Thorez. "Discours à la maison du sport," Arnold ed., *Césaire*, pp. 1510–1527. See also Edwards, Brent Hayes. "Césaire in 1956." *Social Text*, Vol. 28, No. 2 (2010), pp. 115–125.

intellectual forum that will be an important setting throughout this book.[27] The First Congress of Black Artists and Writers, organized by *Présence Africaine* in 1956 and conceived under the sign of the Bandung Conference,[28] attempted to inscribe a different kind of bloc into the map of the Cold War world. Black intellectuals and writers from around the world gathered in Paris to discuss the history, present state, and future prospects of the *monde noir*, a new transnational bloc whose existence the Congress performatively announces. We shall see over the course of this book that worldmaking was a significant element of the political and literary projects Depestre, Césaire, and Alexis (who all stood in solidarity at the Congress), though their worldmaking imaginaries were ultimately circumscribed by Cold War currents.

French Caribbean Literature and Cold War Aesthetic Systems

The global Cold War was conducted, to an unprecedented extent and scale, on the level of culture and ideology.[29] As Susan Buck-Morss argues, the United States and the Soviet Union embodied competing "dreamworlds," utopian visions of mass abundance, whose imaginaries overlapped significantly even though each defined itself in opposition to the other.[30] The United States and the Soviet Union vied with one another through extensive propaganda and cultural diplomacy campaigns to represent themselves as the apogee of progress, the carrier of the torch of

---

27 I borrow this term from Adom Getachew's theory of postwar decolonization in *Worldmaking after Empire: The Rise and Fall of Self-Determination*. Princeton, NJ: Princeton University Press, 2019.

28 This meeting of 29 Afro-Asian nations in Bandung, Indonesia instantiated a global network of South–South relations—the United States and Soviet Union were explicitly not invited to attend. Its organizers, Nasser (Egypt), Sukarno (Indonesia), and Nehru (India), stressed the universal right to self-determination, shared commitment to cultural cooperation and, speaking in the name of two-thirds of the world's population, their refusal to participate in the superpowers' partition of the decolonizing world into armed camps. See Prashad, Vijay. *The Darker Nations: A People's History of the Third World*. New York and London: The New Press, 2007, pp. 31–50.

29 Caute, David. *The Dancer Defects: The Struggle for Cultural Supremacy during the Cold War*. Oxford: Oxford University Press, 2003, p. 1.

30 Buck-Morss, Susan. *Dreamworld and Catastrophe: The Passing of Mass Utopia in East and West*. Cambridge, MA: MIT Press, 2002.

Enlightenment, and the apex of human social, cultural, and technological development. In nearly every sphere of life, the superpowers presented to the decolonizing world alternate models of modernity: free markets vs. central planning, consumerism vs. mass mobilization, individual liberty vs. social justice, cutting-edge technology vs. rapid industrial growth.[31]

Within this global cultural Cold War, literature became a major ideological battleground, and each superpower promoted a particular literary aesthetic—or a reified version thereof—as emblematic of its ideology. For liberal intellectuals in the West, literary modernism "became the talisman of political virtue"[32]; held as the epitome of the individual freedoms enshrined in Western liberal democracy, modernist aesthetics were promoted worldwide by CIA-sponsored cultural diplomacy, subsidizing publishers, cultural foundations, magazines (of which *Encounter* is the most notable), conferences, and radio programs.[33] Perhaps the most influential cultural Cold War institution was the Congress for Cultural Freedom, a CIA-funded organization that, as Andrew Rubin states in *Archives of Authority*, constructed "regimes of consecration" that shaped the canon of what we know today as world literature, privileging works of high modernism.[34] Bhakti Shringarpure distinguishes helpfully between modernism as such and the "diluted version" promoted abroad by US cultural diplomacy and domestically in the US academy, often depoliticized and reduced to techniques of "abstraction, autonomy, fragmentation, [and] indirectness."[35]

In contrast to what it portrayed as the West's decadent formalism, the Soviet Union promoted—indeed, for a time prescribed—the doctrine of socialist realism. This aesthetic emphasized *partinost* (partisanship), proletarian positive heroes, documentation of real social conditions, and optimism about the future, the arc of which must be shown to bend towards Marxism-Leninism.[36] While pressuring cultural cadres

---

31 Westad, *Global Cold War*, pp. 92–93.
32 Caute, *The Dancer Defects*, p. 3.
33 Frances Stonor Saunders' *The Cultural Cold War: The CIA and the World of Arts and Letters* (New Press, 2nd edition, 2013) remains the authoritative work on the CIA's involvement in cultural diplomacy, though her focus is on Europe.
34 Rubin, Andrew. *Archives of Authority: Empire, Culture, and the Cold War.* Princeton University Press, 2012, pp. 8–10.
35 Shringarpure, Bhakti. *Cold War Assemblages: From Decolonization to Digital.* New York: Routledge, 2020, p. 17.
36 Clark, Katerina. *The Soviet Novel: History as Ritual.* Chicago, IL: University of Chicago Press, 1981.

of European communist parties to promote socialist realism, Moscow also courted Third World writers, starting in the 1950s by sponsoring the Afro-Asian Writer's Association, which had its inaugural meeting in the Tashkent (1958) and published the influential magazine *Lotus*,[37] and by awarding the Stalin Peace Prize (renamed the Lenin Peace Prize in 1956) to Marxist and anticolonial writers such as Jorge Amado, Nicolas Guillen, and W.E.B. DuBois.[38] Socialist realism was not prescribed so rigidly to Third World writers (Moscow could hardly enforce such prescriptions, anyway); instead, Soviet literary diplomacy emphasized anticolonial solidarity, and, as Peter Kalliney notes, writers from Afro-Asian countries were able to make relatively free and "creative use of socialist aesthetic theory."[39] As I will discuss below and develop over the course of the book, the authors discussed in this study also turned socialist aesthetics to their own creative uses.

Depestre, Césaire, and Alexis thus chose their own literary aesthetics, but not in conditions of their own choosing. *Cold War Negritude*'s objective is to examine the complex relations of francophone Caribbean writers to what Monica Popescu, in her field-transforming book *At Penpoint* (2020), calls the two "aesthetic world-systems" of the Cold War.[40] As Popescu convincingly argues, realism and modernism were "hijacked by the Cold War superpowers" and charged with ideological overdeterminations in excess of their previous meanings as aesthetic strategies and modes of writing, both "polariz[ing]" and "hierarchiz[ing] them."[41] Another useful way of framing these aesthetic dividing lines is provided by Kalliney, who sets not realism and modernism but the "need for aesthetic freedom" and the "desire to have writing serve practical ends" as the two poles.[42] The emergence of these Cold War aesthetic world-systems forced Antillean authors to reexamine (though

---

37 For discussions of the AAWA, see Popescu, Monica. *At Penpoint: African Literatures, Postcolonial Literatures, and the Cold War*. Durham, NC: Duke University Press, 2020 and Halim, Hala. "*Lotus*, the Afro-Asian Nexus, and Global South Comparatism." *Comparative Studies of South Asia, Africa and the Middle East*, Vol. 32, No. 3 (2012), pp. 563–583.
38 Hammond, *Cold War and Literature*, p. 3.
39 Kalliney, Peter. *The Aesthetic Cold War: Decolonization and Global Literature*. Princeton, NJ: Princeton University Press, 2022, pp. 103–104.
40 Popescu, *At Penpoint*, Ch. 2.
41 Popescu, *At Penpoint*, p. 76.
42 Kalliney, *The Aesthetic Cold War*, p. 10.

not necessarily to abandon) the modernist aesthetics associated with Negritude and to take a side in this Cold War literary debate.

Though they did indeed articulate sometimes intensely polemical stances, the aesthetic alignments that Depestre, Césaire, and Alexis developed were all more complicated than a straightforward choice between "modernism" and "realism." For several reasons, the global debate about literary aesthetics took on specific contours in the Francophone Caribbean context. First, as we have mentioned, the recent history of francophone black poetry as progressively aligned writing that was also ineluctably avant-garde challenged a neat ideological division of modes. Césaire was defiantly pro-surrealist even while he remained in the PCF and, while Depestre and Alexis endorsed some communist critiques of modernism (Alexis went furthest in this direction), they never rejected modernist writing absolutely. The union between surrealism and communism that had still been possible for these writers in the 1940s, however, did indeed become significantly more complicated. Although the PCF's anathema against surrealism perhaps influenced Depestre as he became a young party cadre, Depestre's turn away from surrealism in the postwar decade was not merely a question of party loyalty; it was also a reaction to the failure of the 1946 revolution and the consequent rise of right-wing authoritarianism in Haiti.[43] Surrealists (and ex-surrealists) that Depestre admired—Louis Aragon and Paul Eluard, particularly—were by the 1950s recognized more for their militant antifascist writings during the occupation. Césaire's use of Surrealism also shifted around the time of his split with the PCF, in a different direction: as will be discussed in Chapter 3, he would now harness its spirit of revolt and its antipositivism as a weapon against what he saw as the Party's repressive cultural Stalinism.

Two dissimilar institutions were influential above all upon the authors I study here: to a different extent, and each in its own way, the PCF and *Présence Africaine* functioned as centers of gravity for Depestre, Césaire, and Alexis. This is not at all a straightforward microcosm of the opposition between the overarching aesthetic world-systems—the PCF wielded much greater power and influence and its mediasphere was far more extensive than Alioune Diop's modestly funded publishing house, and in any case the two were not diametrically opposed to one

---

43 Depestre noted as early as the 1940s that, when faced with the struggle against fascism, the Surrealists "hastened to abandon surrealism to adopt a form of expression which was more accessible to a general public" (quoted in Dash, *Literature and Ideology*, p. 159).

another in bipolar fashion, even though (as we shall see) there were significant points of contention. Nonetheless, their connections to the PCF and *Présence Africaine* linked these authors to two distinct international intellectual networks, and different, largely incompatible aesthetic standards prevailed in each domain. While Aragon propounded Soviet socialist realism and the literary doctrine of "national poetry" as PCF cultural policy, and mentored Alexis and Depestre while remaining mostly silent about Césaire, *Présence Africaine* was at the same time enshrining modernism as the unofficial poetics of the *monde noir*, with Césaire and Senghor (and, to a lesser extent, Léon-Gontran Damas) as its canonical figures.[44] The authors studied in *Cold War Negritude* existed between these intellectual constellations, and navigated tactically between them with relative freedom.

A third related but distinct factor specific to the French Caribbean was the controversy that came to surround the concept of Negritude. If the Cold War "hijacking" of modernism had made Surrealism look different in the 1950s than it had in the 1930s, "Negritude" also emerged from the postwar decade significantly transformed. Born in 1935 as a neologism that Césaire coined to capture a spirit of anticolonial, antiracist revolt, by the 1950s the term had been widely disseminated and had come to be associated with a literary and political movement consisting of a specific cohort of pan-Africanist francophone intellectuals.[45] Several black francophone leftists were hostile to the concept because they thought that it reified race into ontological fact and mystified real class conflicts within black societies.[46] Michael Dash argues that Negritude—especially as expounded by Léopold Sédar Senghor—had developed "an almost Classical tendency to prescribe a rigid prosody and thematic

---

44 *Présence Africaine* was more ecumenical than the PCF's cultural policy, publishing black authors of diverse ideological positions (I discuss its high liberal ideological ecumenicism in Chapter 1). However, as I discuss in Chapter 2, the debate over "national poetry" published in its pages was slanted in favor of Césaire's antisocialist realist stance.

45 Besides "Orphée noir," it was perhaps Lilyan Kesteloot's seminal text *Black Writers in French: A Literary History of Negritude* (1963) that did the most to associate "Negritude" with a literary movement rather than a concept.

46 See Fanon, "On the Pitfalls of National Consciousness," *Wretched of the Earth*, pp. 148–205; d'Arboussier, Gabriel. "Une mystification dangereuse: théorie de la négritude." *La Nouvelle Critique* (Jun. 1949), pp. 34–47; and Ménil, René. "Une doctrine réactionnaire: la négritude." *Action: Revue théorique et politique du Parti Communiste Martiniquais*, No. 1 (Aug. 1963), pp. 37–50.

conformity for black writers" and came to function as "an ethnic Pléiade which legislated literary codes for the black world."[47] What is particularly interesting about Dash's critical description of Negritude here is its stark similarity to the standard critique of socialist realism as a doctrine that disciplines writers to conform to prescribed aesthetic norms. The signifier "Negritude" was thus itself a site of Cold War contestation between different visions of solidarity and political belonging. As will become clear over the course of the book, the desire to think through and resolve the tension (not necessarily a polar opposition) between Marxism and Negritude as paradigms of belonging was a preoccupation of all three of the authors I study.

Francophone Cold War/Postcolonial Studies

Much valuable scholarship has emerged recently in francophone postcolonial studies on French Caribbean intellectuals' engagements with global postwar currents. Of these, Gary Wilder's *Freedom Time* (2015) is especially relevant to this book. Wilder argues that Césaire and Senghor should be understood not only as ethnically "rooted" thinkers "influenced" by European thought, but rather as "*postwar* thinkers" who sought solutions "at once rooted and global" to "planetary problems of world-historical transition."[48] Annette Joseph-Gabriel's pathbreaking work on postwar black French feminism in *Reimagining Liberation* (2019) also makes an essential contribution to our understanding of francophone black radical thought, showing that black women were also "political protagonists" who produced progressive alternatives to colonial paradigms of political belonging, civic participation, and identity.[49] In revisiting the Cold War writings of Depestre, Césaire, and Alexis, *Cold War Negritude* builds upon these contributions by excavating and reevaluating progressive aesthetics from this same postwar conjuncture that sought to think black liberation and anticolonialism *together with* solidaristic, universalist class struggle, and not in terms of a straightforward antinomy

---

47 Dash, *Literature and Ideology*, p. 123.
48 Wilder, *Freedom Time*, p. 9.
49 Joseph-Gabriel, Annette. *Reimagining Liberation: How Black Women Transformed Citizenship in the French Empire*. Urbana and Chicago, IL: University of Illinois Press, 2020, p. 19.

between local and global, between class struggle and antiracism, or between particular and universal.

Another related current has been a renewed political criticism of broadly Marxist tendency that questions postcolonial theory's poststructuralist theoretical foundations. From Neil Lazarus' critique of postcolonialism's depoliticizing tendencies to Nivedita Majumdar's recent defense of radical universalism against counter-solidaristic strains in postcolonial theory, there is a growing momentum to move past late twentieth-century postcolonialism's perceived political quiescence and to salvage aspects of the liberationist "grand narratives" of the 1950s and 1960s.[50] In francophone postcolonial studies specifically, this tendency is echoed in Chris Bongie's critique of postcolonialism's bias against "scribal," (i.e., expressly partisan) writing and its privileging of high modernism and the mystified "great writer."[51] Perhaps most notably, Nick Nesbitt has traced and theorized what he calls the "Black Jacobin" tradition in Antillean thought, defining it as claiming "a series of abstract, universal concepts of relevance to all human beings."[52] Drawing inspiration from and building upon these interventions, this book aims to recuperate Marxist aesthetic tendencies of French Caribbean authors that have been dismissed or misunderstood because they do not conform to the parameters of literary valuation that have been predominant in postcolonial criticism.

Cold War Negritude also seeks to bring scholarship on the French Caribbean into conversation with the burgeoning field of global Cold War literary studies that has emerged over the past ten years. For decades, disciplinary boundaries kept the Cold War separate from postcolonial studies: study of Cold War culture was largely confined to US cultural studies, socialist realism limited to Slavic and Russian literature, and the literatures of Africa, Asia, Latin America, and the Caribbean slotted into postcolonial studies.[53] An increasing number of scholars, however, now treat Cold War and decolonization as *one* conjuncture, with the

---

50 Lazarus, Neil. *The Postcolonial Unconscious.* Cambridge: Cambridge University Press, 2012; Majumdar, Nivedita. *The World in a Grain of Sand: Postcolonial Literature and Radical Universalism.* New York: Verso, 2021.

51 Bongie, Chris. *Friends and Enemies: The Scribal Politics of Post/Colonial Literature.* Liverpool: Liverpool University Press, 2008.

52 Nesbitt, Nick. *Caribbean Critique: Antillean Critical Theory from Toussaint to Glissant.* Liverpool: Liverpool University Press, 2013, p. 18.

53 Watson, Jini Kim. *Cold War Reckonings: Authoritarianism and the Genres of Decolonization.* New York: Fordham University Press, 2021, p. 6.

understanding that "decolonization unfolded *through* and *as* the Cold War," in Jini Kim Watson's apt phrase.[54] In addition to the transformational scholarship of Watson, Popescu, and Kalliney in situating world literature within the context of the Cold War, I would also cite Vaughn Rasberry's analysis of African-American intellectuals' appropriation of Cold War geopolitical rhetoric; Cedric Tolliver's study of Cold War African diaspora literary cultures; Julie-Françoise Tolliver's charting of poetic solidarities between Québec, Africa, and the Caribbean; and Duncan Yoon's work connecting Francophone African writers to Maoism.[55] This current has so far been considerably less prominent in French studies than in comparative (mostly anglophone) literature. *Cold War Negritude* is intended as a step towards opening a broader scholarly conversation in French studies about the global Cold War's impact both on francophone cultures and on prevailing scholarly attitudes towards them.

Red Negritude: Recovering French Caribbean Socialist Aesthetics of the Cold War Era

Although the global Cold War is the broadest horizon against which I read Depestre, Césaire, and Alexis, the account I give of Cold War French Caribbean literature in these pages is by no means exhaustive of the subject. There are many significant figures who are mentioned only briefly here: Ménil, who helped found the Martinican Communist Party after Césaire's PCF resignation; Suzanne Césaire, a communist sympathizer, who developed highly original critiques of capitalism; Haitian communist artist and journalist Gérald Bloncourt; Gilbert Gratiant, a communist poet who contributed to Aragon's "national

---

54 Watson, *Cold War Reckonings*, p. 6.
55 Rasberry, Vaughan. *Race in the Totalitarian Century: Geopolitics in the Black Literary Imagination*. Cambridge, MA: Harvard University Press, 2016; Tolliver, Cedric. *Of Vagabonds and Fellow Travelers: African Diaspora Literary Culture and the Cultural Cold War*. Ann Arbor: University of Michigan Press, 2019; Tolliver, Julie-Françoise. *The Quebec Connection: A Poetics of Solidarity in Global Francophone Literatures*. Charlottesville: University of Virginia Press, 2020; Yoon, Duncan. "Figuring Africa and China: Congolese Literary Imaginaries of the PRC." *Journal of World Literature*, Vol. 6, No. 2 (2021), pp. 167–196; and Yoon, Duncan. "Cold War Creolization: Ousmane Sembène's Le Dernier de l'empire." *Research in African Literatures*, Vol. 50, No. 3 (2019), pp. 29–50.

poetry" anthology; Jules Monnerot, who veered hard to the right and became a reactionary anticommunist; and any number of Antillean intellectuals whose alignments were more ambiguous but whose imaginaries were nonetheless touched by the global Cold War. Likewise, there are many important Cold War themes, from atomic weapons testing and mutually assured destruction, to espionage and anticommunist hysteria, that are not discussed at length here. As stated above, I believe that we are at the beginning of the conversation in francophone postcolonial studies about the global Cold War's impact on literatures and cultures of the broader Francosphere, and that there is ample room for further research. I have chosen this group of three, however, because it is they who appear to have had the most extensive Cold War cultural and political entanglements, cutting transversally across all three of its imagined worlds, and to have developed the most sustained aesthetic responses to this world order. For Depestre, Césaire, and Alexis, there is an identifiable cluster of literary writings that engage directly in Cold War aesthetics: Depestre's Aragonian poems, collected in *Minerai noir*; Césaire's poems of the mid-to-late 1950s, collected in *Ferrements*; and Alexis' entire literary oeuvre. There is also a significant body of politico-aesthetic writings between them: the exchanges collectively known as the "Césaire–Depestre debate," Césaire's "Lettre à Maurice Thorez" and the "Discours à la Maison du Sport," Césaire and Alexis' interventions at the First Congress, and a number of texts by Alexis, including "Où va le roman?," "Lettre à mes amis peintres," and *Le Marxisme, seul guide possible de la revolution haïtienne*. These writings form *Cold War Negritude*'s main corpus.

Perhaps the most important element linking Césaire, Depestre, and Alexis is what might be called their Cold War intersectionality: all three were black francophone Antilleans actively involved in the international communist Left. A specific objective in telling the story of Césaire, Depestre, and Alexis' literary aesthetics in the 1950s is to elucidate how each produced original contributions to socialist aesthetics by syncretizing different Marxist literary tendencies from across Cold War worlds. *Cold War Negritude* thus provides a comprehensive account of these authors' engagements with global communist aesthetics and cultural politics, including Soviet, Western Marxist,[56] and other socialist

---

56 I refer specifically to Perry Anderson's definition of Western Marxism as the Marxist intellectual current, lasting from the 1920s until 1968, that emerged from the political defeat of revolutionary politics in Western Europe and whose focus

literary tendencies of the mid-twentieth century. In this respect, it expands upon work such as Claude Souffrant's enduring study of Marxism and Negritude, *Une Négritude socialiste* (1978); David Alliot's excavation of Césaire's PCF connections in *Le Communisme est à l'ordre du jour* (2013); and Jean-Jacques Cadet's genealogy of twentieth-century Haitian Marxist philosophy in *Le marxisme haïtien* (2020). As the PCF was a crucial mediator of French Caribbean intellectuals' connections with the global Left, *Cold War Negritude* also connects to recent scholarship on French Cold War culture, such as Andrew Sobanet's analysis of the French Stalinist mediasphere in *Generation Stalin* (2018). *Cold War Negritude* demonstrates that French Caribbean writers of the 1950s were active and significant participants in what Enzo Traverso calls "the multiform planet of left culture," and argues that our understanding of these authors' aesthetic visions, of francophone Cold War cultures, and of global Marxist thought are enriched by a deeper understanding of their linkages to this international network.[57]

Marxism has never been a monolith, and it was an especially diverse and dynamic ideological universe during the era that *Cold War Negritude* examines precisely because it was so contested. If, as Fanon claims, 1956 marked the conjuncture at which local anticolonial struggles became inextricably plugged in to the bipolar system, it marked a violent disjuncture for the global Left. Like their European comrades, French Caribbean Marxists also became caught up—for better and for worse—in the fragmentation of the international communist movement outside the Eastern bloc in the wake of Budapest and the Khrushchev report. Each of the authors I discuss reacted differently to this shake-up in international communism. Alexis remained aligned, as did a conflicted and shaken Depestre, while Césaire became increasingly attracted to minoritarian tendencies in the communist world: Tito's Yugoslavia, Mao's China, Polish workers and Hungarian dissidents are but a few of these prospective non-aligned comrades with whom Césaire rhetorically aligns himself in the "Lettre à Maurice Thorez."[58] *Cold War Negritude* therefore argues that francophone Caribbean authors were active and

---

was primarily philosophical and aesthetic. See Anderson, *Considerations on Western Marxism*. New York: Verso, 1976.

57 Traverso, Enzo. *Left-Wing Melancholia: Marxism, History, and Memory*. New York: Columbia University Press, 2016, p. 11.

58 "Lettre à Maurice Thorez," Arnold ed., *Césaire*, pp. 1502–1505. For an insightful discussion of Césaire's solidarity with postwar Poland, see Zubel,

significant participants in this global 1950s contestation of Marxist politics and aesthetics.

Cold War Negritude therefore reads canonical French Caribbean authors as actors within what Rossen Djagalov calls the "People's Republic of Letters," after Pascale Casanova's concept of the World Republic of Letters. Djagalov defines the People's Republic of Letters along similar Bourdieusian terms, as a "transnational literary field" with specific actors, structures, resources, and rules organizing the distribution of literary capital; the People's Republic, though, is centered in Moscow rather than Paris, values realism rather than modernism, and works according to the principle of "centrally-administered cooperation" rather than "resource competition among national literatures and individuals."[59] All three authors studied in this book were actors in both Casanova's and Djagalov's literary fields. Césaire attended several Soviet-sponsored peace conferences in the Eastern bloc and was translated in the Soviet review *Literaturnaya Gazeta*. Depestre was sponsored by PCF literary power couple Louis Aragon and Elsa Triolet and, during his exile, built a global network of communist literary connections, including such figures as Jorge Amado, Pablo Neruda, Anna Seghers, and Nazim Hikmet. Alexis, also affiliated with Aragon, was translated into several Eastern European languages, frequented Soviet writers' conferences, and was personally acquainted with both Khrushchev and Mao. Of these three authors, Alexis had perhaps the most literary capital within the People's Republic: Soviet writer Viktor Nekrasov refers to Alexis as a "well-known writer and public figure," and recounts a pleasant afternoon spent with Alexis in Siena, Italy, accompanied by Italian communist writer Carlo Montella.[60] All of these authors, then, did not look only to Paris or the black Atlantic for aesthetic influences; they were also immersed, with varying degrees of ambivalence, in the culture of the socialist world.[61]

Marla. "From Decolonization to Destalinization: Aimé Césaire and the 'Polish Question.'" *Journal of Postcolonial Writing*, Vol. 59, No. 2, pp. 157–171.

59 Djagalov, Rossen. "The Zone of Freedom? Differential Censorship in the Post-Stalin-Era People's Republic of Letters." *The Slavonic and East European Review*, Vol. 98, No. 4 (Oct. 2020), pp. 601–631.

60 Nekrasov, Viktor. *Both Sides of the Ocean: A Russian Writer's Travels in Italy and the United States*. Translated by Elias Kulukundis. London: Four Square Books, 1964, p. 35.

61 Analogously, Keith M. Booker and Juraga Dubravka write that Soviet literature provides "important models" for postcolonial African writers seeking alternatives

Going beyond the well-known thread connecting French Caribbean literature to the libertarian Marxism of the Surrealist movement, *Cold War Negritude* thus seeks to excavate socialist Caribbean aesthetics that have been undertheorized, forgotten, or dismissed entirely. Like old Soviet-era statues of Lenin, the writings of all three authors that are most linked with communism have fallen into neglect, and tend to remain significantly under-read, disavowed as Stalinist errors inauthentic to their true aesthetic visions. Césaire's pre-"Lettre à Maurice Thorez" poems, Alexis' writings in defense of socialist realism, and the products of Depestre's engagement with Louis Aragon's poetics are all examples of texts that tend to be treated as mere Cold War relics. This book instead takes seriously the fact that these authors spent decades of their lives immersed in "orthodox" Marxist thought as communist intellectuals and political actors, and argues that reading these Cold War Marxist aesthetics back into their writings reveals much about their politico-aesthetic visions that has been rendered all but invisible. This book will thus necessarily be preoccupied with Caribbean socialist realism. It was a productive mode of writing in some sense for all three authors during the 1950s: Depestre tried to work out a socialist realist Haitian poetics, Alexis appropriated and syncretized socialist realist conventions with a remarkably free experimentalism, while for Césaire it was mostly a generative *bête noire* to write and think against.[62]

Césaire's metaphor of an "accursed fig tree strangling the poem"[63] for socialist realism's effect on black literary expression has largely prevailed as the hegemonic critical attitude towards the relation of Marxist aesthetics—especially socialist realism, deemed far too "orthodox"—to French Caribbean literature and Negritude. The dismissal of (non-surrealist) Marxism as anything but a straitjacket for colonized writers of color is perhaps less all-pervasive today than it was in the last decade of the twentieth century. Nevertheless, three decades after the Cold War's ostensible end, much in the archive of global

---

to "Western bourgeois aesthetics." "The Reds and the Blacks: The Historical Novel in the Soviet Union and Postcolonial Africa." *Studies in the Novel*, Vol. 29, No. 3, (Fall 1997), pp. 274 and 275–276.

62 Robin D.G. Kelley describes Césaire's poetics of the 1950s as "a rising, a blow to the master who appears as owner and ruler, teacher and comrade." *Freedom Dreams: The Black Radical Imagination* (Boston, MA: Beacon, 2002), p. 181.

63 Césaire, Aimé. "Réponse à Depestre, poète haïtien (Éléments d'un art poétique)." *Présence Africaine*, No. 1 (Apr.–Jun. 1955), p. 114.

Marxist aesthetics remains unthinkable. *Cold War Negritude* aims to broaden the understanding of French Caribbean writers' far-reaching and multifaceted engagements with Marxist aesthetics, and indeed argues that socialist realism in particular was more significant than has previously been acknowledged.

Organization of the Book

Chapter 1 of *Cold War Negritude* pinpoints the First Congress of Black Writers and Artists as the event that crystallized the terms and fault lines of the literary debates traced in subsequent chapters. Diop and the editorial team of *Présence Africaine* organized the meeting under the sign of the 1955 Bandung Conference, emphasizing cultural solidarity of the *monde noir* as a non-aligned, decolonial alternative to the bipolar paradigm. I first trace how the Congress's framing around a capacious definition of culture made culture a screen for the Cold War ideological antagonisms. Within this overall setting of politicized cultural debate, I analyze the contestations of literary form at the Congress, showing how these functioned as the primary Cold War proxy battlefield at the event.

The second, third, and fourth chapters, focusing respectively on Depestre, Césaire, and Alexis, show three parallel trajectories charted between "Budapest and Suez"—that is, three different aesthetic projects that attempted to think the global Cold War together with decolonization. Chapter 2 analyzes René Depestre's 1950s writings through the lens of his alignment with global communism. Depestre's Cold War trajectory was extraordinarily peripatetic: at turns benefiting from his communist ties and at other times suffering for them, Depestre was kicked back and forth across the Cold War worlds more than once. I start by revisiting Depestre's much-discussed debate with Aimé Césaire over "national poetry." Departing from most criticism on the Césaire–Depestre debate, this chapter is framed with Depestre as protagonist. Through close readings of poems from *Minerai noir* (1956), I reconstruct the poetics that Depestre developed through engaging with Aragon's poetry: an aesthetic of class solidarity oriented towards broad political education of a popular audience in contrast to Negritude's avant-garde aesthetics and its vision of political belonging based upon racial solidarity.

Chapter 3 explores the impact of Aimé Césaire's 1956 split with the PCF upon his poetics. Although the "Lettre à Maurice Thorez" is rightly celebrated for its denunciation of Stalinism and its call to Third World progressives to "invent our own route," I argue that Césaire's poetry of this same period offers a significant melancholic counterpoint to the "Lettre à Maurice Thorez." This argument is premised on the claim that Césaire's split from communism was not only a new beginning, but also a loss, by which I mean both an occasion for mourning and the sign of a wider defeat of left aspirations. Césaire's poetry of this period, I argue, tries to think through this loss. The main object of analysis is *Ferrements* (1960), a collection of poems that Césaire wrote over the previous decade at the same time that he was reevaluating his PCF alignment. *Ferrements* tends to be viewed either as reflecting Césaire's disillusionment with radical politics or as a turn away from surrealism. I argue for viewing it instead as a locus of Césaire's rigorous political reflection in a time of ideological disorientation. I conclude that Césaire uses the tools of poetry to map the geopolitical structures and ideological currents of the global Cold War.

Chapter 4 focuses upon Jacques Stephen Alexis' socialist aesthetics. Unlike Depestre and Césaire, who lived to see the fall of communism, Alexis was killed in 1961 by the Duvalier dictatorship. Alexis' entire oeuvre, therefore, was published squarely within the period of "Budapest and Suez." Alexis remained aligned with what he saw as the best chance at emancipation for the majority of the world's population, and viewed literary aesthetics as a political choice between (socialist) realism and (liberal capitalist) modernism. Just as he aligned with communism as decolonizing peoples' best hope, Alexis chose realism, and worked creatively within the constraints of this choice. The chapter provides a systematic account of the socialist aesthetics that develop throughout his oeuvre—from his début novel *Compère Général Soleil* (1955) to *Romancéro aux étoiles* (1960)—as a series of iterative experiments aiming to produce a socialist realism with Haitian characteristics. Although Alexis broadly embraced socialist realist aesthetics, he understood it as prescribing an approach to writing rather than as dictating narrow formal parameters. I show that his experiments in Haitian socialist realism (what he called "marvelous realism") freely combined elements from Soviet, Maoist, and Western Marxist literary tendencies.

CHAPTER ONE

Black Bloc

Reading the First Congress Through a Cold War Lens

"Hanging in the air, as real as the heat from which we suffered, were the great spectres of America and Russia, of the battle going on between them for the domination of world."

(James Baldwin, "Princes and Powers"[1])

"Faisons notre Bandoeng littéraire!"

(Jacques Stephen Alexis[2])

The First Congress of Black Writers and Artists took place in Paris from September 19 to September 22, 1956 at the Sorbonne, the same site where, eight years earlier, Eleanor Roosevelt had announced the Universal Declaration of Human Rights. Organized by Alioune Diop, the Senegalese founder of *Présence Africaine*, the First Congress convened 63 intellectuals from across the black Atlantic, including Aimé Césaire, Léopold Sédar Senghor, Jacques Stephen Alexis, Richard Wright, and Frantz Fanon. In the opening ceremony, Diop announced the following mission: "to enunciate the whole and measure the wealth, crises, and promise of our culture and to offer it for the admiration of the world."[3] In this *mise-en-scène* of the *monde noir*, this ideologically

---

1   Baldwin, James. "Princes and Powers." *Encounter* (Jan. 1957), p. 59.
2   Alexis, Jacques Stephen. "Où va le roman?" *Présence Africaine*, No. 13 (Apr.–May 1957), p. 101.
3   "Discours d'ouverture." Ier *Congrès international des écrivains et artistes noirs (Paris–Sorbonne 19–22 septembre 1956): Compte rendu complet*, *Présence Africaine*, 8–9–10 (Jun.–Nov. 1956), p. 11.

and geographically diverse group of black intellectuals would be united in a collective defense and illustration of global black culture. Diop and his team staged the Congress with two goals in mind: first, to inscribe the *monde noir* into the postwar world map as a distinct bloc; second, to resituate the black person fully within the human, to claim the right of colonized black persons to the enjoyment of universal human rights—their right to have rights, in Hannah Arendt's phrase—despite the fact that many delegates were colonized subjects lacking meaningful political representation by nation-states.[4]

In a 2006 interview, delegate Édouard Glissant refers to the event as "the congress of a poetics … it is not yet the congress of a politics."[5] Glissant puts neatly how the First Congress is usually remembered: the inaugural event of a "black 'cultural renaissance,'"[6] a declaration of "cultural independence"[7] from colonial Europe, demanding that the (white European) world recognize black people as fully human.[8] Yet, as several scholars have noted, Diop and his co-organizers made no concrete political demands, constantly reiterating that cultural regeneration rather than political liberation was the task at hand; and, though the delegates opposed colonialism, most of them could not correctly be described as radical anticolonialists. While the Second Congress (Rome, 1959) is remembered as the more politically oriented gathering, Diop took care that the First Congress would remain centered on black writing, history, and cultural practices.

This chapter investigates the political underpinnings of this gathering that Diop insisted was not about politics. By looking closely at how Diop framed, presided over, and directed the Congress, I draw out its unspoken political project. I first situate the First Congress within the context of the global Cold War and the emergence of postwar human rights discourse, drawing out the competing ideological agendas subtending this foundational event for the *monde noir*. I then analyze the rhetorical and organizational strategies through which a symbolic

---

4 See Arendt, Hannah. *The Origins of Totalitarianism*. Boston, MA, Mariner Books, 1973, Ch. 9.

5 *Lumières noires*. 2006. Directed by Bon Swaim.

6 Jules-Rosette, Bennetta. *Black Paris: The African Writers' Landscape*. Urbana and Chicago, IL: University of Illinois Press, 1998, p. 57.

7 King, Richard H. *Race, Culture, and the Intellectuals*. Baltimore, MD: Johns Hopkins University Press, 2004. p. 236.

8 Fonkoua, Romuald-Blaise and Claxton, Mervyn. "Liminaire / Introduction." *Présence Africaine*, Nos 175/177 (2007), pp. 11–17.

unity was maintained despite political antagonisms among delegates, looking especially at the Congress's iconography. Finally, I examine how debates over literary form on the floor of the Congress became particularly fraught with Cold War political overdeterminations.

Ripples of the Gong Stroke: The First Congress and the Contested "Bandung Spirit"

In a 1998 interview, Malagasy poet and anticolonial dissident Jacques Rabemananjara remembered the First Congress, which he helped organize, in almost messianic terms:

> It was Alioune Diop, with his small and loyal team, who united these people from all over the world [...] We didn't have any money then. But we had faith. And how did these people from all over the world come here to debate these theses, which after all, resulted in some resolutions? I call that a great miracle—the First Congress."[9]

By this account, the "great miracle" of the First Congress was the very fact that it took place, the physical gathering of such a broad caucus of black intellectuals. It marked the first time that the imagined community called the *monde noir* constituted itself as such and manifested in flesh and bone. The Congress can be seen from this perspective as a sort of constituent assembly, the epiphanic moment when a collective body coheres into real existence by representing itself to itself.

In fact, although it is often described as miraculous and unprecedented, the First Congress was not the world's first international gathering of anticolonial black intellectuals. Several Pan-Africanist congresses had already taken place in the first half of the twentieth century, starting with the Pan-African Congress of London, organized by H. Sylvester Williams of Trinidad, in 1900.[10] Nor was the First Congress the first black congress in Paris: in 1919, W.E.B. Dubois had organized the First International Pan-African Congress there. A number of subsequent Pan-African Congresses followed thereafter, culminating in the Fifth Pan-African Congress in Manchester, England in 1945: here,

---

9   Jules-Rosette, *Black Paris*, p. 47.
10 Mouralis, Bernard. *Littérature et développement: essai sur le statut, la fonction et la représentation de la literature africaine d'expression française*. Paris: Agence de cooperation culturelle et technique, Silex, 1984, p. 388.

a politically organized Pan-African Federation, led by George Padmore of Trinidad and Kwame Nkrumah of Ghana, laid out a platform demanding political autonomy for Africa's "subject nations."[11]

The First Congress differs from the earlier Pan-African Congresses in several ways. First, there is the matter of colonial geography: the interwar Pan-Africanists mostly hailed from British territories, whereas the First Congress delegates were overwhelmingly francophone. Second, the Pan-African Congresses—whose delegates included trade unionists and militants as well as intellectuals—did not seem especially concerned with regenerating black culture per se. Instead, they made direct political claims and sought principally to organize cadres for political action.[12] The Pan-African Congresses were avowedly anticapitalist, though not Marxist-Leninist: the Manchester resolutions denounced capitalism along with imperialism, accepting the Marxist view of the latter as a mode of the former.[13] Whereas Manchester's "Declaration to the Colonial Powers" listed specific political demands, the First Congress's final resolution declares a more abstract wish for "various Negro cultures" to be "integrated into the general body of World culture."[14] Finally, the Manchester organizers regretted holding their meeting in a European metropolis rather than in Africa itself, deeming it an unfortunate logistical necessity. Diop, by contrast, made a deliberate symbolic statement by holding the Congress in Paris—and specifically at the Sorbonne—as a performative occupation of the capital city of the world republic of letters, a global black *prise de parole* inscribed in the center of Western high culture.

The 1948 Universal Declaration of Human Rights is another significant event in the genealogy of the First Congress. The UDHR declared a list of inalienable rights shared equally by all human persons; however,

---

11   Legum, Colin. *Pan-Africanism*. New York: Praeger, 1962, pp. 153–158.

12   Although the focus of the Pan-African Congresses was political, they nonetheless included literary figures and featured significant cultural components: the 1900 conference featured performances of the music of Afro-British composer Samuel Coleridge-Taylor (see Jaji, Tsitsi. *Africa in Stereo: Modernism, Music, and Pan-Africanism*. Oxford: Oxford University Press, 2014, Ch. 2) and the 1919 conference featured an influential art exhibition.

13   See Part III, Ch. 1 of Mouralis' *Littérature et développement* for a thorough and systematic treatment of the Pan-African congresses.

14   *Ier Congrès international des écrivains et artistes noirs: Paris, Sorbonne, 19–22 septembre 1956: compte-rendu complet*. Présence Africaine, 8–10 (Jun.–Sep. 1956), p. 364.

as these rights were unenforceable, the UDHR's legitimacy within the postwar global order came to depend upon what Joseph Slaughter calls "vicarious sociocultural modes of substantiation."[15] Colonized African and Caribbean delegates to the First Congress, lacking the power to claim political autonomy for their represented peoples, similarly had recourse to culture: the delegates hoped instead to constitute a black Atlantic public sphere (as I will develop below) through which black personhood would become recognizable as an instance of the modular global "human rights person" posited by the UDHR and broader postwar rights discourse.[16] The choice of the Sorbonne, where the UDHR had been declared, was a symbolic inscription of the *monde noir* into postwar human rights discourse.

However, it was the 1955 Afro-Asian Conference at Bandung, Indonesia that loomed largest by far in the minds of Diop and his co-organizers. Diop explicitly conceived of his cultural congress under the sign of Bandung, where leaders of 25 newly independent African and Asian nations proclaimed their mutual solidarity and their demand for a definitive end to colonialism. Neither the old European imperial powers nor the Cold War superpowers were invited: instead, Bandung established a network of direct South–South relations aimed at initiating a Copernican revolution in international politics, decentering the Euro-American global North on the world stage. In his opening address, Diop thus announces the First Congress as the "second event" of the postwar era, in Bandung's wake.

Bandung, I argue, was one of several *points de capiton*, or unifying master-signifiers, that Diop invoked to give symbolic coherence to the First Congress. There was consensus among delegates upon Bandung's status as event; African Catholics and Antillean communists alike saw it as completing Bandung's promise. At the same time, delegates held mutually incompatible understandings of what this promise entailed. Rabemananjara, for example, sees Bandung as a "gong stroke" announcing a new world order:

> The gong stroke of Bandung has sounded the spectacular end of a monologue lasting several centuries. [...] Only one note is lacking in the concert: the African note. When will the black continent develop in its turn, surrounding the major problems of our time, its own variations,

---

15 Slaughter, Joseph. *Human Rights Inc: The World Novel, Narrative Form, and International Law*. New York: Fordham University Press, 2007, p. 93.
16 Slaughter, *Human Rights*, p. 148.

its melodies of the terroir? On that day, the cycle will be closed and the orchestra complete.¹⁷

Léopold Sédar Senghor, a preeminent Negritude poet and cultural nationalist, saw Bandung as bearing primarily cultural, rather than directly political, significance:

> The Bandung spirit is the concern shown by Afro-Asiatic peoples to firm up—by affirming—their personality, so as not to come empty-handed to the "rendezvous of giving and receiving." [...] And how could one believe that the Bandung spirit that is, for us, primarily a cultural spirit, does not also blow upon the Indians, upon the Negroes of America?¹⁸

Rabemananjara and Senghor, both members of Diop's editorial team, view Bandung as having created the opening that made the First Congress possible. They implicitly conceive of Bandung—and the First Congress by extension—within an idealist Hegelian understanding of History as Spirit coming to understand itself and its relation to the world. Their metaphors of a global "concert" of nations and a "meeting-place" of universal exchange suggest an affinity with French Hegelian philosopher Alexandre Kojève's vision of history as the struggle to realize the human desire for recognition, and the end of history as the achievement of a state of universal mutual recognition.¹⁹ Bandung's "gong stroke" thus introduces a previously inaudible Afro-Asian note within the global harmony, or World Spirit.

Jacques Stephen Alexis had little patience for what he saw as Senghor's depoliticization of Bandung. While agreeing on Bandung's status as a world historical event and sharing the desire to harness the energy it had released, Alexis gives Bandung a more radical significance and takes a far more polemical tone:

> The world—as we have all said—is at a crossroads. It is Bandung, it is a bell that reverberates, that indicates not only that we want our cultures to appear as great and beautiful things but that indicates equally that

---

17 1er Congrès, pp. 21–22.
18 1er Congrès, p. 51.
19 See Kojève, Alexandre. *Introduction à la lecture de Hegel*. Paris: Gallimard, 1947. For a discussion of the influence of Hegelianism—especially the philosophy of Kojève—upon anticolonial Francophone intellectuals of the early- and mid-twentieth century, see Ch. 4 of Nesbitt, Nick: *History and Subjectivity in French Caribbean Literature*. Charlottesville and London: University of Virginia Press, 2003.

peoples want to come to life as constituted bodies [*organismes*]. And it is these constituted bodies [*organismes*] that will be the base of national cultures in formation. Outside this notion, all the declarations of love to culture can constitute nothing but verbal glosses that all do nothing but stifle the problem *(Prolonged applause)*.[20]

For Alexis, Bandung named a new spirit of fraternal solidarity among the world's oppressed peoples against imperial capitalist domination. It was not primarily a shared cultural personality that united these peoples, but a homologous position in the world order and thus a common struggle.

This contestation of the Bandung spirit during the first night's debate session is indicative of what I argue is the fundamental antagonism of the First Congress: the non-identity of the *monde noir* to itself, the ideological fissures between its constituent members that could not be overcome or symbolically integrated.[21] These divisions were compounded by the anticommunism of the US delegates, as well as the latter's hesitancy to identify the African-American situation as colonial. To maintain the cohesion of an ideological field so fraught with internal contradictions, Diop deemed it necessary to repress political antagonism as such: we may therefore read the First Congress' spectacle of a *monde noir* united through cultural affinity as a symbolic act, an "imaginary resolution of real social contradictions."[22]

Sailing on the Sea of the Unstated: Cultural Politics and Consensus Building at the First Congress

A second *point de capiton* symbolically quilting the First Congress together was its very subject: "black culture." Diop deliberately, repeatedly used "black culture" as a consensual term in his addresses, performatively unifying this collective body by addressing the delegates

---

20 I*er Congrès*, p. 71.
21 An ineradicable social antagonism that is constitutive of the social field as such, yet must be repressed in order for the social field to function. See Žižek, Slavoj. *The Sublime Object of Ideology*. New York: Verso, 1989, p. 177. Howlett and Fonkoua define this as division between an "ecumenical" and a "Marxist" universalism (Howlett, Marc-Vincent and Fonkoua, Romuald. "La maison Présence Africaine." *Gradhiva*, Vol. 10 (2009), p. 112).
22 Jameson, Frederic. *The Political Unconscious: Narrative as a Socially Symbolic Act*. Ithaca, NY: Cornell University Press, 1981, p. 77.

as an assembly of "hommes de culture noir." US delegate Mercer Cook, debating Césaire on the second night, protests that Diop had told him the Congress would be "purely cultural"; he asks the delegates whether, despite Diop's assurance, this was in fact merely a "pretext" for political discourse.[23] Like the signifier "Bandung," "black culture" meant something different to everyone in the assembly. James Baldwin, who covered the First Congress for *Encounter* (sponsored by the Congress of Cultural Freedom), writes of "the nearly indefinable complexities of the word 'culture'" as its underlying, unresolved ideological tension; Baldwin concludes that, "the declaration of *political* points of view being [...] prohibited," the Congress's debates over black culture were "in perpetual danger of drowning in the sea of the unstated."[24] However, as I argue, it was precisely this sea of the unstated that grounded Diop and the *PA* editors' consensual political project.

Although the cultural focus was a deft maneuver by Diop intended to keep the superpower struggle off the Congress floor, the Cold War nonetheless loomed over the event from early in its planning. Richard Wright, a friend of Diop, attempted to enlist the CIA-backed Congress for Cultural Freedom as a source of badly needed funding, and he and Diop agreed Wright would warn the US embassy that the Congress threatened to be overrun by communists; the CCF expressed interest in assuring that the Congress did not align with Communism.[25] It was

---

[23] *1er congrès*, p. 213. For a discussion of Mercer Cook's participation in the Congress, see Massé, Guirdex. "Cold War and Black Transnationalism: Aimé Césaire and Mercer Cook at the First International Congress of Black Writers and Artists." *Palimpsest: A Journal on Women, Gender, and the Black International*, Vol. 4, No. 2 (2015), pp. 115–134.

[24] Baldwin, "Princes and Powers," p. 59. Diop does not mention any specific political ideologies on the floor of the First Congress. At the Second Congress in 1959, however, he is more explicit: "Athées ou croyants, marxistes ou non, nous ne nous occuperons pas ici des querelles idéologiques ou confessionnelles qui divisent le monde [...] l'homme de culture [n'a] ni l'obligation de militer dans un parti politique, ni, dans le cadre de notre société [the Société Africaine de Culture], le droit d'entreprendre une propagande idéologique ou religieuse au service de son parti ou de sa religion... Nous sommes donc ici en dehors des querelles politiques qui divisent l'Occident ou nos propres pays." Diop, Alioune. "Le Sens de ce Congrès." *Deuxième Congrès des Ecrivains et Artistes Noirs (Rome: 26 mars–1er avril 1959)*, p. 46.

[25] See Dunstan, Sarah C. *Race, Rights, and Reform: Black Activism in the French Empire from World War I to the Cold War*. Cambridge: Cambridge University Press, 2021, pp. 242–246.

because of this overblown fear of the First Congress going communist that the US State Department denied a visa to W.E.B. DuBois, an invitee, for fear that his intervention would be too openly Marxist (a letter from DuBois was read in absentia). Diop's concern to sideline direct ideological exchanges at the Congress therefore indicates not only his ideological affiliation with postwar liberal internationalism, but also the same skill in taking advantage of Cold War superpower anxieties that Frantz Fanon would later note among the leaders of decolonizing Third World nations.

Jacques Howlett's 1958 article in *Présence Africaine* summarizing international press coverage of the First Congress reveals how the event looked entirely different from different global Cold War perspectives. A Rashomon effect emerges over the course of the article as Howlett demonstrates how each piece of reportage produced its own Congress.[26] The radical right-wing press recognized only a band of savages regurgitating the Marxism of Left Bank rabble-rousers (a *Rivarol* article was disdainfully titled "Le Nègre et le néant"). Moderate right-wing publications viewed the delegates as ingrates airing their ressentiment, viewing the Congress's tone of high intellectuality as proof of the civilizing mission's success. The liberal and non-communist left press came closest to echoing the organizers' vision: Trotskyist journal *Le IVe Internationale* acknowledged the political potential in regenerating Black culture; *France-Observateur* saw the welcome sign of a "black renaissance," and socialist journal *Demain* hailed the "Black cultural Bandung." Howlett notes a paternalist undertone in the qualified praise coming from PCF organs *L'Humanité* and *Les lettres françaises:* their "affirmation, he notes, is clearly also a "warning."[27] Refracted through the prism of the European press, the Congress was represented as either too militant or not militant enough, too political about culture or too cultural about politics, naively universalist or blinkered by particularism.

In addition to avoiding outside political attacks and reprisals, the

---

26 While Howlett groups the press reactions to the Congress according to ideology, he also distinguishes between the European and African presses. "Le Ier Congrès des écrivains et artistes noirs et la presse internationale." *Présence Africaine*, No. 20 (1958), pp. 111–116.

27 In the latter, Jean Marcenac (1913–84), a close friend of Aragon and assistant editor of *Les lettres françaises*, warns the delegates not to get mixed up in "obscure concepts" like Negritude that mythologize cultural difference at the expense of solidarity with *all* of capitalism's victims. Howlett, "Le Ier Congrès," pp. 112–113.

insistence upon culture also served as a screen for ideological antagonisms within the Congress itself. In his opening address, Diop defines culture in deliberately broad terms: "For culture is merely the vital effort by which race and each individual by their experience and aspirations, their work and reflections, reconstruct a world which is filled with life, thought, and passion, and seems to thirst more than ever for justice, love and peace."[28] It is difficult to disagree with this statement, no matter your political stance, precisely because it avoids saying what culture is not. Diop's definition is carefully worded to be capacious and generic, scrubbed clean of any partisan language; indeed, it appears to nod towards both materialists (experience, work, construction of a world) and liberal idealists (the individual, reflections), offering signifiers such as "justice, love, and peace" as vessels that Catholics and Marxists could fill in as they like. Though Baldwin notes the danger of drowning in it, Diop understood this "sea of the unstated" as the foundation upon which the *monde noir* must be constituted if it was to serve its symbolic purpose.

Framing the First Congress's agenda around a capacious definition of culture was thus how Diop established consensus amid political antagonism. Diop was, by many accounts, a gifted consensus-builder. He built the *Présence Africaine* editorial team as a diverse body: himself a Catholic, he brought together cultural nationalist Léopold Senghor, Marxists Aimé Césaire and René Depestre, pan-Africanist Cheikh Anta Diop, and dozens of other figures whom he welcomed at the *Présence Africaine* offices and in his home.[29] At the Congress, through stagecraft and statecraft, Diop leveraged his consensus-building talent and his considerable network to hold the First Congress together. René Depestre recounts a remarkable anecdote as an example of Diop's political acumen. Depestre was preparing to deliver a fiery speech condemning the Soviet Union and PCF, written while still reeling from Khrushchev's speech revealing Stalin's crimes. Diop persuaded Depestre not to give the speech, thus keeping Cold War politics off the Congress floor and avoiding the ideological fractiousness that would tarnish the image of a unified collectivity.[30] I would suggest that Diop's consensual

---

28 Ier Congrès, p. 6.
29 Howlett and Fonkoua, "La maison Présence Africaine," pp. 111–113. See also Verdin, Philippe. *Alioune Diop, le Socrate noir.* Paris: Lethellieux, 2010, p. 255.
30 As Depestre recounts it, Diop warned that his planned speech would "set fire to the powder," sabotaging the fragile consensus that was being built at the

political tactics at the Congress puts his own unspoken political position into relief: Diop becomes visible as the quintessential figure of liberal parliamentary politics: nonpartisan, pragmatist, the consummate parliamentarian able to work out compromise with both sides of the aisle.

Later in his address, Diop makes an ambiguous distinction between culture and politics:

> they are wrong who, in international events and notably in African problems, afford attention only to political action, to the politician. We gladly leave to the latter the stately silhouette with which he adorns himself in the global ruling bodies [...] behind the politician, the man of culture assumes functions no less important and of at least as profound a scope.[31]

This positioning of the man of culture behind the politician can be read in at least two ways. In one sense, it can be understood as suggesting that culture is prior to politics, inspiring political action while remaining a relatively autonomous sphere. It is more interesting, however, to read Diop as implying that culture must *stand in* for politics when direct political action is not (yet) possible. Lacking the "stately silhouette" of the *homme politique*, the colonized *homme de culture* must act as a surrogate, working within the cultural sphere to prepare the way for decolonization.

Diop's liberal politics of consensus is concretized in an iconic image of the First Congress, the portrait of the assembled delegates in the courtyard of the Sorbonne (Figure 1). As a visual representation of the collectivity the Congress was designed to performatively constitute, this image is hardly ideologically neutral. I would suggest, speculatively, that it is no coincidence that several delegates who were ideological adversaries are positioned side by side with one another in the photograph. Senghor and Alexis, who had been adversaries in the first night's debate, sit next to each other in the front row, while Césaire and Depestre, whose contentious exchanges over politics and poetry spanned several issues of *Présence Africaine* (see Chapter 2), stand together in the second row. I am suggesting that this group portrait

---

Congress; he further cautioned Depestre that the Americans would "throw [him] a party" if he used the floor of the Congress to spread anticommunist propaganda. Depestre instead wrote a poem, "Petite lampe sur la mer," that he dedicated "to my black brothers gathered at the Sorbonne." Depestre, René. "Alioune Diop, l'un des pères de la civilité démocratique mondiale." *Gradhiva*, Vol. 10 (Oct. 2009), p. 167.
31 *Ier Congrès*, p. 11.

be read as a *tableau vivant* staged to represent a collective body, a body politic, with ideological contradictions subsumed into the whole just as left and right constitute the poles of a single political field. We may take a moment to compare this *mise-en-scène* of global black unity to the *Spectacle féerique de Gorée*, staged ten years later at the First World Festival of Negro Art in Senegal. Whereas the *Spectacle féerique* would stage the *monde noir*'s historical trajectory through tableaux of key moments, from the beginning of the slave trade to independence, the delegate photo is a choreographed tableau of a single aspirational moment, projected into the near future, when black Atlantic nations would govern themselves.[32] The *Spectacle féerique*, organized diachronically, stages the *monde noir* as a subject in history; the Congress photo's symbolic effect is synchronic, creating an image of the *monde noir* as a collective, self-governing subject in all its internal diversity.

In the delegate portrait and in the special issue's many photographs of delegates debating, convening panels, and delivering speeches, the First Congress also becomes visible as the staging of a cosmopolitan black public sphere. So much the better if political disagreements were expressed within the structure of the Congress; such reasoned debates would only generate more discourse, thus strengthening this public sphere itself. Diop's political agenda is that of what Joseph Slaughter calls a "civicizing mission"; that is, he wants to instill cultural technologies of bourgeois liberal democracy into African nations to come by creating virtual spaces and organizations and by building networks by which such institutions are (re)produced.[33]

There is a fundamental ambiguity in the function of the public sphere as mediator between public and private, citizen and state, and this ambiguity is also present in the First Congress. As Slaughter argues, human rights discourse reifies the public sphere as the place where the individual enjoys and practices rights of speech and assembly and where individuals are protected from the state.[34] The obverse of this protective function, however, is that the public sphere disciplines speech while

---

32 For further discussion of the *Spectacle féerique de Gorée* at FESMAN, see Bush, Ruth. "Performances of the Past at the 1966 World Festival of Negro Arts." In Murphy ed., *The First World Festival of Negro Arts, Dakar 1966*. Liverpool: Liverpool University Press, 2016, pp. 97–112.
33 Slaughter, *Human Rights*, p. 83.
34 Slaughter, *Human Rights*, p. 151.

Figure 1 – Portrait of the delegates to the Premier Congrès des Ecrivains et Artistes Noirs. *Présence Africaine*, 8–10, Sep.–Nov. 1956. © Présence Africaine Éditions

enabling and protecting it: it is not a space of anarchic collective noise but a zone of "mutually regulated and regulatory speech" that establishes and enforces norms for who may speak, what one may say, and how.[35] *Présence Africaine*'s function as a forum for free exchange among black intellectuals corresponds closely to this understanding of the public sphere as an ambiguous mediating institution. This is especially true after the 1955 relaunch of the journal under its "nouvelle formule." In the preface to the inaugural issue of *Présence Africaine*'s new format, Diop describes the agenda of the relaunched journal in the following way: "Free tribune? Yes, but better, a team ... decided, in Europe, not to lose sight that there are circumstances where the singularities of the genius of each individual, particular beliefs [...] cede place to more pressing common alternatives. It is a question of forming a common front to inform Africans, help and encourage creators, denounce impostures."[36] This stated agenda places *Présence Africaine* squarely in the tradition of Enlightenment liberalism: Diop entreats contributors to work toward the goal of building a community in and through discourse, toward emancipation through the public use of reason. Whereas in Habermas' account the public sphere developed spontaneously through the proliferation and sedimentation of conversations in public spaces between private individuals, the *Présence Africaine* project was to build a black public sphere programmatically, by creating the virtual and physical meeting places and by facilitating the discourse that it is made of.[37] If the relaunched *Présence Africaine* served as the virtual space for this incipient black public sphere, the First Congress was its epiphanic moment.

Parliaments and Persons: Liberal Cultural Politics and Political Culture in the Iconography of the First Congress

Looking again at the group portrait (Figure 1), note the delegates' arrangement within the overall composition of the photograph. Sitting front row center in the *place d'honneur* is Haitian ethnologist Jean Price-Mars, whom Diop would introduce as the Congress's "unanimously

---

35 Slaughter, *Human Rights*, p. 153.
36 "Notre Nouvelle Formule." *Présence Africaine*, Nos 1–2 (Apr.–Jul. 1955), p. 7.
37 Diop's vision of the *monde noir* can thus be seen as one of the "sub- and supra-state public spheres in which communal identities are produced and reproduced." Slaughter, *Human Rights*, p. 159.

and spontaneously elected" president. I would suggest that the delegates are arranged according to an order of precedence that recalls portraits of political assemblies. Price-Mars occupies the symbolic position of head of state in the center, while Diop and his editorial team are seated with M. and Mme Price-Mars in the front row. If the latter are positioned as ceremonial figureheads of the Congress, Diop and company occupy the place of prime minister and cabinet, and the remaining delegates complete the portrait of the assembled representatives of the *monde noir*. This photograph represents a collective body, then, but one that is hierarchically organized into differentiated positions and roles—that is, not only a public sphere wherein individual members are imagined as equals. In short, the photo presents the assembly as a sort of black parliament.

Seated next to Price-Mars is his wife, Marie Rose Clara Perez, who stands out as the lone woman in the all-male assembly, a symbolic first lady. Perez's conspicuous dissimilarity to all other figures in the photo indicates the effective exclusion of women at this gathering of black men of culture. Although women were present in the audience, there was not one female delegate at the Congress, an absence criticized by Richard Wright in his speech.[38] Diop would have been familiar with the Nardal sisters, Suzanne Césaire, Mayotte Capécia, and many other *femmes de culture noires*, and his wife Christiane Yandé Diop—who would take over leadership of *Présence Africaine* after her husband's death—played a central role in the Congress's planning. Still, half the population of the *monde noir* remained literally unrepresented at the Congress.[39]

Diop's project consists not only in a liberal cultural politics, but also in rehearsing a liberal political culture. George Shepperson has distinguished between "capital-P" Pan-Africanism, a broad movement with "a single nucleus" such as DuBois or Padmore, and a diverse collection of "small p" pan-Africanisms where "the cultural element often predominates"—he gives Negritude as an example of the latter.[40] I argue that in the First Congress, "small-p" cultural pan-Africanism is combined

---

38 Ier Congrès, pp. 347–348.
39 Massé, Guirdex. "Cold War and Black Transnationalism: Aimé Césaire and Mercer Cook at the First International Congress of Black Writers and Artists." *Palimpsest: A Journal on Women, Gender, and the Black International*, Vol. 4, No. 2 (2015), pp. 115–134.
40 Shepperson, George. "Pan-Africanism and 'Pan-Africanism': Some Historical Notes." *Phylon*, Vol. 23, No. 4 (1962), p. 347.

with what Emily Apter has called, in a very different context, "politics small-p": parliamentary tactics and procedures; coalitions and factions; debates, speeches, and points of order; backroom deals and negotiations.[41] Indeed, reading through the First Congress proceedings, the frequent quibbles over parliamentary procedure and protocol are at times just as striking as the lofty rhetoric of the speeches: Richard Wright's point of order, for example, as to who may address the assembly during debate sessions,[42] Senghor's suggestion that speeches be strictly limited to 20 minutes ("it's a question of discipline," he states),[43] and the more severe suggestion by Horace Mann Bond that rowdy audience members be "disciplined, and disciplined severely."[44] This spectacle of parliamentary culture is another pillar in the *Présence Africaine* "civilizing mission," another clue to the politics behind the Congress's ostensible prioritizating of culture over politics.

Towards this end, Price-Mars was a particularly effective choice for president of the First Congress. Hailed throughout as a symbolic father of the *monde noir*, the author of *Ainsi parla l'oncle* (1928) was a paragon of institutional respectabliity: he had been Haiti's ambassador to the United Nations, a diplomatic chargé d'affaires in Washington, and foreign minister under President Dumarsis Estimé. Price-Mars performed the ceremonial role with appropriate decorum. He remained above partisanship, saying hardly anything with which anyone could disagree: Price-Mars insists in his opening address upon the irreducible uniqueness of black culture, while also reiterating the human rights axiom of universal equality: "Tous les hommes sont l'Homme," a translation of the Haitian Creole proverb "tout moun se moun" that can be understood in this context as a vernacular translation of United Nations universalism. Price-Mars was therefore chosen as president because of his eminence as an *homme de culture*: his scholarship on African cultural practices in Haiti and his institutional capital granted him the stature of an elder statesman, a symbol of this collective body that was, like the master-signifier "black culture," void of determinate political content but that broadly signified sovereignty.

There was another, more radical sense in which Price-Mars was

---

41 Apter, Emily. *Unexceptional Politics: On Obstruction, Impasse, and the Impolitic*. New York: Verso, 2018, pp. 21–36.
42 Ier Congrès, p. 67.
43 Ier Congrès, p. 207.
44 Ier Congrès, p. 208.

recognizable as a political leader. Alexis states during a debate session that he voted for Price-Mars "because, at a moment when the land of Dessalines was occupied once again by foreign forces, one voice was raised that said: 'On this land, there exists a culture, a *national* culture.'"[45] Haitian ethnologist Emmanuel C. Paul also hails President Price-Mars as the father of the indigenist school of ethnology, whose works "have contributed to a great extent to our national reawakening around the years 1919–1930, by consolidating the moral front against the yankee occupier."[46] Alexis and Paul claim Price-Mars not as embodiment of an ecumenical black culture (which Alexis rejects as an abstraction) or instituitional clout but as a figure of resistance to imperial domination—and against the hegemonic capitalist superpower, no less. Price-Mars was thus uniquely situated to embody both the respectable liberal head of state and, simultaneously, the radical national resistance leader.

If Price-Mars is figured as head of state, Diop positions himself as a sort of prime minister, laying out the following agenda for the Congress: "It is up to the writers and the artists to translate for the world the moral and artistic vitality of our compatriots, and at the same time to communicate to the latter the meaning and the flavor of foreign works or of global events."[47] The black man of culture's task is thus to render his people's particularities intelligible to a global public, and then to relate world-historical events back to his people in their idiom. Gayatri Spivak's conjugation of the English word "representation" into the dyad of proxy (*Vertretung*, speaking for) and portrait (*Darstellung*, speaking of) is useful here: Diop's black man of culture is fully a *representative*—like the political representative, he is tasked simultaneously with speaking for his people and speaking of them.[48] The *Présence Africaine* project of nation building through the building of civic culture is thus furthered by the rehearsal of a parliamentary political culture, a model for the state apparatuses of anticipated black Atlantic nations. Diop's Congress was thus not only the concretization of an imagined black public sphere: it was also a dress rehearsal for postcolonial self-governance.

The official First Congress poster (Figure 2) also figures centrally in *Présence Africaine*'s iconography. This image, however, emphasizes

---

45 Ier Congrès, p. 69.
46 Ier Congrès, p. 152.
47 Ier Congrès, p. 17.
48 Spivak, Gayatri Chakravorty. *Critique of Postcolonial Reason*. Cambridge, MA: Harvard University Press, 1999, pp. 256–266.

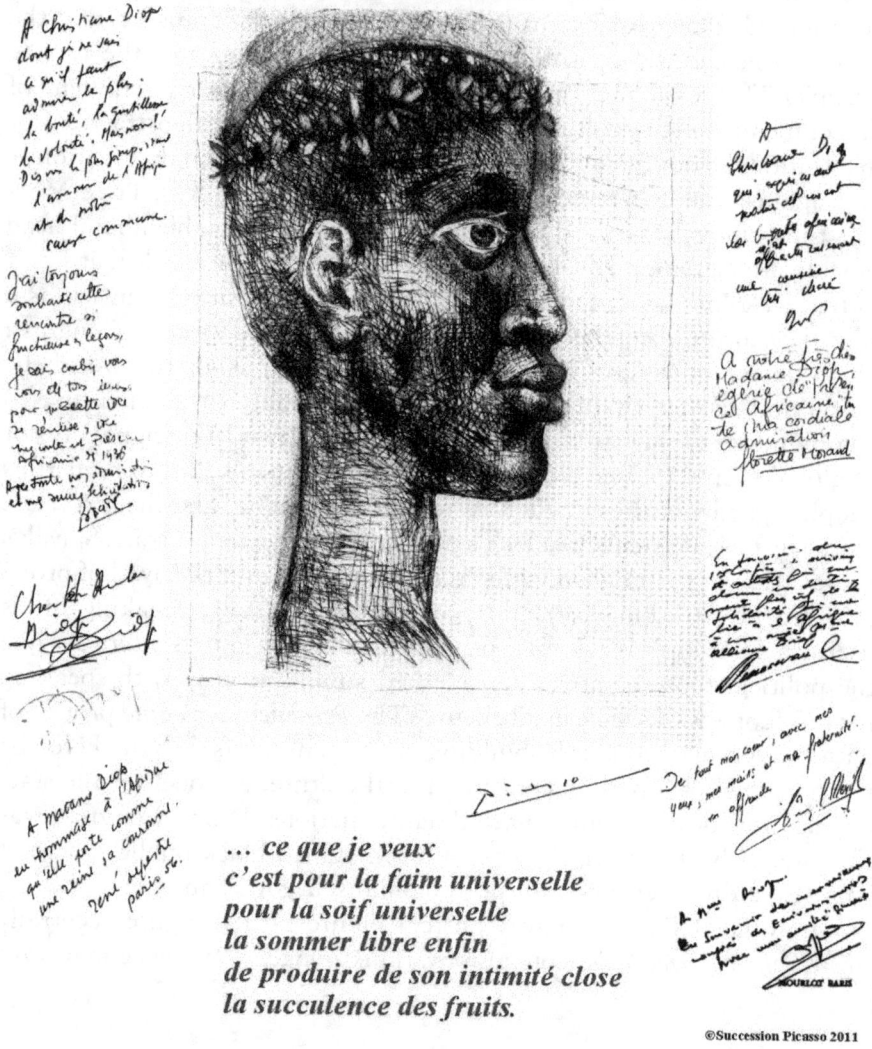

Figure 2 – Official poster for the Premier Congrès, with image by Pablo Picasso and text from Césaire's *Cahier*. © Présence Afraine Éditions

individual personhood rather than the body politic. The poster's central figure is a sketch by Pablo Picasso, entitled "Le poète couronné," of a black man in profile wreathed in laurels. The laurels immediately recall the figure of the *vates,* or poet-prophet whose song expresses the aspirations of his people; indeed, several delegates explicitly hailed Césaire as such a vatic figure in their speeches.[49] The crown of laurels also functions, however, as a symbol of sovereignty: in addition to conferring distinction upon him as a poet laureate, the crowning of this black poet also grants him the symbolic authority to speak as a fully autonomous person. We may even recognize in Picasso's sketch an allusion to the symbol of the UN itself, the map of the world, representing the totality of the human race, wreathed in olive branches.

Beneath Picasso's sketch is a quote from Aimé Césaire's *Cahier d'un retour au pays natal,* republished in its "definitive edition" in 1956 by *Présence Africaine* and invoked several times by other delegates (I will have more to say about this in the following section). The quote reads:

> ce que je veux
> c'est pour la faim universelle
> pour la soif universelle
> la sommer libre enfin
> de produire de son intimité close
> la succulence des fruits

It is as if Picasso's laureled black poet were speaking these lines himself, the *homme noir universel* (an alternate title for Picasso's sketch) given body and voice through this prosopopoetic pairing of image and text. The citation of this specific passage—as opposed to any number of more militant, even violent passages from the *Cahier*—makes the black subject speak in the liberal universalist idiom of human rights. The official poster of the First Congress thus provides the unified image of a black person, not so much endowed with an individual personality as partaking in a generic, universal personhood. The subject of the First Congress, as engendered by its official poster, is the purely abstract subject of formal rights.

Despite Diop's consensus-building efforts, there were some delegates who rejected the First Congress's rights-based frame, especially its solemn focus on recognition and respectability in lieu of a clear and forthright anticolonialism. The strongest internal critique of the liberal

---

49 Sartre also refers to Césaire as a *vates* in "Orphée noir" (p. xv).

humanist spectacle of the Congress came from Frantz Fanon. His speech, "Racism and Culture," performs a radical critique of the abstract universalism he sees in the Congress platform—that is, of its depoliticization of anticolonial sentiment in favor of a cosmopolitan discourse of rights, civility, recognition, and identity. Fanon's "non-compromising" speech referred primarily to structures of oppression used by the French in Algeria, although he did not utter this name.[50] In his peroration, Fanon lays out a path to universality that is quite different from the "concert of nations" envisioned by Rabemananjara: "The occupier no longer understands. The end of racism begins with this sudden incomprehension. The spasmodic and rigid culture of the occupier, liberated, finally opens itself to the culture of the people become actually fraternal. Universality resides in this decision to recognize the reciprocal relativism of different cultures, once the colonial status is irrevocably excluded."[51] Fanon's speech represents the radical limit of the Congress's symbolic unity, the frank militancy of his comments going well beyond the two poles of what we might call the Congress's mainstream political spectrum. As David Macey notes, Fanon's speech was met with an uncomfortable silence both in the press and on the floor of the Congress itself, effectively marginalizing his view.[52] Paulin Joachim, interviewed in Bob Swaim's documentary *Lumières noires* (2006), recalls Fanon's demeanor as "deranged" and "bloodthirsty." The violent struggle that was prerequisite, in Fanon's view, to any later flourishing of disalienated culture was the troubling Real about which the Congress could not speak.

Both Alexis and Fanon's critiques of the hegemonic discourse at the Congress about rights, culture, and belonging identify a number of political limits to the First Congress's cultural–political paradigm. Above all, they anticipate Samuel Moyn's trenchant criticism of the ideology of human rights as a depoliticized, ultimately conservative "substitute" for "a collective entitlement to self-determination."[53] We shall see that Depestre, Césaire, and Alexis' egalitarian political imaginaries go beyond such abstract claims about formal rights and inclusion within a generic human personhood. However, the very fact

---

50 Macey, David. *Frantz Fanon: A Life*. New York: Picador, 2001, pp. 286–287.
51 *Ier Congrès*, p. 161.
52 Macey, *Fanon*, p. 289.
53 Moyn, Samuel. *The Last Utopia: Human Rights in History*. Cambridge: Belknap Press, 2010, p. 45.

of Fanon and Alexis' presence and participation in the First Congress suggests that Diop's liberal project nonetheless held political potential that radicals sought to harness and fight out from inside rather than critique from the outside.

Formal Debate: Literary Form and Cold War Antagonisms at the First Congress

This section considers literary form as a proxy battlefield at the First Congress. Having established that the Congress's repressed political antagonisms were displaced onto cultural debates, I argue here that literary form was the principle site of this displacement. Seeking recognition of the *monde noir* on the world stage was a question not only of geopolitics but also of literary aesthetic concerns like figuration, fabulation, genre, mode, register, and focalization. How should the *monde noir* be made recognizable, and for whom—in whose name, and to whose benefit?

Since Aristotle, literary form has been theorized as a hierarchical system of distinction between subjects and voices: the hero of tragedy is noble, while the protagonist of the *Bildungsroman* is the young bourgeois professional. At the First Congress, debates around literary form were similarly a question of distinction and placement. As Romuald Fonkoua notes, the primary question that the First Congress posed was that of "the place of the Black person [*Nègre*] in the history of humanity."[54] In Rancierean terms: should black intellectuals claim a determinate place within the global distribution of the sensible, or was the point to contest this distribution itself?

In this section, I analyze several speeches and debates at the Congress about literary form. When delegates debated forms of literary expression, they were also simultaneously—explicitly or implicitly—debating political alignments and forms of political organization. Roughly following the Congress's program, this section will first analyze speeches and debates having to do with black poetry: as we shall see, delegates with different ideological coordinates ascribed vastly different political meanings to black poetry. I then move on to consider discussions regarding prose, arguing that Diop and his team organized the event to tell a particular narrative of development of the *monde noir*.

---

54 Fonkoua, "La maison *Présence Africaine*," p. 116.

Poetry was the most widely recognized form of black literary expression at the Congress, among delegates and observers alike. Césaire's *Cahier* was overwhelmingly the most cited and mentioned work; excerpted on the poster and quoted by delegates of varying ideological coordinates, the *Cahier* became the shared foundational text of the *monde noir*. In the words of Paulin Joachim: "the *Cahier*, it was our Bible."[55] Not coincidentally, 1956 was the year that a revised, "definitive" edition of the *Cahier* was published by *Présence Africaine*, thus solidifying the official status of the text as keystone of the *monde noir*'s literary canon. Such reverential invocations of the *Cahier* conform to Diop's politico-cultural agenda as he explains it in his opening speech: "The classics of a people have the need to be renewed and thus rethought, reinterpreted in each generation. It must be thus with our classics."[56]

Several delegates argued that poetry was the most culturally authentic form of literary expression for black writers. Baldwin's reaction to the speech of Nigerian poet E.L Lasebikan on "The Tonal Structure of Yoruba Poetry" exemplifies this tendency. Lasebikan's speech blended performances of poems in the Yoruba language, accompanied by drums, with analysis of their prosody. Baldwin notes being particularly moved by this performance, though the formal analysis was lost on him: "I doubt that I learned much about the tonal structure of Youriba [sic] poetry," Baldwin writes, although he did retain a strong impression of "the sensibility which had produced it," the "style of life" that the poetry evoked, the "peaceful, rhythmic domesticity" of the poem about the "pounding of yams."[57] Poetry is portrayed as ideally suited to broadcasting lived experience, communicating the rhythms and tonalities of being: the expository portion of Lasebikan's speech was significant only as pretext for the poetry to be performed, and was quickly forgotten anyway. For Baldwin, Lasebikan's Yoruba poetry contained a capacity to cut across linguistic and cultural divides, to make itself understood in a way that his analytic prose (in English) could not.

Martinican writer Gilbert Gratiant, in his contribution entitled "La Place du 'créole' dans l'expression antillaise," adds another dimension to the Congress debate over black poetry in arguing that Martinican Créole is a language of living poetry compared to abstract, prosaic French. Créole

---

55 *Lumières noires* (2006).
56 *Ier Congrès*, p. 16.
57 Baldwin, "Princes and Powers," p. 54.

communicates "a remarkably alive idea of attitude, sentiments, gestures, movements."[58] Acknowledging Créole's relative "poverty in vocabulary," he insists nonetheless that "French has its domain, and Creole has its own," associating Créole with the popular classes and spontaneity, and the French language with empirical description, functionality, and reasoned discourse: "Creole is therefore an instrument of easy liberation in our Antilles, a reserve of poetry, a vehicle of the popular humor."[59]

Léopold Sédar Senghor's intervention offered one of the the most systematic and developed treatises on black poetry at the Congress. In his speech "L'esprit de la civilization ou les lois de la culture négro-africaine," he seeks to define the singular genius of the *nègre*, different from and complementary to Western rationalism and scientific thought. This genius is, he argues, essentially a *poetic* one. He delivers this treatise on the *nègre*'s poetic nature in high academic prose, however—Senghor deploys the philosophical language of phenomenology in his account of Black culture, which he calls a "physiopsychologie du nègre."[60] In a word, Senghor posits that the *nègre* is primarily a sensorium: he is "firstly sounds, odors, rhythms, forms and colors ... He feels more than he sees."[61] Senghor insists that he is not arguing—as Gobineau and other nineteenth-century race scientists did—that "sensual" Black people are therefore devoid of reason. Rather, for him, black sensibility is a different mode of consciousness: intuitive and participatory where white reason is analytic, concrete and embodied compared to white reason's abstraction, vital where white thought is instrumental.[62] Literature and art are everywhere in the *nègre*'s lifeworld, not restricted to theaters or museums as in Europe but integrated into daily social life. All forms of black African literary expression, furthermore, are essentially poetic according to Senghor: from the work song to the Griot's teachings, poetry binds the *nègre* to his community, and to nature.

As I have been implying, the above discussions of black poetry all share—in effect, if not explicitly—an essentially Heideggerian understanding of

---

58 Gratiant, Gilbert. "La place du 'créole' dans l'expression antillaise." *Présence Africaine*, Nouvelle série, Nos 14–15, *Contributions au Ier Congrès des Écrivains et Artistes Noirs* (Jun.–Sep. 1957), p. 253.
59 "La place du 'créole,'" p. 253.
60 Ier Congrès, p. 52.
61 Ier Congrès, p. 52.
62 For a discussion of Negritude and philosophical vitalism, see Jones, Donna V. *The Racial Discourses of Life Philosophy: Negritude, Vitalism, and Modernity*. New York: Columbia University Press, 2010.

poetry.[63] Baldwin's reaction to Lasebekan's incantations of Yoruba poetry emphasizes a quality evoked by poetic expression that is close to Martin Heidegger's notion of the "manifestness of Being" in poetry, a concept that Roxanna Curto ties convincingly to Senghorian Negritude.[64] Senghor's Heideggerianism is evident in his speech, borrowing significantly from Heidegger's notion of poetry as a "primitive" antidote to the anomie of modern technological life.[65] This quasi-Heideggerian view of poetry was one distinct tendency in the literary debates at the Congress. It was not a view that went unchallenged.

During the first evening's debate session, Jacques Stephen Alexis challenged Senghor's "laws of Negro-African civilization" as idealist mystification, offering his own materialist account of Black cultural production:

> if we are talking, in one measure or another, about making culture into a vague fact, a fact that would be purely spiritual, that would not be tied to history [or] to life, it seems to me that this is committing a crime against these peoples who are suffering and are fighting to arrive at their individuality [...] We must therefore pose the problems of culture in function of national independence—in function of the formation of nations. (Prolonged applause.)[66]

Alexis argues that any demand for recognition for the *monde noir* should be understood in explicitly political and agonistic terms, not in taxonomic civilizational terms. If Senghor's version of black African civilization is centered on a vitalist reflection upon black life, Alexis critiques Senghor's prescriptions precisely because they lack a concrete engagement with the struggles of real black people living in determinate social relations. What could Senghor's mystical poetry have to say to the black South Africans being worked to death in the diamond mines, whose lived experience is closer to Zola's *Germinal*?[67] While Senghor promotes a poetry of Being that brings communities into closer proximity, Alexis counters by promoting the realist novel as a truer and more politically efficacious mode of writing, arguing that literature's function is to map structural relations of power.

---

63 See Heidegger, Martin, *Poetry, Language, Thought*.
64 Quoted in Curto, Roxanna. *Inter-Tech(s): Colonialism and the Question of Technology in Francophone Literature*. Charlottesville: University of Virginia Press, 2016, p. 69.
65 Curto, *Inter-Tech(s)*, p. 71.
66 Ier *Congrès*, p. 70.
67 Ier *Congrès*, p. 70.

In a rhetorically shrewd rebuttal, Senghor engages Alexis on the topic of literary form and politics. He begins with a (possibly apocryphal) anecdote: "I saw in the course of an electoral campaign, an orator just having finished a very nice speech about the constitution; he collected only meager applause. A poet coming up, on the same subject, singing and commenting on his song, made people cry. He got through to them!"[68] Senghor builds upon this parable by explaining that the people will not understand political prescriptions, whatever their content, if they do not employ a rhetoric of *pathos* in the correct idiom: "if the works that discuss this didn't respond to the black African aesthetic, they couldn't be tasted."[69] In a surprising gambit, Senghor deploys Marxist discourse against Alexis:

> I'm going to give you an example that's significant in this matter: the example of Mao Zedong. Read his *Speech to the Writers*. Mao Zedong tells us that one has to write for the people. We agree. I demonstrated to you that in Africa literature was made *by* everyone and *for* everyone. Mao Zedong says then that you have to write, you have to speak *to* the people about the preoccupations *of the people*. Only, he tells you that you have to stylize—that, precisely, if you don't stylize, you can't please the people. Mao Zedong tells us that you have to stylize by relying on national tradition—as it happens, in that which concerns us, on black art and black culture.
>
> But why? If, tomorrow, you speak to the people about very current problems, about the strike, the struggle against colonialism, etc., etc., if you employ a haughty style, you won't touch the people.[70]

There is considerable irony in Senghor's rebuttal, which was not lost on Alexis. In fact, as we will see in Chapter 4, Alexis devotes much of his novel *Les arbres musiciens* to exactly this question of modernism's ostensible connection to the people—his protagonist Carles Osmin, a Haitian *poète maudit*, tries and fails to achieve the connection that Senghor is describing. Senghor, however, turns Mao's argument about the intellectual's revolutionary vocation on its head. In the *Talks at the Yenan Forum on Literature and Art* (1942)—a text that influenced Alexis, as will also be discussed in Chapter 4—Mao calls for intellectuals to "go among the masses," to immerse themselves in the culture of the peasantry, to listen to the people to find the adequate language for giving

---

68   *Ier Congrès*, p. 71.
69   *Ier Congrès*, p. 71.
70   *Ier Congrès*, p. 71. Emphasis in original.

voice to their struggle. It is this element of aligning oneself with the people, of becoming their instrument—what Depestre, as we will see in the next chapter, calls the people's "handyman"—that Senghor occludes in his invocation of Mao: instead, he uses Mao to make a claim about securing and reproducing the people's consent to be governed by the one who speaks to and for them. The poet-*homme de culture* slips into the figure of the poet-statesman.

Alexis' riposte to Senghor's cultural nationalism is one of resolute universalism. It is also defiantly opposed to cultural politics defined in racialized or (synonymously, for Alexis) civilizational terms. At this point, Alexis drops the pretense of literary debate entirely:

> In our epoch, there is something called the new humanism, that is just as much from the West as it is from Asia. Precisely, it's the product of a sorting [*un tri*], of a conscious choice of all men of culture, of all the nations of the earth, as to what will be this human culture to come, because the humanity that lives on this little planet called "Earth," at one moment or another in its evolution, will be brought towards having a common culture, because it will have, at that moment, common conditions of existence.[71]

Several aspects of Alexis' rebuttal are worthy of note here. First is the concept of culture as *tri* (Depestre uses this same vocabulary in response to Césaire, as we will see in the next chapter). The "new humanism" that Alexis envisions is neither Western nor black nor Asian, but a transversal selection of progressive cultural expressions cutting across these reified taxonomic groups. To borrow from Timothy Brennan, Alexis counters Senghor's model of a "culture of being" with that of a "culture of belief,"[72] viewing culture as the product of intentional human behavior, or production, rather than the natural expression of an essence. Stressing that people have a choice in the forms of culture that they wish to produce—just as they may choose how production is organized in the broader political economy—Alexis envisions culture as dynamic, not identical to itself but always being (re)produced In response to Senghor's

---

71 *Ier Congrès*, p. 76.

72 Brennan's broader argument that contemporary theory is unduly centered on the "politics of being," whereas "the problem is that belief, too, although arguably chosen rather than inherited, confers on its holders a *culture*." Brennan argues, not unlike Alexis, that liberal formulations of cultural politics have led to prejudices against "left belief cultures" and the "censoring [of] an earlier and still viable Left." *Wars of Position*, pp. xi–xii.

admonition that we "must take a cultural inventory," Alexis replies that "we must take the inventory of our people and our nations, *in formation*."[73] Culture is production for Alexis, in a way that it is not for Senghor.

Overall, this debate between Senghor and Alexis demonstrates with particular clarity how literary aesthetics were ascribed implicit political logics at the Congress, ideas about literary composition formulated and understood as interventions in an ideological contest. These politico-aesthetic associations were less often flatly declared than ascribed to political adversaries: Alexis viewed Senghor's modernism as false populism and reactionary mystification, while Senghor viewed Alexis' realism as clunky dogma that, for all its professed radicalism, was too scholastic and generic to connect to those it sought to move. As we shall see below, Diop also took part in this Cold War politicization of literary aesthetics, though less polemically than Senghor and Alexis. Diop's preferred literary aesthetic is visible in practice, in the very structure of the Congress itself.

Plotting the *Monde Noir*: The First Congress as *Bildungsroman*

In his opening speech, "Europe et nous," Jacques Rabemananjara posits two different ways of giving an account of black culture, using two texts by Aimé Césaire to illustrate this point. First, Rabemananjara notes that Europe has long recognized and even admired black "lyricism." This conforms perfectly to the white supremacist's invented image of the black race, he argues, and such recognition of the lyrical in black culture costs Europe nothing at all: "No contestation if it's only a matter of putting us on the charts as artists, poets, dancers, athletes, boxers."[74] Dubbing Césaire the "*aoidos* of Negritude," Rabemananjara cites a passage from the *Cahier*—the first of many delegates to do so—that positively revalues the stereotype of black people as a historical nullity:

> Eia pour ceux qui n'ont jamais rien inventé
> pour ceux qui n'ont jamais rien exploré
> pour ceux qui n'ont jamais rien dompté
> mais ils s'abandonnent, saisis à l'essence de toute chose.[75]

---

73   *Ier Congrès*, p. 76.
74   *Ier Congrès*, p. 25.
75   Quoted in *Ier Congrès*, p. 25.

Colonial Europe cannot get enough of such images of black people, Rabemananjara argues; it "regrets having only ten fingers to clap with."[76] Europe recognizes in this figure the very image that it itself has confected as the Other of Western reason, a figure of the child-like authenticity that the West left behind when it got civilized. Rabemananjara argues that these lines express the colonial stereotype of "the attitude of the black person before nature" and "situate so well the only place," in colonial Europe's eyes, "to which he should aspire in the human hierarchy."[77] Though he recognizes black poetry's value, Rabemananjara suggests that it cannot be the final word on black culture.

Rabemananjara claims that black intellectuals must now speak and write in a different register. He counters the figure of poetic blackness with another Césaire quote, this time from the *Discours sur le colonialisme*, that enumerates a long list of black African civilizations that Europe has refused to recognize and concludes that the "idea of the barbarian is a European invention."[78] The erudite, critical, and polemical tone of this "same Césaire," he argues, is far more unsettling to white European audiences because it contests the place that Europe has assigned to the *nègre* within the hierarchical racial distribution of talents and forms. Rabemananjara thus constructs Césaire's expository writing—and by extension, critical and theoretical discourse by black writers—as a more mature stage in the development of black consciousness. He is particularly emphatic about the urgency of generating discourse at the Congress: "Mesdames et messieurs, causons!" is Rabemananjara's closing exhortation.[79]

Rabemananjara also makes a sharp critique of the colonial ideology implicit in discourse about European culture. He frames the Congress and the speech community it inaugurates as an ideological apparatus that would further a black civic culture as an antidote against the European *mission civilisatrice*. "The inventors/contrivers [*inventeurs*] know how to use the voice of Mars as well as that of the siren," he states, developing this metaphor into a lexical field of duplicity and two-facedness: Janus, the Gorgon masked as Venus, the stone hidden by the lily. Rabemananjara is not simply saying that Europe's sirenic, Venusian face—its cultural superstructure—is a false one; he is making

---

76 *Ier Congrès*, p. 25.
77 *Ier Congrès*, p. 25.
78 *Ier Congrès*, p. 26.
79 *Ier Congrès*, p. 27.

the finer point that Europe reproduces its domination of the colonized world both through direct repression and through ideology. His speech explicitly frames the Congress's project as fighting the anticolonial struggle on the level of ideology, and, in his glossing of the two Césaire quotes, implicitly suggests that in the present context the expository is the more useful weapon in this struggle than the lyrical "arme miraculeuse."

Rabemananjara's association of prose with development, I would argue, is echoed both in Diop's speeches on the stakes of the Congress and in his organizational scheme. The official agenda for the Congress, though leaving ample room for different kinds of interventions from the delegates, in effect imposed a set of generic conventions upon the event, guiding both Congress spectators and readers of the Congress proceedings towards reading the event in a specific way. Each day was organized around a specific temporal theme: on the first day, a cultural inventory of black African cultural forms throughout history; the second day was devoted to the "current crisis" of black culture; and the final day was to address prospects for the future development of black culture. Overall, the Congress tells an almost Whiggish narrative of the progressive trajectory of black culture, from past benightedness to present liberation to future modernization and development.

The order in which the delegates spoke also indicates the narrative logic of the Congress's organizational scheme. On the first day, devoted to the "cultural inventory" of the *monde noir* (that is, its past), poetry is the recurrent theme. Rabemananjara spoke first after Diop's opening comments—as we have seen above, Rabemananjara's speech argues that it is time to move on from lyrical poetic expression to reasoned political discourse, from the *Cahier* to the *Discours*. Following Rabemananjara were Paul Hazoumé, who spoke on Dahomeyan devotional poetry; Lasebekan's discourse on Yoruba poetry; and Senghor's speech claiming a "poetic" cultural essence across the *longue durée* of black African culture. The day devoted to what came *before* the present moment, therefore, was devoted to discussing poetry, and framed by a speech that located such poetic expression in the *monde noir*'s past.

Poetry was hardly discussed on the second day. Davidson Nicol's report on Anglophone West African literature, "The Soft Pink Palms," notes with relish the modern innovations in African literary production of the preceding decade. He singles out Nigerian novelist Amos Tutuola for praise—the latter "is to be congratulated" for having "certainly put West Africa on the map of the literary world" when, only ten years earlier, "it was doubtful whether any novel by a West African had been published."[80] Nicol's survey quickly glosses over traditional West African poetry—"there is much poetry and song in the local languages. These will [...] reach only those who know the language"—and goes on to discuss efforts to produce modern translations into English of Yoruba-language poetry. The second day's final speech is Césaire's soaring "Culture et Colonisation," wherein Césaire makes his famous call to linerate the "demiurge" who will organize the "chaos" of colonized culture into a "new synthesis," with Césaire crying out, "Let black peoples enter the great stage of history!"[81]

By the third day, devoted to the *monde noir*'s future, poetry had all but disappeared. Besides Alexis' "Du réalisme merveilleux des Haitiens" and George Lamming's "The Negro Writer and his World," most speeches focus on the social sciences: Cedric Dover's "Culture and Creativity," A. Wade's "L'Afrique doit-elle élaborer un droit positif?," and James Ivy's "The NAACP as an Instrument of Social Change." The final speech, "Tradition and Industrialization," given by Richard Wright, considers the conditions under which decolonizing peoples of the Third World might modernize their societies. Wright's argument is that colonial elites must be given "carte blanche" to modernize their nations rapidly: "an irrational Western world helped, unconsciously and unintentionally, to smash the irrational ties of religion and custom and tradition in Asia and Africa! THIS, IN MY OPINION, IS THE CENTRAL HISTORIC FACT!"[82] Though one can imagine that this specific point of Wright's may not have been universally accepted, it is continuous with the main thread of the final day's speeches in situating the traditions catalogued on the first day definitively in the pre-modern past.

The First Congress's official program, I would argue, thus has a clear plot. It is a narrative, framed by Diop and collectively performed by the delegates, of the development of black personhood. We get a strong hint that Diop conceived of the Congress as such a narrative in his preface to the second volume of Congress proceedings. Here, Diop discusses the significance of the First Congress precisely in terms of cultural development. There is room in Diop's master signifier of "culture" for technical development: "technique, when it is taken on

---

80 Ier Congrès, pp. 112–113.
81 Ier Congrès, p. 205.
82 Ier Congrès, p. 354.

[*assumée*] and thought by a people, becomes an element of its culture."[83] Diop notes that, at this moment in history when the superpowers compete over technology of all sorts while Europe is overhauling its educational programs to produce more engineers, "the people who are the most disinherited (but the richest in raw materials) *would be misguided to content themselves with poetry and dance, with music and metaphysics.*"[84] What the *monde noir* needs is not more poetry, he suggests, but rather the technical knowledge needed to initiate the people of the *monde noir* into modern life. The *monde noir* cultural traditions that Diop seeks to consecrate are framed, from the moment of this inaugural event, as *past* traditions, a shared canon conferring symbolic capital upon the nation-building development projects that Diop envisions.

Implicitly, therefore, Diop structures the First Congress as a novel of development: specifically, it is structurally and thematically figured as a *Bildungsroman*. Slaughter explains that the *Bildungsroman* was the literary form *par excellence* of the postwar era, bound up with the liberal discourses of human rights and national development that were codified in this period.[85] Just as the conventional *Bildungsroman* traces a young protagonist's trajectory from a state of innocence to rebellion against social norms towards final integration into normative social institutions, the overall narrative of universal human rights and development has to do with the trajectory of newly born nations towards political self-determination, social and cultural modernity, and economic self-sufficiency.

This connection between the First Congress and the liberal human rights ideology of *Bildung* runs even deeper. Slaughter ascribes a "convoluted teleological–tautological plot logic"[86] to the *Bildungsroman*, the first-person narrator narrating her coming-of-age from a point in time when she has already come of age—that is, when she has gone through the process of disalienation and integration. He argues furthermore that this temporal logic and that of the postwar human rights

---

83 "Nos tâches." *Contributions au Ier Congrès*, p. 3.
84 "Nos tâches." *Contributions au Ier Congrès*, p. 5, emphasis mine.
85 The UN's official "Development Decade" was not inaugurated until January 1961. However, as Diop's preface exemplifies, "development" was by 1956 already a keyword among intellectuals looking forward to decolonization and towards improved material conditions.
86 Slaughter, *Human Rights*, p. 215.

regime are one and the same: "the conventional form of first-person, retrospective *Bildungsromane* closely approximates the tautological form and hypothetical (or aspirational) character of human rights law, which pretends to legislate for tautological (self-same and sovereign) subjects in the hope of realizing such human rights subjects."[87] I would argue that there is a similar "tautological–teleological" temporality at work in Diop's discussion of the *monde noir*'s independence: in one paragraph of his preface to the Congress proceedings, he writes that "the national independence stage of our people is far from having been crossed"; in the very next paragraph, however, he states to the contrary that "this independence stage we can also say that it has already been passed, in the sense that it is inevitable."[88] We see here the same tautology–teleology that Slaughter associates with the *Bildungsroman* and with human rights law: Diop filters the *monde noir*'s trajectory of independence and modernization through the narrative trajectory of the *Bildungsroman*, orienting the delegates towards a moment in the future when modernized and independent African nations will be able to represent and govern themselves, and behaving, in the meantime, as if this has already been achieved.

Conclusion

There are limits to the cultural politics implicit in the First Congress's organization and staging, many of which were articulated by various critics on the floor of the Congress itself. Despite Diop's maneuvers to keep radical delegates inside the tent, critiques by Fanon and Alexis elaborate the dangers of "precipitous revalorization"[89] of culture and of its mystification as "vague" and "purely spiritual."[90] It is tempting to label Diop a precocious postcolonialist in his prioritization of cultural politics and in the privilege he accords to elite cultural cadres to represent (speak of and speak for) colonized peoples.

I am not convinced, however, that the First Congress falls into the same "disastrous confusion of spheres" that philosopher Peter Hallward

---

87 Slaughter, *Human Rights*, p. 215.
88 Diop, *Contributions au Ier Congrès*, p. 5.
89 *Ier Congrès*, p. 130.
90 *Ier Congrès*, p. 70.

diagnoses as the great failure of postcolonial theory.[91] The First Congress reminds us, first of all, that there is power in the principle of the united front. In the First Congress and the Société Africaine de Culture that arose from it, Diop managed to build and hold together a coalition of anticolonial black intellectuals; though they may have agreed on little else, these intellectuals could physically stand together against the common adversary of European colonialism at a moment when it seemed possible to defeat it. The First Congress is also radical—perhaps despite Diop's own intentions—in that, in its performance, it throws the limits of liberal human rights discourse into relief. The *monde noir* constituted by the First Congress was, after all, comprised precisely of those human communities that, in the postwar era as in today's era of neoliberal globalization, had no voice within the global order and no share of the global distribution.

A quiet consensus-builder and backroom negotiator rather than a fiery orator or militant theorist, Alioune Diop nonetheless emerges as a singular agent of decolonization through his planning, organization, and management of the First Congress. In organizing the First Congress, Diop and his editorial team set up a stage upon which colonized black subjects from Africa and the Caribbean acted nonetheless *as if* they were fully integrated members of a truly cosmopolitan and inclusive public sphere, *as if* they fully enjoyed the human rights that the colonial republics proudly declared to be universal but denied to them in fact. In this sense, the First Congress stages what Jacques Rancière calls dissensus, a performance creating a sensible manifestation of the gap between law and fact.[92] This international gathering of black global citizens—most of whom in fact had no nation and did not in fact enjoy the rights of citizenship—made visible that these colonized black subjects "have not the rights that they have, and have the rights that they have not."[93]

The cultural politics of the First Congress is ultimately not a sterile pseudo-politics; it is, rather, a practical and constructive program of building civil practices and institutions, with the express purpose of organizing apparatuses and networks that could be used in the process

---

91 Hallward, Peter. *Absolutely Postcolonial: Writing Between the Singular and the Specific*. New York: Palgrave, 2001, p. xix.
92 Rancière, Jacques. "Who Is the Subject of the Rights of Man?" *The South Atlantic Quarterly*, Vol. 103, Nos 2–3 (2004), p. 301.
93 Rancière, "Who Is the Subject of the Rights of Man?," p. 302.

decolonization. It is a high liberal cultural politics that, despite its limitations, is centrally concerned with experimentation and creation: of institutions, of networks and virtual spaces, of discourses and spheres, and ultimately of free nations.

CHAPTER TWO

Comrade Depestre

The National Poetry Debate and René Depestre's Cold War Aesthetic Solidarities

> "Yet what force on Earth is weaker than the feeble strength of one
> But the union makes us strong."
> ("Solidarity Forever," lyrics by Ralph Chaplin)

> "Poetry is at its very root tendentious."
> (Vladimir Mayakovsky)

> "Not me. Us."
> (Bernie Sanders)

Introduction

The debate between René Depestre and Aimé Césaire over *poésie nationale*, a literary aesthetic promoted at the time by PCF poet Louis Aragon, has long been considered a watershed moment in the literary history of Negritude. Depestre triggered this debate in 1955—probably inadvertently[1]—via the publication of a letter to his comrade Charles Dobzynski in the PCF cultural organ *Les lettres françaises*, wherein he offered some preliminary reflections upon Aragon's *Journal d'une poésie nationale* (1954) and endorsed the latter's promotion of a

---

1 Depestre claimed to David Alliot that he had meant for the letter to remain private and that Aragon, perhaps intending to promote the young poet, published it without consulting him. Alliot, *Le communisme est à l'ordre du jour*, Ch. 5, para. 5.

new "national poetry" grounded in classical French meter and form.[2] This proposed turn towards classical, expressly non-modernist forms appealed to Depestre as a way to help his efforts to eliminate "formal individualism" in his own writing. "Aragon [...] lights the path that we, Haitian poets, must take," he writes, expressing hope that Aragon's ideas might guide him towards a "realist" poetics adequate to the demands of the ongoing anticolonial and class struggle in Haiti.[3] In this letter to a comrade, Depestre envisions—schematically—a regenerated national Haitian poetry that would syncretize classical French forms with popular Haitian cultural forms of African descendance.

Césaire, who had long considered Aragon an adversary, published a sharp riposte to Depestre in *Présence Africaine* in the form of a poem entitled "Réponse à Depestre, poète haïtien," written archly in the very modernist style that Aragon's *poésie nationale* rejected.[4] Addressing Depestre as a fellow black Caribbean poet, and casting Aragon as an Other in more than one sense, Césaire literally tells Depestre not to give a damn about what Aragon says:

> que le poème tourne bien ou mal dans l'huile de ses gonds
> fous t'en Depestre fous t'en laisse dire Aragon[5]

Césaire's poetic polemic occasioned an extensive debate in *Présence Africaine* on the question of *poésie nationale*'s relevance to black writers in an era marked by the burgeoning hope of Third World decolonization and an intensifying Cold War. This series of exchanges has come to be known as the Césaire–Depestre debate.

And yet, reading most critical accounts of this *querelle*, one can scarcely speak of an actual debate at all. While Césaire's most stinging

---

2   The book is an anthology of poems—almost all sonnets—submitted to *Les lettres françaises* and selected by Aragon. The poems are interspersed with critical essays by Aragon on poetry; aside from the sonnet form, many of the poems share communist themes such as international peace, denunciation of the US atomic weapons program, and opposition to NATO.

3   Depestre, René. "Lettre à Charles Dobzynski." *Les Lettres françaises*, No. 573 (Jun. 16–23, 1955), p. 5.

4   This feud dates back to Aragon's split with Surrealism and embrace of socialist realism in the 1930s. For a comprehensive discussion of the 1930s literary feud between Césaire and Aragon, see Noland, Carrie. *Voices of Negritude in Modernist Print*. New York: Columbia University Press, 2015, Ch. 5.

5   Césaire, Aimé. "Réponse à Depestre, poète haïtien (Éléments d'un art poétique)." *Présence Africaine*, No. 1 (Apr.–Jun. 1955), p. 114.

lines are quoted admiringly, Depestre's position in the Césaire–Depestre debate is quickly schematized and dismissed.[6] It is as if the signifiers "formal individualism" and "Aragon" triggered some ideological content filter and automatically discredited Depestre's argument as mere Stalinist *langue de bois*. Indeed, a significant critical consensus still holds that Depestre's argument is that of a naïve useful idiot—that is, implicitly, that the argument is not even Depestre's, only a parroting of the apparatchik Aragon, who is himself parroting some Moscow party line. In perhaps an even graver transgression, Depestre's apparent deference to Aragon marks, for some, an obsequious choice by a black writer to remain under a white European poet's tutelage, thus subordinating authentic black poetic expression to a colorblind, Eurocentric Marxist dogma with no poetry in it.[7] In nearly all such discussions, Depestre's letter is rarely cited except in decontextualized fragments, and his considerably more developed essay "Réponse à Aimé Césaire (Eléments d'un art poétique haïtien)" is hardly mentioned at all. The debate tends to be remembered, then, almost as a melodrama: the hero Césaire rescues a talented young black poet from the villain Aragon, who threatens to impose a Stalinist formalism that would reduce the poem to a machine and bind black poetry to—of all things—the old, white, French sonnet.

Césaire's intervention in—indeed, his apparent instigation of—this *querelle* with Depestre is also often treated, implicitly or explicitly, as a prelude to his "Lettre à Maurice Thorez," a masterful denunciation of the Stalinist authoritarianism that prevailed in the postwar PCF and an

---

6   There are notable exceptions. J. Michael Dash touches briefly upon Depestre's argument in *Literature and Ideology in Haiti* (p. 176). Kaiama L. Glover's "'The Francophone World Was Set Ablaze': Pan-African Intellectuals, European Interlocutors and the Global Cold War" (*Postcolonial Studies* (2021), pp. 1–20) and Maryse Condé's article "Fous-t'en Depestre, laisse dire Aragon" (*Romanic Review*, Vol. 92, No. 1–2 (Jan.–Mar. 2001), pp. 177–184) both provide even-handed and nuanced treatments of the Césaire–Depestre debate.

7   Dominique Combe, for example, refers unqualifiedly to Aragon as Depestre's "master in poetry as in politics" (Preface. Hiddleston, Jane and Crowley, Patrick eds. *Postcolonial Poetics: Genre and Form*. Liverpool: Liverpool University Press, 2011, p. ix). Philip Kaisary also writes of Depestre's 1967 *Un arc-en-ciel pour l'occident chrétien* as marking a "new beginning," a sign that the poet "had found his own way" after rejecting Aragon's socialist realism. Kaisary, Philip, *The Haitian Revolution in the Literary Imagination: Radical Horizons, Conservative Constraints*. Charlottesville: University of Virginia Press, 2014, p. 58.

indictment of the party's condescending, "fraternalist" attitude towards colonized peoples of color outside the *Héxagone*.[8] This connection between the Césaire–Depestre debate and Césaire's courageous dissent is certainly legitimate, and there is much to admire in Césaire's split with the PCF in 1956, which I discuss at length in the next chapter. What I want to do in this chapter, however, is argue that reducing the Césaire–Depestre debate to an episode in the heroic narrative of Césaire's anti-Stalinism erases a significant contrapuntal narrative: that of Depestre's own serious attempt, both in the debate and in his contemporaneous poetic writing, to work out an engaged communist poetics that would avoid some pitfalls he identified in the avant-garde modernism hegemonic in Negritude poetry. Framing the Césaire–Depestre debate as a foreshadowing of Césaire's self-emancipation from Eurocentric Marxism requires—or has thus far required in effect—reducing Depestre's own, differently conceived project of poetic emancipation to a Stalinist straw man. Césaire's dissident project is commemorated and affirmed, while Depestre's aligned project is rendered unthinkable.

Departing from most criticism on the subject, this chapter focuses on Depestre's position in the debate, the position that almost no one—not even Depestre in later years, for the most part—has seen fit to defend. My aim is not so much to give an apologia for Depestre's position as to excavate its logic from the post-Cold War dustbin of history, thereby enabling us to consider its insights and potential utility. I do not simply claim that Depestre was right and Césaire was wrong (this is not exactly my view, in any case). Instead, I reconstruct the point of view that remains foreclosed by residual Cold War ideology: the specifically communist politico-aesthetic thought of the René Depestre who wrote the "Lettre à Charles Dobzynski" and aligned with Aragon, and who envisioned an engaged poetry oriented towards the political education of a broad popular audience (albeit a speculative one) in lieu of Negritude's avant-garde aesthetics and cultural politics of racial authenticity. A proper articulation of Depestre's point of view will better throw into relief the scope—and indeed, certain limits—of Césaire's much-vaunted position. It will also allow us to consider aspects of Depestre's reflections on poetry and politics that, I contend, contain useful insights for

---

[8] "Fraternalisme" is a neologism that Césaire coined in "Lettre à Maurice Thorez" to describe the specific characteristics of Stalinist cultural imperialism, that talk of "fraternity" with colonized people of color masks the superior, coercive attitude of an authoritarian Big Brother.

thinking about the role of poetry and the poet within anticolonial and anticapitalist struggles.

In the revisionist account I offer of the Césaire–Depestre debate, I reorient the way in which Depestre's aesthetic argument, articulated in his debate interventions and informing his poetry, is understood. To do this, I will need to begin by elucidating the ideological underpinnings and geopolitical determinants of *Présence Africaine*'s editorial framing of the debate. After retelling the story of the Césaire–Depestre debate with Depestre as the protagonist, I proceed by considering how Depestre's contemporaneous poetry—especially in *Minerai noir* (1956)—reflects an attempt to practice the aesthetics he developed through engaging with Aragon's *poésie nationale*. Though not uncritical of Depestre, my readings are deliberately sympathetic to his intentions. A following section reads the title poem of *Minerai noir* as an attempt by Depestre to work through—and develop a realist and materialist alternative to—what he understood to be the dominant aesthetic treatment of race in Negritude poetry. The final section explores Depestre's intellectual connection to Aragon. Treating this connection as an influence stemming from freely chosen alignment rather than blind allegiance, I explain the Depestre–Aragon connection as a specific kind of political relation that was known to Depestre and fellow communists as *comradeship*.

"A Nonsense and a Utopia": Realigning the Césaire–Depestre Debate

It is an obvious fact, but it must nonetheless be stated, that the Césaire–Depestre debate did not simply happen spontaneously; rather, it was organized and staged by *Présence Africaine*'s editorial team, led by Alioune Diop, the great doyen of postwar Negritude whose anticolonial cultural politics are discussed at length in Chapter 1. However, the fact that the Césaire–Depestre debate was staged by *Présence Africaine* almost simultaneously with the 1956 Congress of Black Writers and Artists (Césaire's poem appears in 1955, and the debate is closed in 1957) carries several less obvious ideological implications, particularly when we consider the debate in the context of the global cultural Cold War. Before turning to Depestre's interventions, it is necessary to make these Cold War underpinnings visible, as it is largely the original editorial framing of the Césaire–Depestre debate in *Présence Africaine* that came to determine—and indeed, still does determine—how the debate and main participants would be remembered.

We may first note that the issue of *Présence Africaine* in which the opening salvo of the debate, Césaire's poem "Réponse à Depestre, poète haïtien," appears is the first issue in the journal's "New Series." The editorial page of its 1947 premiere issue had featured a patronage committee that included the names of prominent white French intellectuals such as André Gide, Emmanuel Mounier, and Jean-Paul Sartre as imprimaturs conferring legitimacy upon the endeavor. However, as Nick Nesbitt explains, in the January 1955 launch of its New Series, these European intellectual patrons have been "purged" in a symbolic act of decolonization and replaced with a collective, all-black "comité *Présence Africaine*." Nesbitt sees this relaunch as a significant "gesture of independence" on the part of Diop and the journal's editorial team, heralding a "mature phase of the decolonization movement in the sphere of cultural production."[9] Césaire's poem performs a similar decolonizing gesture to this purge of the *Présence Africaine* masthead, insisting upon black poets' independence from white European patrons, guides, and masters, and chastising Depestre for seeking one in Aragon: "et pour les grognements des maîtres d'école/assez."[10]

Once Césaire had fired this first shot, *Présence Africaine* organized a "Débat sur la poésie nationale chez les peuples noirs," the proceedings of which appeared in Issue 4; it undertook this endeavor precisely under the sign of its Bandung-inspired decolonial project of independence and cultural autonomy.[11] The issue's editorial note, entitled "Entre l'Est et l'Ouest," explicitly frames this national poetry debate as a front in the larger struggle towards a non-aligned pan-African cultural awakening: "A great debate has opened before the consciousness of Africans: that regarding the Africanization of our means of expression, against assimilation. Poets open this [debate] in this issue, seizing upon a doubly opportune occasion offered to Aimé Césaire by an article that appeared

---

9 *Voicing Memory*, p. 106. See also Chapter 1 of this book for an extended discussion of *Présence Africaine*'s cultural Cold War positioning.
10 "Réponse à Depestre," p. 113. There is a slippage in the poem between "maître d'école" and "maître à fouet," one that has tended to go unremarked.
11 *Présence Africaine* did organize an in-person debate on national poetry in Paris on July 5, 1955. The irony that Depestre could not attend due to his exile in Brazil was not lost on Depestre himself, who noted with sarcasm that he had heard of the debate and the critiques of his position only "grâce au magnétophone." Depestre, René. "Réponse à Aimé Césaire (Introduction à un art poétique haïtien)." *Présence Africaine*, No. 4 (Oct.–Nov. 1955), p. 44.

in a large weekly magazine."[12] An introductory note also reproduces excerpts of Depestre's letter to Dobzynski, the editorial voice explaining that this letter had triggered Césaire's vexed rebuke. The note specifies that "the root of the problem" in the following debate was not the question of national poetry as such, nor the merits of Aragon's theory on their own terms, but rather "the authenticity of the cultural expression of our writers."[13]

In thus framing the debate's terms, the editorial note transplants and translates Depestre's remarks on Aragon into an interpretive community and a discursive framework significantly different from their original publishing context. Depestre himself claims in a 2009 interview that his letter to Dobzynski was intended as an intervention in a broad discussion of *poésie nationale* among several French leftist poets, including Tristan Tzara, Guillevic, Claude Roy, Pierre Seghers, and others.[14] Depestre's mentions of "Aragon's lessons" and of Aragon "lighting the path" thus take on connotations in the pages of *Présence Africaine*—where his interlocutors are fellow black intellectuals ("our writers")—that they did not have in the pages of *Les lettres françaises*, where his comments are addressed to communist comrades. Aragon is visible in the pages of *Présence Africaine* not as a comrade but as an Other—a white poet and "master," not one of "us" (unlike in the *Les lettres françaises* context, where Aragon is fully one of that particular "us"), but one of "them."

The discussion continued in four subsequent issues of *Présence Africaine*, with interventions by a number of prominent black francophone intellectuals. Reading these essays together, one can discern a dynamic akin to the present-day social media pile-on. Senegalese poet-statesman Lépold Sédar Senghor explicitly seconds Césaire's anti-Aragon position, and faults Depestre for imposing an ideological "a priori" upon black poetry that would stifle its free, autonomous development (presumably, towards surrealist modernism).[15] Gilbert Gratiant, while sympathizing

---

12 "Liminaire: Entre l'Est et l'Ouest." *Présence Africaine*, No. 4 (Oct–Nov. 1955), pp. 3–4. The "article" referred to is Depestre's "Lettre à Charles Dobzynski," published in *Les Lettres françaises*.

13 "Introduction: Un débat autour des conditions d'une poésie nationale chez les peuples noirs." *Présence Africaine*, No. 4 (Oct–Nov 1955), p. 36.

14 Depestre, "Alioune Diop," p. 164. The discrepancy between this account by Depestre and his explanation to Alliot (see p. 165), though not necessarily discrediting of either of Depestre's comments, must be noted.

15 Senghor, Léopold Sédar. "Réponse." *Présence Africaine*, No. 5 (Dec. 1955–Jan. 1956), p. 79.

with Depestre politically—Gratiant had even contributed a poem to Aragon's anthology—reproaches Depestre for wanting to "meditate" upon classical French forms, arguing that this is an arbitrary question of technique and that the "practice of the sonnet is neither obligatorily nor automatically enriching."[16] Bernard Dadié argues that black African poets, not having had the time to develop their own modern prosodies, should not "limit ourselves by the adoption of a form. We would discourage our own."[17] Amadou Moustapha Wade's tone is much sharper, even irked: declaring the whole question to be a "false problem," he asks what "we, blacks living in 1956, have to do with some 'return to the sonnet"; of Depestre, he says that he "regret[s] that Depestre has made Aragon's views his own," and that he no longer recognizes the young man he had regarded as "a Haitian friend."[18] Georges Desportes, for his part, rejects Aragon's *poésie nationale* as the reduction of poetry to "lyric propaganda" and dismisses "a socialist realism proclaimed in France" as "a nonsense and a utopia" with no relevance to black writers.[19] The general thrust of these interventions is twofold: dismissal, on the one hand, of Depestre's interventions (and of Aragon's vision of "national poetry") in tones ranging from bemusement to outrage, and—on the other hand—enthusiastic praise of the new (modernist) black poetry in French, with Césaire as this canon's central laureate figure.[20]

The debate is closed in Issue 11 (December 1956–January 1957), the closing remarks explicitly stating the editorial line on the debate and explaining its significance. The outcome, according to this coda, is unambiguous: Césaire won, Aragon lost, Depestre admitted defeat

---

16 Gratiant, Gilbert. "D'une poésie martiniquaise dite nationale." *Présence Africaine*, No. 5 (Dec. 1955–Jan. 1956), pp. 87–88.
17 Dadié, Bernard. "Le fond importe plus." *Présence Africaine*, No. 6 (Feb.–Mar 1956), p. 117.
18 Wade, Amadou Moustapha. "Autour d'une poésie nationale." *Présence Africaine*, No. 11 (Dec. 1956–Jan. 1957), p. 84.
19 Desportes, Georges. "Points de vue sur la poésie nationale." *Présence Africaine*, No. 11 (Dec. 1956–Jan. 1957), p. 88.
20 Césaire's centrality to this emergent black francophone literary field was already established, but it was cemented in the year 1956 with three major achievements: the "Lettre à Thorez"; the First Congress of Black Writers and Artists, where Césaire gave his "Culture and Colonialism" speech and where he was repeatedly praised and cited by other delegates; and *Présence Africaine*'s publication of the definitive edition of Césaire's master work, *Cahier d'un retour au pays natal* (see Chapter 1).

and was brought back into the fold. Depestre is quoted as having been convinced by Césaire and the First Congress: "regarding lyricism, nothing, absolutely nothing could separate me from the aesthetic position that Césaire defined last year."[21] The editorial voice expresses the hope "that these lines [from Depestre] will appease the concerns" that Depestre's many detractors had expressed, and declares the debate closed, a victory won against cultural assimilationism. As Anne Douaire-Banny astutely puts it, the "Conclusion" stages a return of the prodigal son: Depestre has been duly subjected to criticism, has performed a satisfactory autocritique in accepting the correct view and deferring to Césaire, and consequently has been "called in."[22]

In other words, the metalinguistic editorial framing of the debate scrambles Depestre's position, stages it as a deviation corrected by the debate's happy ending. Subsequent writing on the Césaire–Depestre debate has tended not to make much distinction between the other participants' criticisms of Depestre's arguments and Depestre's own words. The participants' various criticisms of Aragon's prescriptions are certainly valid: Aragon does fall into an unfortunate ideological formalism in his reification of the sonnet, which he refers to as a "rigorous thought machine" driven by the "mighty French tractor of the *alexandrin*."[23] However, valid as they are against Aragon, most of these criticisms do not appear to correspond to any of *Depestre's* claims, either in his letter to Dobzynski or in his more extensive essay "Réponse à Aimé Césaire." Depestre does not even mention the sonnet form, for example, let alone propose that black poets from Martinique to Senegal scrap their free verse and start writing only in rhymed quatrains and sestets.

As is often the case in literary debates of this period, the *Présence Africaine* debate over *poésie nationale* reveals itself upon scrutiny to be overdetermined by the Cold War–influenced political alignments of its organizers and participants. Depestre seems to have been a target of opportunity; Depestre's role in the debate is thus cast as a sort of

---

21 "Conclusion." *Présence Africaine*, No. 11 (Dec. 1956–Jan. 1957), p. 101.
22 Douaire-Banny, Anne. "Sans rimes, toute une saison, loin des mares. Enjeux d'un débat sur la poésie nationale." Mar. 20, 2011. http://pierre.campion2.free.fr/douaire_depestre&cesaire.htm. Nesbitt views this as a necessary concession by Depestre, "yielding to a poetic alpha male, submitted to [Césaire as] a new figure of cultural authority." *Voicing Memory*, p. 109.
23 Aragon, Louis. *Journal d'une poésie nationale*. Lyon: Les écrivains réunis, 1954, p. 36.

heel, the editors constructing Depestre the Stalinist as the Other of the collective *hommes de culture noirs*. It was quite easy to cast Depestre specifically in this role: the younger poet was a relatively new figure on the Parisian literary scene and occupied a marginal position in the field compared to a Césaire, a Senghor, or an Aragon. His position was rendered even more precarious by his status as a political exile; his reliance upon Aragon's patronage, furthermore, made him susceptible to charges of assimilationism in a way that these more established figures were not (Césaire's earlier promotion by Sartre and Breton, for example, does not come under similar suspicion).[24] For these reasons, it was both easy and convenient to ascribe to Depestre—even to project upon him—the false universalisms of Eurocentric assimilationism and Stalinist orthodoxy, all the better to denounce them, *through* him, under the sign of anticolonial racial solidarity.[25]

This is not to suggest that Depestre was a victim of some sort of francophone cancel culture *avant la lettre*; he appears to have suffered no serious material consequences for his debate interventions, and, indeed, after duly professing his *mea culpa* he subsequently became even more closely aligned with *Présence Africaine* (though not uncritically, as we shall see). Nor do I wish to question the emancipatory value of *Présence Africaine*'s campaign for pan-African cultural autonomy or its turn towards a non-aligned Third-Worldism.[26] I would simply note that *Présence Africaine* was not neutral ground, somehow free of ideology, and that its editorial line had—like nearly any intellectual journal in the postwar French literary field, as scholars such as Frances Stonor Saunders and Gisèle Sapiro have established—ideological coordinates that informed its protocols of literary valuation.[27] *Présence Africaine*'s political alignment was significantly at odds with the PCF and with communism more broadly;

---

24 See Sartre's "Orphée noir" and Breton, André. "Martinique, Charmeuse de serpents: Un grand poète noir," *Tropiques*, No. 11 (May 1944), pp. 119–126.

25 Depestre himself suggests that the *Présence Africaine* editorial team framed his debate with Césaire as a prelude to the First Congress: "Le débat de 1955 devait donc marquer un nouveau départ et une nouvelle cohésion autour de la revue qui rendit possible la réussite du congrès de la Sorbonne en septembre 1956." (Depestre, "Alioune Diop," p. 48).

26 To the contrary, in Chapter 1 I argue precisely *for* the emancipatory potential of *Présence Africaine* editor Alioune Diop's cultural politics in the context of the Cold War in the 1950s.

27 Sapiro, Gisèle. *The French Writers' War, 1940–1953*. Translated by Vanessa Doriott Anderson and Dorrit Cohn. Durham, NC: Duke University Press, 2014.

an expressly communist-aligned Depestre could only appear as an Other in such a forum.[28] Nevertheless, Depestre was able to articulate a coherent materialist rebuttal to the dominant current in the debate, one worth analyzing systematically because it constitutes a productive counterpoint to the pro-Césaire consensus.

It is no small irony, given Depestre's marginalization, that the most rigorous critical intervention in this entire debate was made by Depestre himself, in his unjustly ignored essay "Réponse à Aimé Césaire (Éléments d'un art poétique haïtien)." While the essay is not free of a certain Communist Party scholasticism, it would be reductive to view it as mere boilerplate that obeys, zombie-like, the cultural *ordre du jour* from PCF headquarters. To the contrary, in the context of the debate, Depestre's essay is the lone voice of dissent against the consensus in favor of Césaire (and, more broadly, of what the latter represents in this context: a liberal emphasis upon cultural authenticity and the full development of individual subjectivity in literature).[29] Depestre's "Réponse à Césaire" is also at times a masterful polemic, and it contains what is still today perhaps the most extensive critical analysis of Césaire's now famous poem. Depestre's objective is not simply to rebut Césaire's charges; rather, he aims to develop more formally and systematically the thoughts about national poetry that he lays out only schematically in his letter to Dobzynski. Rather than focus on how Depestre's positionality limits him, my rhetorical analysis of the "Réponse à Césaire" aims to restore to the critical discussion a number of significant and underappreciated insights that the essay provides into a few ideological limitations of the consensus position in the Césaire–Depestre debate.

From its opening paragraph, Depestre's essay takes on a high rhetorical register. Aware of the readership he is addressing, Depestre begins his response in a conciliatory tone, explaining that he had written to Dobzynski informally and in confidence, and explaining why he thought Aragon's *poésie nationale* relevant to progressive writers of color in the

---

See also Saunders, Frances Stonor. *The Cultural Cold War. The CIA and the World of Arts and Letters*. New York: The New Press, 2001, Ch. 8.

28 In his 1963 polemic against Négritude, René Ménil describes *Présence Africaine* and the affiliated Société Africaine de Culture—most ungenerously—as "orientées et dirigées avec souplesse par des catholiques." See "Une doctrine réactionnaire: la négritude," p. 38.

29 Among the other participants in the debate, as Nesbitt notes, "[n]one [...] offers a critique of Césaire's fundamental position." *Voicing Memory*, p. 111.

first place. He explains that he had wanted to preempt any charges of assimilationism by insisting, "au départ," that a Haitian national poetry must not simply imitate classical French prosody, but instead must integrate the latter with the "African component" of Haitian culture. He acknowledges the vitriolic response to his letter as evidence that he should make his position clearer. After this rhetorical concession—in effect, a counter-accusation that he had been deliberately taken out of context—Depestre pivots to a systematic critique of Césaire's promotion of Negritude's avant-garde aesthetics and, relatedly, of what he views as a reified vision of racial belonging and a mystified understanding of culture at work in Césaire's poem.

The concept of Negritude itself is Depestre's first target. His defense of national poetry begins by defending the "national" frame precisely as a materialist alternative to Negritude's racial/civilizational frame.[30] "Outside this national light," Depestre argues, "we risk falling into the basket of 'negritude' which denies the diversity of the material conditions of evolution, which considers the creative sensibilities of black people as a homogenous cultural bloc, without frontiers, interchangeable in its expressive manifestations."[31] The "national light" for Depestre is a specific set of material conditions, losing sight of which leads to idealist abstractions. Depestre rejects Negritude as a mystification that evacuates real differences between the various collectivities, individuals, and socio-economic relations grouped under the ascriptive identity of "nègre," and that would treat all black people—everywhere and of every social position—as if they spontaneously shared a single corporate interest.[32] Depestre's overall attitude towards Negritude is more nuanced than this

---

30 Though Depestre does not define "nation" explicitly, his discussion of a "community of culture" based in "communities of territory, language, economic life, and psychic formation" ("Réponse à Césaire," p. 45) reflects a standard Marxist-Leninist conceptualization of national character. See Stalin, Joseph. "Marxism and the National Question" [1913]. Marxists Internet Archive, https://www.marxists.org/reference/archive/stalin/works/1913/03.htm (accessed Aug. 5, 2021).

31 Depestre, "Réponse à Césaire," p. 45.

32 Depestre's is not the first such materialist critique of Negritude—Senegalese communist Gabriel d'Arboussier does this in his article "Négritude: une mystification dangereuse" (*La Nouvelle critique* (Jun. 1949))—but it does anticipate subsequent better-known critiques of Negritude by African intellectuals such as Jean-Marie Ndengue (*De la négritude au négrisme* (1970)) and Stanislas Adotevi (*Négritude et négrologues* (1972)) by more than a decade.

sharp rejection, as I will develop in the next section. In this polemical text, however, Depestre's concern is to throw into relief the internal contradictions within the dominant strain of Negritude discourse that make it unwieldy both as a paradigm of political belonging and as a way to understand the social role and responsibility of the poet.

Depestre devotes the remainder of his essay to rebutting Césaire in detail through an attentive close reading of the "Réponse à Depestre" poem. His critique can be divided roughly into three movements, each addressing a different contradiction he diagnoses in Césaire's poem. First, he contests the meaning of Césaire's neologism, *marronner*, a term coined to denote a radical emancipatory act of subtraction; second, he critiques Césaire's racialized mode of address to the younger poet; finally, and relatedly, he finds fault with Césaire's deployment of tropes related to popular Afro-Caribbean religious practices.

First, in reclaiming and repurposing Césaire's neologism, *marronner*, Depestre contests the meaning of the very lines that are often cited as Césaire's moment of triumph. This term that Césaire coins here is, without a doubt, what the poem is best known for: the poem itself reappears under the title "Le verbe marronner" in Césaire's collection *Noria* (1976), and the term has received the attention of numerous scholars, from A. James Arnold to James Clifford to J. Michael Dash.[33] It appears in the poem as a first-person inclusive imperative:

> marronnons-les Depestre marronnons-les
> comme jadis nous maronnions nos maîtres à fouet[34]

The verb *marronner* is, of course, an explicit historical reference to the Caribbean Maroons, enslaved people who escaped from their slavers to form free communities outside the plantations, often in mangroves and hills.[35] The verb therefore signifies "to run away," but in a sense that

---

[33] Clifford, James. *The Predicament of Culture*. Cambridge, MA: Harvard University Press, 1988; Arnold, A. James. *Modernism and Negritude: The Poetry and Poetics of Aimé Césaire*. Cambridge, MA:Harvard University Press, 1981; and Dash, J. Michael. "Aimé Césaire: The Bearable Lightness of Becoming." *PMLA*, Vol. 125, No. 3 (2010), pp. 737–742. See also Rosello, Mireille. "'The Césaire Effect,' or, How to Cultivate One's Nation," *Research in African Literatures*, Vol. 32, No. 4 (2001), pp. 77–91; and Roberts, Neil. *Freedom as Marronage*. Chicago, IL: University of Chicago Press, 2015.

[34] Césaire, "Réponse à Depestre," p. 114.

[35] For a thorough discussion of *marronnage*, see Price, Richard. *Maroon Societies: Rebel Slave Communities in the Americas*. Baltimore, MD: JHU Press, 1996 and

emphasizes the self-emancipating agency of the enslaved black subject. Rather than running away *from* slavers, *marronner* is something you do *to* them, subtracting your own freedom by leaving the masters behind.[36] Césaire expands upon this metaphor of the slave plantation later in the poem, comparing the Aragonian sonnet to the industrial byproduct of (enslaved) sugar production:

> C'est vrai ils arrondissent cette saision des sonnets
> pour nous à le faire cela me rappellerait par trop
> le jus sucré que bavent là-bas les distilleries des mornes
> quand les lents boeufs maigres font leur rond au zonzon des moustiques[37]

Cloying, mechanically produced, excremental, and lacking nutritive value, Aragonian "poésie nationale" is a sort of ideological effluvium for Césaire, a nasty byproduct of the Stalinist doctrine of literature-as-heavy-industry. It also constitutes, by implication, a kind of intellectual plantation work for black poets, a coerced labor performed for a white master in Europe—and using the master's tools, to recall Audre Lorde's famous line. As Dash argues, Césaire valorizes "the poetic word as the ultimate form of *marronnage*," captured in his image of vodou priest Boukman's "insane song," a purely transgressive outcry "that has little to do with" founding a collective social order.[38]

Depestre ratifies Césaire's call to *marronnage* as a salutary decolonial gesture, but then immediately contests the term's meaning: who or what, asks Depestre, ought to be the direct object of this transitive verb? For Depestre, defining the referent of the object pronoun "les" in Césaire's imperative phrase "marronnons-les" in broad racial or civilizational terms is dangerously indiscriminate: "We must limit as much as possible the risks of making a mistake, in aesthetics and at all the crossroads of knowledge, the risks of marooning [*marronner*] the radiant visage of our own hopes."[39] Here, Depestre is directly challenging Césaire's apparent rejection of classical French prosody as irrelevant to black poets writing in French. To the contrary, Depestre argues, *everyone* has the right to appropriate classical French literature, Haitians all the more so precisely

---

Diouf, Sylviane. A. *Slavery's Exiles: The Story of the American Maroons*. New York: NYU Press, 2014.

36 Kaiama Glover translates Césaire's line, accurately, as "let's free ourselves from them Depestre." See "'The Francophone World,'" p. 11.
37 Césaire, "Réponse à Depestre," p. 114.
38 Dash, "Bearable Lightness," p. 740.
39 Depestre, "Réponse à Césaire," p. 44.

because the majority of Haitians have historically been *denied* this right to the written word in French. Further in the essay, Depestre draws an analogy to how African-American writers relate to the US literary canon, and counters the gesture of *marronnage* with that of *triage*:

> Is it not an advantage for American Negroes, when they are able to go to school, to jump right into Anglophone culture and immediately to start sorting [*faire le tri*] between that which is stained by racist obscurantism and that which emits humanist waves, between the medieval Ku Klux Klan and Walt Whitman, between the various mystical opiates and Howard Fast, between Ezra Pound and Langston Hughes, between what is already dead and what is already born, between the moribund heirs to the slave ships and the eternal youth of the eternal beating of the Shakespearian heart!"[40]

Depestre's almost Dantean sorting out of canonical literary historical figures into the (progressive) saved and the (reactionary) damned is not uncommon among Cold War intellectuals.[41] What is interesting about such *triage* in this context, though, is that Depestre offers it as a corrective supplement to Césairean *marronnage*, a means of shedding the racist mysticism and obscurantism of European written traditions without denying oneself the use of what is still living and serviceable within these traditions.[42]

By far the most pointed section of Depestre's rebuttal, however, consists of Depestre taking issue with how Césaire addresses him. Here, Depestre responds specifically to the following lines from Césaire's poem:

> Depestre j'accuse les mauvaises manières de notre sang
> est-ce notre faute
> si la bourrasque se lève
> et nous désapprend tout soudain de compter sur nos doigts

---

40 Depestre, "Réponse à Césaire," p. 52.

41 Aragon performs a similar *tri* in selecting the poems anthologized in *Journal d'une poésie nationale*, choosing classical poets over the nineteenth-century "poètes maudits," especially Mallarmé (*Journal*, pp. 70–73). See also Bhakti Shringarpure's discussion of the "Cold War paradigm" of canon formation in the US academy, which favored specific modernist aesthetic tendencies (*Cold War Assemblages*, Ch. 4).

42 Jean-Jacques Cadet writes similarly of Jacques Stephen Alexis' appropriation of Marxism, and of Western thought more broadly, as a "tri intellectuel et idéologique." *Le marxisme haïtien*, p. 22.

> de faire trois tours de saluer
>
> Ou bien encore cela revient au même
> le sang est une chose qui va et qui revient
> et le nôtre je suppose nous revient après s'être attardé
> à quelque macumba. Qu'y faire? En vérité
> le sang est un vodoun puissant.[43]

The "nous" that Césaire conjures is without question a racialized collective subject, a *nous* grounded explicitly in shared blood. To critique this way of grounding political belonging, Depestre performs a deft rhetorical gesture, following the immanent logic of Césaire's address: "I therefore beg Césaire and our friends [...] not to be angry with me for harboring drops of blood from another man under my left breast. Aragon's blood, which is the brother of ours, how can you doubt it my friends, even if in its comings and goings it hasn't 'stopped over at some *macumba*.'"[44]

With a good dose of rhetorical irony, Depestre tries to catch Césaire in the act of recapitulating a mystification of blood that hearkens back to nineteenth-century race science (and further back to folk attitudes about blood).[45] Depestre inhabits the collective subject from Césaire's poem ("nos amis") to expose its ideological roots in racialist discourse, sarcastically pleading to be accepted as a true member of the race though he harbors drops of impure blood in his veins, implying that Césaire's objection to his affiliation with Aragon—the "autre homme"—follows the same formal logic as the ideology of miscegenation. According to Depestre's critique, there is a dangerous elision from political to racial ontology in Césaire's poem: his rejection of Aragon on aesthetic grounds slides into a paradigm of belonging that conjures hoary notions of racial essence. What Depestre reproaches in Césaire's poem is that Césaire has slipped into what Barbara and Karen Fields have named "racecraft": practices that reproduce the ideology of race by treating race as if it were a natural category of human distinction.[46]

Depestre develops his critique of Césaire's uncharacteristic slippage into racecraft by questioning Césaire's deployment of Haitian *vodou*

---

43 Césaire, "Réponse à Depestre," p. 114.
44 Depestre, "Réponse à Césaire," p. 54.
45 For a thorough account of the racial mystique of blood, see Fields, Barbara J. and Fields, Karen. *Racecraft: The Soul of Inequality in American Life*. New York: Verso, 2012, Ch. 2.
46 Fields and Fields, *Racecraft*, Introduction.

and Afro-Brazilian *macumba* as signifiers of shared racial belonging. Both religions are indeed practiced by New World descendants of enslaved Africans, and syncretize African, indigenous American, and European religious practices. What Depestre objects to is Césaire's erasure of the *class* provenance of these religions, his evacuation of their status as cultural expressions of the exploited peasantries of Haiti and Brazil (Depestre's place of exile, as Césaire knew). He reframes *vodou* as "a mass religion, an incubator protected from absorption into the dominant ideology (foreign clergy, American sects, pan-Americanism)" that shelters popular Haitian "national characteristics and psychological particularities."[47] *Vodou*, Depestre reminds Césaire, is a cultural form opposed equally by American capitalists and their missionaries, foreign Catholic Church authorities, and the Haitian ruling class.[48] The force of Depestre's critique is his insistence upon grounding his understanding of popular Haitian practices in political economy. Depestre reframes these folk traditions, making them visible as those of a class rather than those of a race.

Depestre sharpens this line of critique by calling out Césaire for effectively posing as a *vodouisant* himself:

> if effectively our blood comes back to us after having lingered at some *macumba* or some *vaudou*, we must consider this a historically dated tragedy of unhappy conscience. Our blood's own way of playing mystical hookie. Must we today, when we as intellectuals have the means of rising to a theoretical and practical intelligence regarding the national question, resign ourselves to this opium?[49]

Depestre's point is, in one sense, a perfectly straightforward Marxist (and even vulgar Marxist) one: even an authentically popular Afro-Caribbean religion such as *vodou* remains, qua religion, an ideological mystification in the final instance. Depestre makes a more suggestive point, however, by identifying a certain bad faith in Césaire's invocations of *macumba* and *vodou* rituals: for Césaire—an eminent member of the Parisian intelligentsia, a *normalien,* and a sitting member of the

---

47 Depestre, "Réponse à Césaire," p. 54.
48 It must be noted here that there is a significant—and unfortunate—dose of Stalinist historical stagism in Depestre's account of *vodou* in this essay: Depestre acknowledges *vodou*'s revolutionary potential "at certain phases of the national struggle," while still viewing it as a superstition to be ultimately discarded. Depestre, "Réponse à Césaire," p. 55.
49 Depestre, "Réponse à Césaire," p. 54.

Assemblée Nationale, not to mention an avowed atheist—to pantomime taking part in folk religious practices of the Haitian and Brazilian peasantry strikes Depestre as faux-populist imposture. Again, Depestre changes the terrain of the debate, attempts to realign its central terms from cultural (i.e., racial) authenticity to class antagonism: his counter-measure to Césaire reminding him that he, too, is black ("our blood") is to remind Césaire that he, too, is bourgeois ("we as intellectuals").

Depestre's final criticism is to admonish Césaire that his public fight with Aragon is politically irresponsible. Césaire's "fous-t-en Depestre laisse dire Aragon" line, he warns, will become a "boomerang"—that is, it will recoil upon the broader left: "Ah, these ironic rhymes, *cher* Césaire, I know people who will make an *arc de triomphe* out of them. I know others who will use them as a master-key to open the door to all sorts of impostures."[50] This argument is not at all dissimilar to Jean-Paul Sartre's reproach to Albert Camus only four years earlier, in 1952, over the latter's public interventions against revolutionary politics: "I did not want to reply to you. Who would I be convincing? Our enemies, certainly, and perhaps my friends. And you—who do you think you are convincing? Your friends and my enemies. To our common enemies, who are legion, we shall both give much cause for laughter. That much is certain."[51] Depestre's reproach to Césaire, like Sartre's reproach to Camus, is more directly an expression of anti-anticommunism in this context: Depestre is reminding Césaire that such airing of dirty laundry among leftists will only redound to the benefit of reactionaries who are no friends to peoples of color, communist or otherwise. Whereas Césaire, addressing himself teasingly to "Camarade Depestre," cajoles Depestre like a mischievous schoolboy enticing his uptight friend to play hookie with him, Depestre addresses Césaire as a comrade with the full weight of obligation implicit in that term, reminding the latter of his political responsibility and calling him to discipline.[52] We may view this as a direct response to the attitude of *désinvolture* that runs throughout Césaire's poem, particularly in the latter's call to leave the "school-masters" behind and to "look at the springtime." Comradeship conceived

---

50 Depestre, "Réponse à Césaire," p. 56.
51 Sartre, Jean-Paul. "Reply to Albert Camus." *Portraits (Situations IV)*. Translated by Chris Turner. London: Seagull, 2009, pp. 123–172.
52 As this debate occurred prior to Césaire's demission from the PCF, Césaire was indeed officially a comrade when Depestre's response was published.

as a disciplining relationship is an important thread in Depestre's poetry to which we will return in this chapter's section.

Having established how Depestre's poetic vision is articulated with his political commitments, we can now perhaps see beyond the various anticommunist caricatures of Depestre's mid-1950s interventions. Rather than merely "toeing the party line" (to use the standard cliché), Depestre is arguing in favor of aesthetic standards that do not conform to the modernist protocols that were dominant in the orbit of Césaire. We can also better comprehend the political logic—including both the strengths and limitations thereof—in Césaire's much-celebrated defense of poetic freedom in "Réponse à Depestre," thrown into relief by renewing our attention to Depestre's extensive critical reading of the poem. In the sections that follow, I examine the alternatives to these modernist aesthetics of postwar Negritude that Depestre develops in his 1956 collection *Minerai noir*: first, his historical materialist poetic treatment of the racial question in *Minerai noir*, and, in the final section, his study of the poetics of Louis Aragon.

Passing Through Negritude in *Minerai noir*

If Depestre remained suspicious towards the predominant tendency in Negritude thought, it would be a mistake to assume that Depestre was therefore opposed to all aspects of Negritude. We shall see in this chapter's final section that Depestre's solidaristic poetic vision is indeed conceived as a materialist alternative to the avant-garde modernism practiced by many (if not all) poets of the emergent postwar Negritude literary canon. In this section, however, we shall see that Depestre's attitude towards the prevailing understanding within Negritude of the politics of racial belonging is more nuanced. I argue overall in this section that Depestre's attitude towards race is not some vulgar Marxist "class reductionism," but rather an attempt to think race through a materialist lens as an alternative to what he views critically as the idealist tendencies within Negritude.

Depestre's longstanding wariness towards Negritude is well-known. It should always be remembered that Depestre's skepticism towards race-based paradigms of political belonging stems not from Marxist dogma, but rather from personal experience as a Haitian left revolutionary in the wake of the Haitian Revolution of 1946. Depestre witnessed the rise of the Griot movement in Haiti, the right wing of which articulated a reactionary political ideology based upon a racialized mystique of Haitianness emphasizing black African cultural purity and racial authenticity.[53] Michael Dash succinctly describes *noiriste* ideology as "the rationale for a black cultural dictatorship,"[54] which is precisely what prominent Griot François Duvalier would install upon being elected President of Haiti in 1957.[55] Though Depestre would not see firsthand the ravages of Duvalierism until his brief return to Haiti in 1958, his antagonism towards the Griots predates this return. For Depestre, then, the sometimes caricatured Marxist understanding of race as an ideological weapon deployed by reactionary forces to rationalize their class power and thwart progressive efforts at building popular solidarity was not simply a party zealot's article of faith; to the contrary, it was an assessment borne out by his observation of the rise of fascist tyranny in his own country.[56]

However, although Depestre had concrete reasons to distrust black movements defined around racial authenticity, his view of Negritude is not that of a typical PCF intellectual. Later in life, Depestre has more than once affirmed his agreement with Jean-Paul Sartre's theory of Negritude, which the latter lays out in "Orphée noir."[57] As we have seen in the Introduction, Sartre's existentialist view is that Negritude, a black consciousness most fully expressed in the "new black poetry," is an "antiracist racism" that constitutes a necessary *point faible* in a dialectical process of deracialization. In short, Negritude, according to Sartre, is a phase to be traversed in order to produce the negation of the negation, a truly egalitarian human society that has rid itself of the ideological belief in hierarchized subspecific human groups called "races."

---

53 For more on the racial ideology of the Griots, see Smith, *Red and Black*, Ch. 4.
54 Dash, *Literature and Ideology*, p. 96.
55 Smith, *Red and Black*, Chs 4–5.
56 Smith, *Red and Black*, p. 57 and *passim*. See also Depestre's discussion of the capture of Haiti's Bureau d'Ethnologie by reactionary *noiriste* cadres in Bonniol, Jean-Luc. "Entretien avec René Depestre." *Gradhiva*, Vol. 1 (2005), pp. 11–13.
57 Here is the full quote of Depestre's views on Sartre's theory of Negritude: "Je me suis toujours méfié du concept de race, bien que moi-même j'aie pense, et je ne regrette pas de l'avoir fait (je rejoins la position de Sartre par rapport à la négritude), qu'on ne pouvait pas du jour au lendemain se débarrasser, dans notre conscience d'écrivain, de cette affaire raciale en un tour de main, qu'il fallait l'assumer sur le plan de la création elle-même: du point de vue philosophique, il fallait l'utiliser comme une médiation, il fallait en passer par là" (Bonniol, "Entretien," p. 20).

In francophone communist intellectual circles of this period, a significantly more dismissive, even hostile, attitude towards Negritude appears to have prevailed. Most notably, Senegalese Marxist politician Gabriel d'Arboussier wrote a sharp denunciation of Negritude entitled "Une dangereuse mystification: théorie de la négritude" (1949) in the PCF-affiliated review *La Nouvelle Critique*. In it, d'Arboussier lays out several criticisms of Negritude's understanding of race that are representative of standard attitudes within the PCF in the period. Though d'Arboussier's polemic mostly targets Sartre, his argument offers useful points of comparison with Depestre's perspective on Negritude. D'Arboussier's polemic against Sartre is centered on what he sees as false "mystifications" about race and blackness. To begin with, d'Arboussier indicts Sartre's existentialism as a false idealism: "In all this mess, it is all about nothing but consciousness, subconsciousness, the state of the soul, metaphysics."[58] Denunciations of existentialism were certainly not uncommon in the PCF mediasphere, but d'Arboussier's charge is specifically that the existentialist philosophical approach is inadequate to understanding racial oppression. Sartre, he argues, has reified race by defining it as a quasi-metaphysical category of being, in Manichean opposition to a quasi-metaphysical whiteness. Relatedly, he repudiates Sartre's flattening out of myriad different human communities into the abstracted category of "nègre"; he points out, for example, the absurdity of Sartre associating Parisian sophisticates such as Senghor and Damas with an ostensibly essentially black "poésie d'agriculteurs" ("Damas, Senghor, agriculteurs? *Allons donc!*").[59] Finally, d'Arboussier denounces Sartrean Negritude as promoting a fundamentally counter-solidaristic paradigm of political belonging that risks driving a wedge between white workers and workers of color in France and in the colonies.

We can observe several congruities between d'Arboussier's critique of Negritude and Depestre's rebuttal to Césaire. Depestre is especially aligned with d'Arboussier's refusal to evacuate class antagonisms among black people, his suspicion towards racial belonging as such, and his

---

58 d'Arboussier, "Une mystification dangereuse," p. 37.
59 d'Arboussier, "Une mystification dangereuse," p. 37. Emphasis in original. Another example that d'Arboussier gives of Sartre's evacuation of internal differences among people categorized as "nègre" is that Sartre posits chattel slavery as the definitive historical experience of the black subject; although this may be true of black peoples in the Antilles and the Americas, d'Arboussier argues, most sub-Saharan African people do not share this historical experience.

prioritization of transracial working-class solidarity. However, where d'Arboussier's attitude towards Negritude is dismissive and oppositional, Depestre's is ambivalent and multifaceted, if still very critical. It should be noted that, despite having argued against Césaire and others in *Présence Africaine*, Depestre, unlike d'Arboussier, did not declare himself an outright adversary of Negritude; to the contrary, he maintained close ties with Diop, Césaire, Senghor, and other members of the journal's editorial board.[60] Indeed, it was *Présence Africaine* that published *Minerai noir* in 1956.

Depestre's critical but not hostile relationship to Negritude was not simply a question of maintaining a literary network; it also reveals something about Depestre's political imaginary. Although Depestre seems consistently to look forward to a time when race-thinking has been cast off for good, he never goes as far as d'Arboussier's utter rejection of Negritude's "antiracist racism." In fact, as I will now discuss, Depestre takes seriously the Sartrean argument that Negritude must be *traversed*. In a 2005 interview, Depestre says that although he has "always been wary of the concept of race," he also believes that one "could not rid oneself overnight [...] of this racial business in a flash," and that the black writer "had to take it on board on the level of [literary] creation itself."[61] Explicitly endorsing Sartre, Depestre claims that "speaking philosophically, one had to use [race] as a mediation, one had to pass through it."[62]

I argue that Depestre takes on the task of "passing through" Negritude deliberately in his 1950s poetry and, above, all in the title poem of *Minerai noir*. I am interested in using this framework of "passing through Negritude" as a way to better understand Depestre's thinking about how to articulate antiracism with a socialist political vision. This section is therefore dedicated to interpreting Depestre's materialist revision of Negritude. I tease this out via a close reading of "Minerai

---

60 It was Senghor who, according to Depestre, secured him and his wife asylum in Vienna in 1953 after the young couple was denied a visa to reenter Paris. See Depestre, René. *Bonsoir tendresse, autobiographie*. Paris: Odile Jacob, 2018, Ch. 4.
61 Bonniol, "Entretien," p. 20.
62 Bonniol, "Entretien," p. 20. Similarly, Nick Nesbitt writes of Césaire telling him, à propos of a discussion between the latter and Senghor on Hegelian dialectics, that "to arrive at the Universal one must immerse oneself in the Particular!" *Voicing Memory*, p. xiv.

noir," the work that Depestre later mentions as his literary attempt to "pass through Négritude."[63]

"Minerai noir" is a narrative poem that recounts the history of the transatlantic slave trade. In retelling this history, however, the poem situates this bloody economy of extraction, exploitation, and extermination within the broader context of the rise of the capitalist mode of production. The imagery throughout the poem is centered on concrete material relations and processes: historical processes of development, industrial processes of extraction and production, social relations of exploitation and violence, economic relations of supply and demand, and ideological processes of racialization and commodification. Importantly, the poem is *not* about individual subjects—nor, to recall d'Aroussier, is it about consciousness, or the unconscious, or states of the soul, or metaphysics.

Two epigraphs preface "Minerai noir," each paratext announcing a different facet of the poem to follow. Gérard Genette writes of the "epigraph-effect" as "a signal (intended as a sign) of culture [read: erudition], a password" by which the author "chooses his peers and thus his place within the pantheon."[64] For Depestre, the epigraph serves an analogous function, but it is a sign of alignment rather than of positioning within a canon; it is a mechanism by which the author chooses his comrades and thus his place within a *political* community. The first epigraph is excerpted from the Franco-German surrealist poet Yvan Goll's poem "Jean sans terre à son frère noir":

> Auprès de toi ton ombre semble claire
> L'or du soleil s'assombrit dans ton oeil
> Toute la vie tu portes le suaire
> Ta nudité ressemble à un long deuil.
> ....
> Toi qui caches le charbon millenaire
> De ta douleur dans la nuit de ton corps.[65]

Besides the obvious message of fraternity communicated in the title, it is above all the material imaginary of Goll's poem that accounts for Depestre's selection of this excerpt. The substances it introduces will

---

63 Bonniol, "Entretien," p. 20.
64 Genette, Gérard. *Paratexts: Thresholds of Interpretation*. Translated by Jane E. Lewin. Cambridge: Cambridge University Press, 1997, p. 160.
65 Quoted in Depestre, René. *Rage de vivre: œuvres poétiques complètes*. Paris: Seghers, 2007, p. 104. Ellipses in the original.

appear prominently in Depestre's poem: gold, sweat, but, above all, the "millenary coal" that Goll deploys as a symbol for the accretion of centuries of black pain. As we will soon see, Depestre will make this fossilized suffering the very ur-substance of "Minerai noir."

The poem's second epigraph is, not coincidentally, a quote from none other than Aimé Césaire: "We are black people, but above all, men equal to all other men, and that alone counts; and we also want to have our place in the trains that you exalt, the trains you launch upon the rails of your pride: the train of liberty, the train of equality, the train of fraternity."[66] This citation, rarely quoted since, is from a 1949 pamphlet by PCF intellectual Dominique Desanti entitled *Nous avons choisi la paix*, a collection of speeches made by French communist intellectuals at the 1948 International Peace Conference in Wroclaw, Poland. Given the context of the Césaire–Depestre debate, it is tempting to note something arch in Depestre's selection of this particular Césaire quote—a relatively obscure one, after all, and at a moment, too, when citing the *Cahier d'un retour au pays natal* was a widespread practice. To recall his rebuttal to Césaire, Depestre appears to be calling a comrade to discipline through his inclusion of this Césaire quote as paratext, reminding Césaire of the ineluctably universalist dimension of the communist project to which they have both professed commitment. Taken together, both epigraphs introduce Depestre's poetic rendition of transatlantic slavery by framing it within a universalist vision of antiracist socialist fraternity, performatively signaling the poet's left alignment.

The poem's first lines situate the mass kidnapping and enslavement of African people within the political–economic context of Spanish mercantilism's extraction of precious metals from Spain's New World colonies. The poem opens at the exact historical moment when the slave trade began:

> Quand la sueur de l'Indien se trouve brusquement tarie par le soleil
> Quand la frénésie de l'or draina au marché la dernière goutte de sang indien
> De sorte qu'il ne resta plus un seul indien aux alentours des mines d'or
> On se tourna vers le fleuve musculaire de l'Afrique
> Pour assurer la relève du désespoir[67]

In choosing the temporal preposition *quand* as the poem's opening word, Depestre announces an insistent focus upon the determinate

---

66 Quoted in Depestre, *Rage de vivre*, p. 104.
67 Depestre, *Rage de vivre*, p. 105.

historical forces that gave rise to the slave trade. We also see Depestre immediately taking up the same base materials introduced in the Goll epigraph—sweat and gold, to which Depestre also adds blood—and reworking them into his poem, placing them, as commodities, within a dynamic of market forces. Relatedly, these first lines also introduce the economic equilibrium of supply ("la dernière goutte," "il ne resta plus") and demand ("la frénésie de l'or," "assurer la relève"); indeed, this tension between supply and demand will become the motor of the poem. It is the exhaustion of the indigenous labor supply that creates the economic incentive—the impersonal pronoun "on" refers to economic forces—to exploit the "fleuve musculaire" of Africa.[68]

The poem continues, pinpointing this exhaustion of indigenous enslaved labor in the Americas as the proximate cause of the rise in demand for African enslaved labor. Depestre figures this turn as the equivalent of a gold rush:

> Alors commença la ruée vers l'inépuisable
> Trésorerie de la chair noire
> Alors commença la bousculade échevelée
> Vers le rayonnant midi du corps noir
> Et toute la terre retentit du vacarme des pioches
> Dans l'épaisseur du minerai noir[69]

What I wish to emphasize about this passage is the striking difference in the material imaginary of "Minerai noir" compared to that which can be found elsewhere in the Negritude corpus. From Aimé Césaire's declared wish to "become a tree" in the *Cahier* to Suzanne Césaire's Frobénius-inspired description of black African civilization as "vegetal"—a trope picked up and developed by Senghor as essential to African civilization, by surrealists such as André Breton, by Sartre in his discussion of black "being-in-the-world," and many others—a prevailing current in Negritude has associated blackness figuratively with plant life, vegetation, and agriculture. Aside from Negritude, Depestre's poem is also a departure from Marx's metaphor of Europe's transformation of Africa into a "preserve for the hunting of blackskins."[70] Depestre instead

---

68 The adjective "musculaire" here suggests the actual substance—human muscle, and, more precisely, the labor-power it represents—of the African "river" that the emergent Atlantic slave economy will seek to exploit.
69 Depestre, *Rage de vivre*, p. 105.
70 Marx, Karl. *Capital. Volume One*. Translated by Moore and Aveling. Edited by Friedrich Engels. Marxists Internet Archive, p. 395. For an extensive discussion

categorizes blackness under the third material kingdom in Linnaean taxonomy: the material stuff of Depestre's poem, introduced in the Goll epigraph and the title but sustained throughout, is consistently mineral. Depestre figures the slave trade as the systematic extraction and processing of human bodies as raw material, a substance dug out of the earth with pickaxes; Africa's reserves of black flesh are referred to as a "treasure trove"—"O couches métalliques de mon peuple," the poet later cries out in an apostrophic lamentation.

I would suggest that, in this figurative shift from vegetal to mineral, Depestre is contesting how Africa, Africans, and black people more broadly are often represented in the modernist literary imagination. Rather than hark back to an idealized, bountiful, agricultural and vegetal Mother Africa as a lost homeland, Depestre figures African land as a site of capitalist extraction, a terrain possessing natural resources—including "black ore"—that carry value on the world market. It is a remarkable figuration of the mass enslavement of Africans, one through which Depestre connects this proto-capitalist practice of extracting and consuming human beings directly to imperial capitalism's insatiate extraction of Africa's vast mineral resources in the twentieth century (a process that continues today). Depestre figures Africans as mineral in order to argue that the racialization of enslaved African populations as "black" is a process related to the capitalist logic of resource extraction and commodity production.

The poem's longest movement consists of a grotesque and frankly harrowing enumeration of commodities made out of this "black ore," literally from the flesh, blood, and bones of enslaved black people:

> Et tout juste si des chimistes ne pensèrent
> Aux moyens d'obtenir quelque alliage précieux
> Avec le métal noir tout juste si des dames ne
> Rêvèrent d'une batterie de cuisine
> En nègre du Sénégal d'un service à thé
> En massif négrillon des Antilles
> Tout juste si quelque curé
> Ne promit à sa paroisse
> Une cloche coulée dans la sonorité du sang noir
> Ou encore si un brave Père Noël ne songea

of Marx's writings on slavery, see Anderson, Kevin B. *Marx at the Margins: On Nationalism, Ethnicity, and Non-Western Societies.* Chicago, IL: University of Chicago Press, 2010.

> Pour sa visite annuelle
> A des petits soldats de plomb noir
> Ou si quelque vaillant capitaine
> Ne tailla son épée dans l'ébène minéral
> Toute la terre retentit de la secousse des foreuses
> Dans les entrailles de ma race
> Dans le gisement musculaire de l'homme noir

The images in this long passage are of black bodies processed into trinkets and household items; they are hyperbolically grotesque, horrific in a way that recalls the postwar rumors of household products made from the flesh of those murdered in the Nazi death camps. Scholars in critical race theory such as Saidiya Hartman and Hortense Spillers have written in different contexts of "fungibility" as a determining characteristic of enslaved black bodies. While it is true of the wage-worker under capitalism that their labor-power becomes alienated and commodified, the enslaved black person is distinct in that their body itself is treated as a commodity, measured, weighed, and reduced to quantity.[71] Depestre's poem acknowledges precisely this dehumanizing fungibility as definitive of the situation of enslaved black people, and he renders it with horrific literality.

What Depestre emphasizes, however, is that the dynamo motivating this monstrous machine that renders and processes black life, labor, and flesh is Western capitalist commodity production. These bourgeois Europeans do not dream of torture or domination per se, but rather of having nice things: new metallic alloys, fancy tea sets, a new church bell, little toy soldiers for the children, a decorative sword. One is reminded of historian Barbara Fields' famous critique of the tendency to discuss slavery "as though the chief business of slavery were the production of white supremacy rather than the production of cotton, sugar, rice and tobacco."[72] It was the feverish rise of consumer demand in early capitalist Europe that motivated the slave trade, the poem argues, as opposed to the quasi-metaphysical force of racism as such.

The incipit of Depestre's later book-length treatise *Bonjour et adieu*

---

[71] Spillers, Hortense. "Mama's Baby, Papa's Maybe: An American Grammar Book." *Diacritics*, Vol. 17, No. 2 (1987), pp. 64–81. See also Hartman, Saidiya. *Scenes of Subjection: Terror, Slavery, and Self-Making in Nineteenth Century America*. Oxford: Oxford University Press, 1997.

[72] Fields, Barbara J. "Slavery, Race, and Ideology in the United States." *New Left Review*, Vol. 181 (May/Jun. 1990), p. 99.

à la negritude (1980) figures the enslavement of black people in very similar terms to the poetic imagination of slavery in "Minerai noir":

> There was once a category of human beings whom colonization generically and pejoratively baptized Black (*nègres*). Thus named, the Africans, members heretofore of ethnicities and peoples with diverse cultures, were reduced to the state of a biological combustible. The combustion of Black people in plantations in the plantations and workshops of the Americas made possible the age of enlightenment, steam and electricity, and the other conquests of the modern world's first industrial revolution.[73]

"Minerai noir" makes this same argument in lyrical form, and through precisely the same figuration of slavery as a process whereby inhabitants of Africa were racialized as black, extracted by force, and consumed like coal or oil ("numbered, measured, classed, and killed," to recall Césaire), allowing the accumulation of capital that fueled the development of Europe's industrial revolution.[74]

Depestre's rendering of enslaved Africans as fossil fuel—a metaphor bearing especially ominous undertones for twenty-first-century readers that it perhaps lacked in the 1950s—is unusual, and it is worth unpacking here because it adds a further layer to Depestre's figuration of black life as mineral rather than vegetal. Fossil fuels are the dead remains of once-living matter transformed by heat and pressure over time into a substance whose use-value lies in its combustibility. A fossil fuel is a zombified substance, in this sense, the dead—or those in a state of social death, to recall Orlando Patterson's famous phrase—preserved in undeath to be exploited by the living. Crucially, it is non-renewable: it is not grown or cultivated but extracted and consumed. Here, Depestre's metaphor draws another major distinction between the black slave and the exploited European wage worker under industrial capitalism: whereas processes existed to ensure the reproduction of the labor power of the European worker, the same was not true for New World slaves, who, in colonial Saint Domingue, for example, often died from disease or overwork within a matter of years, the slave population constantly replaced by additional enslaved Africans freshly extractred and shipped across the Atlantic.[75]

---

73 Depestre, René. *Bonjour et adieu à la négritude*. Paris: Laffont, 1980, p. 7.
74 This account is quite similar to Marx's assertion that "the veiled slavery of the wage workers in Europe needed, for its pedestal, slavery pure and simple in the new world." *Capital*, Vol. 1, p. 400.
75 See Dubois, Laurent. *Avengers of the New World*. Cambridge, MA: Harvard

Depestre develops his metaphor of enslaved black people as human fossil fuel in the poem's final lines. Here, the poet apostrophizes this racialized collectivity as a "people":

> Peuple dévalisé peuple de fond en comble retourné
> Comme une terre en labours
> Peuple défriché pour l'enrichissement
> Des grandes foires du monde
> Mûris ton grisou dans le secret de ta nuit corporelle
> Nul n'osera plus couler des canons et des pièces d'or
> Dans le noir métal de ta colère en crues[76]

Extending the metaphor of "human combustible," Depestre envisions a future revolutionary explosion of oppressed black people as a natural process, a combustion reaction as spontaneous as firedamp's reaction with fire. The coda to the poem is thus, in one sense, a figuration of Marx's claim that "capitalist production begets, with the inexorability of a law of Nature, its own negation."[77] Revolution is an industrial byproduct. It is also worth noting that, having begun in the gold mines of the sixteenth century, the poem ends in a modern coal mine. Instead of treating race as a transhistorical essence, Depestre traces the *longue durée* of a process of racialization and exploitation across historical periods and modes of production, from Spanish mercantilism to the eighteenth-century boom of slave-produced commodities to the modern capitalist fossil fuel economy.

Overall, although Depestre is sometimes sharply critical of the way in which race is commonly discussed and figured within Negritude, the above reading of "Minerai noir" demonstrates that he is far from what is known in today's parlance as a "class reductionist." In "Minerai noir" he does not insist upon seeing "class, not race," or even upon prioritizing "class first"; rather, his consistent stance is to view race and racialization through a historical materialist lens. If he ultimately agrees with d'Arboussier's assessment of Negritude as a "mystification," this is not to reject it entirely but rather, as Marx set out to do for Hegel, to turn it right side up.[78]

University Press, 2005, p. 14 and *passim*.
76 Depestre, *Rage de vivre*, p. 106.
77 Marx, *Capital*, Vol. 1, p. 402.
78 Marx, Preface to the Second Edition, *Capital*, Vol. 1, p. 15. Depestre uses this same language in the "Réponse à Césaire": "On a surtout parlé de 'poésie noire', de la poésie nationale 'chez les noirs', de 'formalisme noir' opposé au 'formalism

"Aragon's Lessons": Depestre's Poetics of Comradeship

In his recent autobiography *Bonsoir tendresse* (2019), Depestre reflects upon his Cold War *querelle* with Césaire more than 60 years after the event. Really existing communism has, by this point, been defunct for three decades; Césaire himself has been dead for more than a decade, and Depestre, now a nonagenarian, has become a radically different figure from the young communist poet of the 1950s. In the 65 years since his debate with Césaire, Depestre has explicitly renounced the authoritarian communism of the Soviet bloc and condemned Zhdanovian "socialist realist" aesthetics several times over. He has reinvented himself as a novelist—especially with the Renaudot-winning *Hadriana dans tous mes rêves* (1988)—and, while he has never given up on radical politics as such, his later work has been more centrally preoccupied with themes of "solar eroticism" and what some have called a "magical realist" aesthetic informed by cultural practices deriving from Haitian *vodou*.

Remarkably, however, in this recent reflection upon his debate with Césaire, Depestre still—although admittedly not without qualification—defends Aragon. When he begins to discuss his younger self's support for *poésie nationale*, the older Depestre adopts a significantly defensive tone. In defense of his earlier position, Depestre insists that he never intended to promote "formal sectarianism," nor to criticize free verse per se, nor to suggest that the sonnet was somehow the "summit of poetic form."[79] Rather, as the older writer explains it, he found Aragon's critique of formal individualism "not unfounded" and postulated that, "being of French expression" himself, he "ought to reflect on all aspects of French prosody." Was he guilty of the charge of assimilationism that Césaire and others leveled against him? No, he insists, since Haiti had its own tradition of classical verse, composed by writers who "happened to be good, Haitian poets."[80] This later reflection is largely consistent

---

blanc', de 'négritude', de 'l'aliénation culturelle des nègres', toutes catégories insaisissables, qui ou, sont fausses par définition, ou, marchant sur la tête comme la dialectique chez Hegel, ont besoin d'être remises sur leurs jambes historiques" (p. 44).

79 Depestre says—incorrectly, as one can easily see by reading the poems collected in *Minerai noir*—that "all my poems were in free verse." *Bonsoir tendresse*, Ch. 8.

80 *Bonsoir tendresse*, Ch. 8. Depestre is referring here to the Haitian poets associated with the nineteenth-century Cénacle movement—including Ignace Nau, Coriolan Ardouin, Massilon Coicou, and, later, Oswald Durand—who did indeed

with Depestre's interventions in 1955–56, although the senior *homme de lettres* of *Bonsoir tendresse* significantly lacks the fervor and enthusiasm that come through so clearly in the letter to Dobzynski and the "Réponse à Césaire."[81] Though this later recollection strikes a guarded tone in place of the younger poet's defiant apologia, he still ultimately defends his original position vis-à-vis Aragon. There is something in this aesthetic alignment, then, that has survived the demise of really existing communism and Depestre's own complicated belief in it.

Several critics have sought to account for Depestre's alignment with Aragonian *poésie nationale* beyond the clichéd pseudo-explanation that he was merely toeing the party line. Romuald Fonkoua points to the material support that Aragon and Elsa Triolet provided in Depestre's early years as a student poet in Paris.[82] Anne Douaire-Banny concurs, and further suggests that Depestre's support for Aragon reflected an attempt to gain standing in the Parisian literary field and within the PCF mediasphere.[83] Indeed, Depestre did benefit from the patronage of Aragon and (especially) Triolet as part of the Groupe des jeunes poètes, although Aragon was but one of several established cultural figures—not all of them PCF-affiliated—upon whom Depestre came to rely in the 1950s.[84]

As Maryse Condé convincingly argues, Aragon's antifascist *bona fides* also appealed to Depestre: Depestre admired Aragon as a Resistance poet who had deployed his nation's cultural patrimony in the service

---

write in alexandrine verse, though about Haitian cultural themes. It is too tempting to resist mentioning here the title of Coicou's 1892 collection poems in alexandrine verse: *Poésies nationales*.

81 Depestre's recent defense of Aragon is, however, in sharp contrast to his denunciations of Marxism in a 1997 interview, in which he blames his earlier Marxist commitments for "nearly destroy[ing] my integrity as a citizen and a writer." ("Interview with René Depestre: Between Utopia and Reality," *UNESCO Courier*, Dec. 1997, p. 48).

82 Fonkoua, Romuald. *Aimé Césaire (1913–2008)*. Paris: Perrin, 2010, p. 171.

83 Douaire-Banny, "Sans rimes, toute une saison, loin des mares."

84 As part of Aragon and Triolet's entourage, Depestre frequented the couple's home and met many Parisian intellectual celebrities; he recalls feeling frequently starstruck (*Bonsoir tendresse*, Ch. 8). However, Depestre also frequented *Présence Africaine*, and also viewed decidedly non-Communist figures such as Alioune Diop and Léopold Senghor as mentors, along with Césaire the de-aligned Marxist (*Bonsoir tendresse*, Ch. 8).

of resistance to foreign occupation.[85] Haiti, however, unlike France vis-à-vis postwar Germany, remained under the indirect domination of its former occupier, the United States, and this continued subjugation of Haiti by the United States points to another reason for Depestre's 1950s Aragonian alignment: the latter's steadfast opposition to US and NATO imperialism. In many of his writings from this period—especially in the collection *Les yeux et la mémoire* (1954), which Depestre singles out for praise—Aragon denounces the *yankee* as the new occupier of France (via NATO), expresses horror at the destructive power of the US atomic bomb, and condemns US interventions from Guatemala to Korea. This antiimperialist and internationalist political affinity between the two communist writers runs deep, although it still does not fully account for the specifically *aesthetic* affinity that Depestre expresses for Aragon in the 1950s.

We can begin to understand Depestre's aesthetic alignment with Aragon by situating it within the context of the young poet's lived experience of the postwar decade. This was a tumultuous period of exile and displacement for Depestre that saw Depestre and his then wife Edith Sorel tossed back and forth across the borders of the three Cold War worlds in an uncommonly peripatetic itinerary. Indeed, the chapters of his memoir in which he discusses this period read at times like excerpts from a John Le Carré spy novel (only, as far as one can tell, without any actual espionage). Expelled from Haiti by President Estimé for having participated in the revolution that ousted his predecessor Elie Lescot, Depestre was sent to "study abroad" in postwar Paris, where he lived for years until he was expelled from France for his PCF affiliations.[86] A timely telephone call by PCF-aligned poet Paul Éluard to the Czechoslovakian ambassador secured the Depestres asylum in Prague. Finding life behind the Iron Curtain intolerable—the couple was subject to constant surveillance by Czechoslovakian secret police, who suspected them of being NATO spies—the Depestres found asylum within their ostensible place of asylum when they befriended Brazilian novelist Jorge Amado and Chilean poet Pablo Neruda, both fellow communists. An internationally renowned literary figure with significant cultural capital, Amado was able to hire Depestre as an assistant and help the couple

---

85 Condé, "Fous t'en Depestre; laisse dire Aragon," pp. 179–180.
86 Depestre was offered a university scholarship to study in Paris as a pretext; he makes it clear, however, that all parties were aware that this supposed study abroad was a means of neutralizing Depestre politically. *Bonsoir tendresse*, Ch. 2.

relocate to the Bohemian castle where Amado resided, thus sparing them the police harassment they had endured in Prague.[87]

I wish to draw a few insights from this remarkable chapter in Depestre's biography that will be useful in contextualizing his postwar thinking about literary aesthetics, and that will help to elucidate the stakes of his aesthetic alignment with Aragon. First of all, Depestre's traumatic experience living under really existing communism in 1950s Prague suggests that his ideological disillusionment with Stalinism likely preceded the grim revelations of 1956: the notion that Depestre remained aligned with Aragon in 1955 due to some presumed naiveté about state communism is belied by the fact of Depestre's miserable sojourn in Prague.[88] Depestre maintained his political commitments despite being repelled—even horrified—by most of his interactions with communist state apparatuses, and also at the expense of his and his wife's enjoyment of political rights and personal security.

The elder Depestre provides an illuminating explanation for why he did not split with communism in the 1950s: over and over again, Depestre found that he could depend on comrades. Though these comrades were often also friends, such as Neruda and Amado, Depestre also identifies as comrades fellow communists who were complete strangers to him: for example, the Italian lawyer who helped Depestre and his wife obtain temporary Italian visas to reenter France clandestinely by train after his plan to seek asylum in Cuba fell through.[89] What kept Depestre connected to the communist project, despite its disappointments and even the crimes committed in its name, was precisely this sense of comradeship:

> What, then, kept me from breaking [with Communism]? It was above all the fraternal bonds I had woven [...] with people of such quality as [Jorge] Amado and [Pablo] Neruda [...] In our Eastern European exile, they embodied to my eyes the hope for a solar, human *us [nous]*, who would one day blossom into a cheerfully universal *us*. [...] They treated me without condescension, like a friend, a comrade, a true comrade.[90]

---

87 This skips over several episodes in Depestre's Cold War odyssey, which also included brief sojourns in Vienna, East Berlin, Genoa, and an abortive trip by sea to pre-revolutionary Cuba. *Bonsoir tendresse*, Ch. 3 and Ch. 4.
88 This is speculative, of course, as Depestre's recollections of his sojourn in Prague were all made decades after the fact.
89 Depestre, *Bonsoir tendresse*, Ch. 4.
90 Depestre, *Bonsoir tendresse*, Ch. 4.

I want to argue here that, for Depestre, "comrade" denotes a specific form of relationality, one defined in expressly political terms. Political theorist Jodi Dean provides a theory of the "comrade form" as precisely such a form of *political* belonging: "The term *comrade*," Dean argues, "indexes a political relation, a set of expectations for a common goal. [It is] a generic figure for the political relation between those on the same side of a political struggle."[91] As a term denoting the specific relation that exists between "those on the same side," the comrade form "abstracts from socially given or naturalized identities as it posits a common field of equality and belonging."[92] The common political field posited by the comrade relation is thus indifferent to racial, cultural, national, or civilizational forms of belonging. Dean is careful to specify, furthermore, that comrade is *not* a form of individual subjectivity; to the contrary, "the individual, as a locus of identity, is the 'Other' of the comrade."[93] The "solar, human us" in which Depestre believed was precisely this kind of political relation: Depestre's comrades provided him with a field of belonging and a horizon of possibility, even in the face of really existing communism's failures. "Comrades," writes Dean, "are the zero point of possibility, what is left after everything else is gone, remainders existing in ruins, at the negative place of beginning."[94]

In so far as Depestre's political adherence to global communism in the 1950s stems from his commitment to (and trust in) comrades, I would argue that this specific form of political belonging also significantly elucidates Depestre's engagement with Aragon's communist aesthetics. Parallel to Depestre's politics of comradeship is an aesthetics of comradeship that Depestre tries to work through by appropriating and using elements of Aragon's *poésie nationale*. The close readings that follow in this section tease out the specific qualities of Depestre's comradely poetics; they also place Depestre's poems in direct dialogue with Aragon's theoretical and poetic writings, therefore suggesting an engagement and influence that go substantially farther than what scholars have thus far acknowledged.

Depestre's poetic reflection upon comradeship does not begin with his letter on Aragon; indeed, comradeship is a preoccupation that

---

91 Dean, Jodi. *Comrade: An Essay in Political Belonging*. New York: Verso, 2019, pp. 2–3.
92 Dean, *Comrade*, p. 26.
93 Dean, *Comrade*, p. 77.
94 Dean, *Comrade*, p. 54.

cuts across his early poetry. All of the poems collected in *Végétations de clarté* (1951), for example, are odes to comrades. Among those Depestre lauds in this sequence of odes are (alas) Joseph Stalin ("Je chante un homme en fleur"); Maurice Thorez ("Le commissaire de l'espérance"); Turkish poet and political prisoner Nazim Hikmet ("Nazim l'invincible"); French antiwar activist Raymonde Dien ("Billet à Raymonde Dien"); and Henri Martin ("Le soldat bien-né"), a French soldier who deserted in protest against the Indochina War.[95] The final poem, "Tombés au champ de la clarté," is an elegy for a group of 18 Nigerian miners murdered in 1950 for having organized a strike for higher wages. The very title of *Végétations de clarté* contributes to the volume's organizing thematic of comradeship. In the field of botany, "vegetation" denotes the sum total of interconnected plant life in a given biome, considered collectively; it is a general term, therefore, focusing on collective life without regard to particular taxa. The comrades of *Végétations de clarté* are just such a plural, interconnected proliferation of life. *Végétations de clarté* thus brings together as one collective subject an international network of men and women, workers, intellectuals, soldiers, and leaders from numerous racial and ethnic groups, united by the fact of being on the same side; in doing so, the collection exemplifies the solidaristic, transindividual imaginary implicit in the comrade relation as theorized by Dean.[96]

If *Végétations de clarté* reflects a comradely imaginary, the poems of the collection *Minerai noir* (1956) reflect an attempt by Depestre to develop a poetic style and a prosody anchored by this political imaginary. Though critics rarely discuss the collection in any context—and none appear to have discussed it in the context of the *poésie nationale* debate—it is in *Minerai noir* that Depestre experiments most extensively with applying what he calls "Aragon's lessons" to his own poetic style, particularly Aragon's prescriptions regarding classical French verse.

---

95 I thank Gül Bilge Han for sharing with me the delicious anecdote that Depestre's poem was transmitted clandestinely to Hikmet in the latter's prison cell, stuffed by an anonymous comrade into a piece of bread.

96 The epigraph to Depestre's ode to Stalin in *Végétations de clarté*—a collection to which Aimé Césaire wrote the preface—is a quote from Aragon's *L'Homme communiste*: "L'homme communiste, ouvrier, paysan, intellectuel, c'est l'homme qui a une fois vu si clairement le monde qu'il ne peut pas l'oublier, et que rien pour lui désormais ne vaut plus que cette clarté-là, pas même ses intérêts immédiats, pas même sa propre vie." *Rage de vivre*, p. 63.

The volume contains 18 poems in total, of which nine are written in alexandrine meter, mostly in an unrhyming *alexandrin blanc* that is not always strictly maintained.[97] Despite Aragon's emphasis on the sonnet, there does not appear to be a single poem in Depestre's collection that could reasonably be identified as one; rather, the alexandrine meter itself seems to be of primary interest to Depestre in *Minerai noir*, not simply because it *is* classically French or because Aragon promoted it but rather, I would argue, because of what Depestre thinks it may be able to *do*, how it may be able to help him give form to thought.

Depestre's concern to develop a prosody in harmony with his Marxist political vision is most direct and apparent in the poem "La Liberté raconte sa vie." This is the finished version of a poem that had appeared alongside the letter to Dobzynski in *Les lettres françaises* under the title "Pour que lèvent les blés humains" as a sort of proof of concept for Depestre's appropriation of *poésie nationale*.[98] It is a several-page dramatic monologue in *alexandrin blanc*, written in the voice of an allegorical, female-gendered "Liberté." Liberté, a sort of personified World-Spirit, speaks from the point of view of the present moment, when she has acquired consciousness of herself and is thus able to recount the linear history of her coming into self-consciousness. Liberté's view of history is squarely Marxist-Leninist:

> Je n'ai pas été donnée à l'homme comme
> Un attribut profond de son moi fabuleux
> La fleur la plus intime de son essence humaine;
> Je suis le fruit douloureux de ses conquêtes,
> Le chant qu'il a gagné à la sueur de son cœur,
> Chaque étape de ma vie a eu ses martyrs,
> Héros tombés avec mon soleil sur leurs lèvres.[99]

Liberté's recounting of her life takes the form of a materialist dialectic whose motor is class struggle, a history scattered with progressive heroes

---

97 The poems in *Minerai noir* written in alexandrine are "Mon cinéma d'enfant noir," "Sous les ponts de l'amour," "Complainte des mères malheureuses," "Le maïs qui lève," "Au large d'Edith," "La Liberté raconte sa vie," "les armes de mon sang," "Le chercheur d'or," and "Les Gués de l'amour." "Lettre à ma mère" contains several dodécasyllabic lines interspersed with free-verse stanzas, ans thus does not sustain the meter throughout.
98 "Pour que lèvent les blés humains (fragments)." *Les lettres françaises*, No. 573 (Jun. 16–23, 1955), p. 5.
99 *Rage de vivre*, p. 122.

and martyrs who, sometimes unknowingly, pushed history towards its socialist *telos*.[100] Liberté's history also appears to align neatly with the Stalinist theory of stagism: there is nearly a one-to-one ratio of stanzas to historical stages, from primitive communism through ancient slavery and feudalism, continuing through various phases of capitalism, and arriving at the present moment where socialism appears finally on the horizon. She reserves harsh words for the bourgeois class, which has sorely disappointed her initial hopes for it ("O bourgeoisie ...").[101] Overall, it would seem that Depestre employs the classical French *vers héroïque* here in order to afford the materialist account of History the highest possible register, composing high epic verse with History itself succeeding the demigod, the prince, and the bourgeois individual subject as hero.

The alexandrine meter does considerably more ideological work, however, in the poem's final stanza, wherein Liberté performs her peroration. Here, the poem comes to a crescendo, ending in a long, rapid enumeration of exploited people across the world, all viewed through Liberté's eyes:

> Oh mes amis je suis celle dont la chair saigne
> Chaque fois que sur cette terre un peuple
> A en sang le doux visage de son espoir
> Il n'est pas au monde de patrie torturée
> En qui je ne devienne un cri de torture
> Il n'est pas au monde un esprit insulté
> Un paysan volé un ouvrier opprimé
> Un soldat méprisé un employé gifle
> En qui mon coeur ne voie une aurore humiliée.
> L'histoire de ma vie est celle de mes enfers
> Et il n'est pas au monde un être affamé
> Un nègre lynché un enfant abandonné
> Une femme prostituée un innocent condamné
> En qui je ne reconnaisse mon propre faim
> Mon lynchage et mon abandon
> Ma prostitution et ma condamnation.[102]

---

100 See the discussion of socialist realist conventions in Clark, *The Soviet Novel*, especially Ch. 1.
101 *Rage de vivre*, p. 122.
102 *Rage de vivre*, p. 123.

The alexandrine meter is tightest in this final stanza, nearly every line dividing neatly into two equal hemistiches of six syllables each:

> Il n'est pas au monde / de patrie torturée

In addition, there is semantic and syntactic coherence to each rhythmic unit: in nearly every line, at least one hemistich consists of an indefinite article, a noun denoting a person, and a past participle used as an adjective: "un esprit insulté," "[u]n paysan volé," "un ouvrier opprimé," "un soldat méprisé," "un employé giflé," and so on. Each hemistich therefore names one kind of oppressed person (the indefinite article implying genericity, that there are many of each), and specifies the particular exploitative or oppressive action done to each. Note also the regularity of the distribution of stresses in these hemistiches, each divided into two anapests:

> un es *prit* / in sul *té*

The final stanza thus achieves an almost perfectly regular rhythm, nearly without syncopation. In this poetic enumeration of the *damnés de la terre*, each of the oppressed and exploited is thus allotted the same slot of six syllables, and is made to fit into the same syntactic and rhythmic structure, literally placed side by side with one another. To further this overall aesthetic of genericity, in the ninth line of the stanza Liberté even coins a generic term to encompass all those listed, quantity becoming quality: to her eyes, each is "une aurore humiliée," "a dawn humiliated." Without erasing the diverse specific identities of the enumerated subjects, the poem's structure is indifferent to these differences, seeking not to oppose or contrast the various oppressed and exploited subjects it enumerates but rather to posit a set of which each of the poet's enumerated subjects is a member, each counting as one within the structure of the poem—and, implicitly, within the emancipatory political movement.[103] An injury to one, in other words, is an injury to all, even to Liberté herself.

In its way of portraying a collection of multiples united in and by common struggle within a situation, the poem takes part in a longstanding tradition of militant socialist art. For example, the poem's generic, regular structure achieves the same solidarizing energy as the refrain to Bertolt Brecht's 1936 "Workers United Front Song": "To the left, two, three! To

---

103 Similarly, Dean locates the etymological origins of the term "comrade" in the lexicon of architecture; it a repeatable structure" that produces "an inside separate from outside." *Comrades*, p. 3.

the left, two, three!/ Comrade, there's a place for you/ Come and join the Worker's United Front/ For you are a worker, too."[104] It also calls to mind the sublime finale of Jean Renoir's Front Populaire propaganda film *La vie est à nous* (1935), where diverse crowds of working people—young and old, male and female, beautiful and ugly, sick and healthy, urban worker and rural peasant—coalesce into a single collective subject, singing "L'Internationale" in unison with fists raised. These are unapologetically equalitarian works that seek to reach and politically educate a mass audience, works that address the vast majority as a collectivity united by common interests. They stress, furthermore, what Alain Badiou names the communist hypothesis, the axiomatic declaration that "there is only one world," a "single world of human subjects," between whom "an infinite set of differences exist," and wherein all human subjects therefore "exist exactly as I do."[105] Depestre's poem inscribes itself in this very same fighting tradition of solidaristic socialist aesthetics.

The solidaristic impulse of "Liberté racontant sa vie" is carried further in other poems collected in *Minerai noir*. In "Le maïs qui lève," also written in *alexandrin blanc*, there is a sequence very similar in structure to the stanza quoted above. Here, though, it is not a self-aware Liberté who speaks, but the impersonal voice of the poet, who assigns to himself a set of directives for his poetry (which he addresses as "mon vers" and "mon chant"):

> Lève-toi aussi mon vers ta place est dans la rue
> Sois l'homme à tout faire de la paix du monde [...]
> Crie crie à perdre haleine le danger qui pèse
> Sur ses jours crie-le au nom de tous les arbres
> Crie-le avec la force de ton premier baiser
> Pour que sur la terre il n'y ait pas un seul homme,
> Pas un seul bras de mère pas un soleil de femme
> Pas une trille d'oiseau pas un banc d'amoureux
> Pas une poignée de main pas un sommeil d'enfant
> Pas un morceau de pain pas une goutte de sperme
> Qui ne soient allumés du désir torrentiel
> De défendre la paix leur couronne de rois![106]

---

104 Brecht, Bertolt. *Collected Poems of Bertolt Brecht*. Translated and edited by Tom Kuhn and David Constantine. New York: Liveright, 2018, p. 671.
105 Badiou, Alain. "The Communist Hypothesis." *New Left Review*, Vol. 49 (Jan.–Feb. 2008), pp. 38–39.
106 *Rage de vivre*, p. 117.

As in "Liberté racontant sa vie," the individual poet—and, more broadly, the individual subject—is subordinated to the transindividual, collective project. The same generic (one might also say democratic) structure, traversing differences and counting as one anyone on the same side, is repeated here. Furthermore, Depestre, by placing his verse in the street—in contrast to Césaire's call to escape "far from the fens" ("loin des mares") and to "look at springtime" ("regarder le printemps")—would have the poet immerse his poetry in the collective struggle. Depestre cries out for his poetry to ground itself in what Mayakovsky called a "social command."[107] As Alain Badiou has written of Aragon, Depestre's poetry requires an *object-cause*, meaning both that his poetry cannot be gratuitous but must respond to a material cause and that his verse must draw its force and momentum from serving a cause.[108] His political imaginary here is not centered on subjectivity or consciousness; rather, it is transindividual (note the "Pas un" anaphora) and rooted in a shared struggle whose objective is not disalienated individual subjectivity per se but the production of a universal fraternal relation: *la paix du monde*.

The transindividual vision that drives these poems can be further elucidated by exploring Depestre's engagement, beyond the theory of *poésie nationale*, with Aragon's poetic writings from this period. Indeed, a major facet of the Depestre–Aragon connection that usually goes unmentioned is Depestre's explicit praise in the "Lettre à Dobzynski" for Aragon's poetry collection *Les Yeux et la mémoire* (1954). Depestre writes that he cannot stop listening to his recording of *Les Yeux et la mémoire*, and that the collection is all the rage among the Brazilian poets and intellectuals he frequents. Depestre thus credits not Aragon the theorist, but rather Aragon the poet for providing him what he calls an "école de gammes,"[109] or a lesson in musical scales.

What becomes visible, then, if we consider Depestre vis-à-vis Aragon *the poet* rather than Aragon the cultural commissar? In one of the most gushing passages in Depestre's letter to Dobzynski, he writes that "Aragon's book spills over the frontiers of French poetry. It is the

---

107 "The presence of a problem in society, the solution of which is only conceivable in poetical terms." Mayakovsky, Vladimir. "How Are Verses Made?". *Volodya: Selected Works. 1926*. Edited by Rosy Carrick. London: Enitharmon Press, 2016, p. 231. Depestre uses Mayakovsky's term "social command" explicitly when outlining his vision of Haitian national poetry in "Réponse à Césaire," p. 51.
108 Badiou, Alain. *Radar poésie: Essai sur Aragon*. Paris: Gallimard, 2020, p. 3.
109 "Lettre à Dobzynski," p. 5.

opportunity for numerous Brazilian poets to illuminate their path by applying Aragon's method to the conditions of development specific to the poetry of their country."[110] It is explicit in the letter that the book that Depestre is referring to is *Les Yeux et la mémoire*, not *Journal d'une poésie nationale*. If we put Depestre's poetry in dialogue with this poetic text by Aragon, we can imagine a poet working through an aesthetic thread in his own writing through immersing himself in the writings of another poet, rather than a doctrinaire young Stalinist cadre counting proverbial angels on the head of a pin.

Take, for example, the congruity between "Le maïs qui lève" and a few stanzas from Aragon's poem "Les vêpres interrompus":

> Est-ce un crime vraiment de dire ce qu'on voit
> Partager son amour chanter chercher des rimes
> Je ne sais pas vraiment ce que l'on veut de moi
> Est-ce vraiment vraiment un crime
>
> De rêver au bonheur dans la gueule du loup
> Et de dire à minuit que l'alouette est proche
> Mes amis mes amis que cela soit de vous
> Pourtant qu'en vienne le reproche
>
> Le paysage Allez je sais ce que l'on dit
> *Il faut peindre l'histoire il faut peindre la lutte*
> *Et que nous venez-vous en pleine tragédie*
> *Jouer un petit air de lutte*
>
> C'est la charrue et l'homme ici que je veux voir
> Connaître exactement la date de vos neiges
> Qui tient la terre et qui la travaille et savoir
> Ce que signifie ce manège[111]

Aragon performs a sort of poetic self-criticism in these stanzas, giving voice to the "social command" from which the poet receives guidance and correction and who tells the poet the imperatives ("*Il faut ... il faut*") and priorities of the cause to which the poet is committed, what the cause requires from him and from poetry. This collective voice of the poet's comrades is set off in italics. Similarly, Dean writes of the comrade form as an "ego ideal," a Lacanian term that in this context denotes "the point from which party members assess themselves as doing important,

---

110 "Lettre à Dobzynski," p. 5.
111 Aragon, Louis. *Les Yeux et la mémoire*. Paris: Gallimard, 1954, p. 39. Italics in original.

meaningful work."[112] As in Depestre's poem, Aragon's verse has its place in the streets, furnishing the people with a "little fighting tune" rather than a useless, escapist poem with no connection to the lifeworld of the people.

There is further thematic congruity between *Minerai noir* and *Les Yeux et la mémoire* around these texts' shared poetic ideal of solidarity, figured in both volumes as a transindividual commitment that transcends subjectivity and identity. We have seen above how Depestre expresses this transindividual political vision, through typographically and prosodically organizing the oppressed into harmonized ranks. In "Nocturne des frères divisés," Aragon expresses a similar vision of the many becoming one:

> Je songe à l'unité lente que nous gagnons
> Etoiles Ressouder les feux qui se scindèrent
> Inaugurer enfin le grand jour solidaire
> Et faire un soleil de tous ces lumignons[113]

As we have seen, Depestre's solidaristic poetics is born of the same concern to win a "slow unity," to "mend" or "resolder" ("Ressouder") disparate struggles, to amalgamate the disparate "dim lights" of the wretched of the earth into a single sun—a "solar, human *us*."

Another, broader aspect of Aragon's poetics in *Les Yeux et la mémoire* with which Depestre aligns himself is what Depestre calls "la technique du vers."[114] By the French word "technique," not only style is implied but also a broader understanding of poetry, and of writing, as technical—and even technological—rather than as organic or natural. There is a sense in which, for Depestre, seeing the poem as technological—perhaps even as mechanical, despite Césaire's objections—is desirable. As Roxanna Curto establishes in her book *Inter-Tech(s)*, technology was very much at the forefront of the imaginaries of Francophone writers of color in the early Cold War/decolonization era; many such writers viewed "Western technologies [as] capable of being dissociated from" the Western colonizer's culture, and these authors consequently came to "equate their acquisition with liberation from the Old Order" of colonialism.[115] As Curto argues convincingly,

---

112 *Comrade*, pp. 4, 19, 36.
113 Aragon, *Les Yeux et la mémoire*, p. 47.
114 Depestre, "Réponse à Césaire," p. 59.
115 Curto, *Inter-Tech(s)*, p. 3.

literary forms, genres, and techniques came to be widely understood as cultural "technologies" that could be appropriated and repurposed by the colonized.[116]

I would suggest that a similar understanding of form as technical rather than organic is at work in Depestre's engagement with Aragon's socialist poetics. The metalinguistic reflection upon poetic technique in "Le maïs qui lève" is also a major thread running throughout *Les Yeux et la mémoire*. In "Comment l'eau devint claire," for example, Aragon similarly makes explicit the ideological rationale for his production of alexandrine verse: "j'ai réglé mon pas pour que ceux qui m'écoutent/ En scandent la chanson sur le pas ouvrier."[117] In "Sacre de l'avenir," Aragon even submits this choice to autocritique:

> C'est possible après tout qu'à parler politique
> Sur le rythme royal du vers alexandrin
> Le poème se meure et tout soit rhétorique
>   Dans le langage souverain[118]

Aragon again gives a justification of his aesthetic choices, demonstrating his accountability to the cause:

> Nous aurons des métros comme des basiliques
> Des gloires flamberont sur les toits ouvriers
> Et le bonheur de tous sur les places publiques
>   Psalmodiera son Kyrie[119]

His intent, he explains, is to socialize the classical tradition, to reclaim it for the proletariat as the great Moscow metro stations were meant to achieve in the domain of architecture.

Depestre and Aragon's guide in their parallel reflections upon poetic technique is Mayakovsky, who sees the writing of poetry as production. Depestre, like Mayakovsky and Aragon, wants "to write about poetry as a practitioner."[120] Depestre expresses a desire in his response to Césaire to undertake an apprenticeship, to study and practice (here he quotes Mayakovsky directly) "the methods of all poetic work, studying

---

116 Curto further argues that "appropriating technology [meant] not to overturn colonial hierarchies but to instigate progress and economic development in their nations." Curto, *Inter-Tech(s)*, p. 17.
117 Aragon, *Les Yeux*, p. 76
118 Aragon, *Les Yeux*, p. 89
119 Aragon, *Les Yeux*, p. 90.
120 Mayakovsky, "How Are Verses Made?" p. 226.

the practices of this industry, which help to create others."[121] We might thus understand his production of alexandrine verse as the acquisition of a technique that might potentially be aesthetically and conceptually useful, as a musician, actor, baker, or dressmaker might learn a technique for the purposes of a specific project.

The desire to weed out "formal individualism" that Depestre first expresses in his letter to Dobzynski may now look less like mere *langue de bois* and more like a desire to articulate his aesthetics with his solidaristic political imaginary. The alexandrine poems of *Minerai noir* insist upon a disciplined but capacious solidarity, the poet organizing a broad and diverse multiplicity of subjects into the same structure, setting the rhythm for their common march forward. With "Aragon's lessons" as a starting-off point ("à partir les leçons d'Aragon"), Depestre ultimately constructs an alternative image of the poet to the one prevalent in the pages of *Présence Africaine*, and to that in Sartre's "Orphée noir": rather than the Césairean *vates*—or the "aiodos of Negritude," as Jacques Rabemananjara calls Césaire[122]—Depestre offers a competing vision of the poet as handyman of the cause.

Conclusion

When asked recently about the literary legacy of communism, Depestre gave a measured answer. After saying that only a small number of communist writers had been able to write aesthetically successful works, he said that, on the other hand, "one can't purely and simply throw everything that has been marked by the experience of the October Revolution into the garbage. There were things that were magnificent because they were lived in authenticity."[123] This chapter has argued that this also holds true for Depestre's own poetic, critical, and polemical writings of the 1950s, and has sought to contribute to salvaging these texts that have indeed long been subject to "pure and simple" discarding. Un-forgetting Depestre's communist poetics of the 1950s, with its insights as well as its shortcomings, opens French Caribbean literature to being

---

121 Depestre, "Réponse à Césaire," p. 61.
122 *Ier Congres*, p. 26. See discussion of Rabamananjara in Ch. 1.
123 Depestre proceeds immediately to list 18 different Communist or fellow-traveling authors he deems to have succeeded in this way, including "sans doute Aragon, quoi qu'on dise." Bonniol, "Entretien," p. 9.

reconnected with the vast archive of global leftist cultural production, making visible aesthetic influences and solidarities beyond the quite well-known, though certainly important, connection to surrealism.

The René Depestre that I have sought to recover, because of his unapologetically universalist political vision and orthodox Marxist theoretical coordinates, functions as something like a dissident within postwar Negritude, at least vis-à-vis the consensual account of this thought tradition. Of course, Depestre was not repressed by the dominant tendencies within Negritude in the same way that the term "dissident" connotes, yet the perspective he expresses in his 1950s writings was rendered unthinkable almost immediately upon its publication, and has remained so for decades. For Negritude, viewed in all the generative contradictions it contains as an aesthetic, political, and philosophical movement, Depestre's poetry and criticism of the 1950s offers a trenchant and underappreciated contrapuntal voice. Excavating Depestre's communist aesthetics also affords the opportunity to challenge certain orthodoxies—anti-Marxist ones, in this case—concerning how literary works still tend to be evaluated in postcolonial studies, including francophone postcolonial studies. Such tendencies implicitly value rupture over solidarity, the dissenter over the comrade, indirectness over intensity, and being on a margin over being on a side. I have suggested in this chapter that, as the end of the Cold War grows ever more distant, perhaps it is not Depestre's communist writings themselves that are Cold War relics, but rather the illegibility of these writings and the critical reproduction of their illegibility.

CHAPTER THREE

Poetry of the Césaire–Soviet Split
The Melancholy Geopolitical Vision of Aimé Césaire's Cold War Poems

"*De la politique? (Soupir.)*"

(Aimé Césaire[1])

"*We have no wish to be dependent on anyone. We do not want to be small change.*"

(Josip Broz Tito[2])

"*During the Cold War, we lived in coded times when it wasn't easy and there were shades of grey and ambiguity.*"

(John Le Carré[3])

When Aimé Césaire split with the PCF on October 24, 1956, in an open letter to PCF chairman Maurice Thorez, he ended a political alignment that went back at least to 1945. During the long postwar decade, Césaire had been an active Cold War warrior. Elected to the Assemblée Nationale in 1946, Césaire served for a decade as a PCF deputy; ever a gifted rhetorician, he gave speeches praising the Soviet Union's economic development of Central Asia, and opposing the building of NATO bases in the French Antilles, and against the extension of the European Economic Community into the Caribbean.[4] As a

---

1 Césaire, Aimé. "Interview." *L'Express*, May 19, 1960.
2 Quoted in Prashad, *The Darker Nations*, p. 97.
3 "Interview. John Le Carré at the NFT." *The Guardian*, Oct. 5, 2002. Online.
4 In a speech at the Assemblée Nationale, Césaire stated: "Alors que, dans nos territoires, la misère, l'oppression, l'ignorance sont de règle, nous voyons, en Union

cultural and political figure of international reputation, Césaire was also a significant figure in Cold War cultural diplomacy, participating in Soviet-sponsored peace congresses in Wroclaw (1948), Bucharest (1949), Paris (1949), and Vienna (1952), and traveling to Moscow in 1953 to attend Joseph Stalin's state funeral.[5] He wrote an ode to Thorez, praised Stalin in the Soviet journal *Literaturnaya gazeta*,[6] contributed to the PCF tract *Pourquoi je suis communiste* (1947), and praised the Soviet Union's "fraternal development of diverse peoples" in a speech opposing a mutual defense treaty between France and NATO.[7] In the *Discours sur le colonialisme* (1950), today Césaire's most widely read prose text, he argues that only socialist revolution can save an "indefensible" Europe.

Césaire's "Lettre à Maurice Thorez" marks a definitive renunciation of this political alignment: citing Khrushchev's "secret speech" that admitted Stalin's myriad brutalities (and the PCF's failure to admit them), and expressing sympathy with the vanquished Hungarian Revolution and suppressed worker revolts in East Germany, Césaire recasts Stalinism as one more outgrowth of European colonialism and called for people of the Third World to "abandon all the old routes" and to forge their own paths towards socialism.[8] Césaire was one of hundreds of French intellectuals to split with the PCF over the revelations of 1956, but as an elected deputy and a prominent black party member, his demission was significantly embarrassing to the Party, warranting a flummoxed response by Thorez in *Les lettres françaises* and a number of rebuttals

---

soviétique un développement magnifique, un développement fraternel de peuples divers, de toutes races et de toutes nationalités, un magnifique développement des peuples, même de ceux qui étaient considérés comme les plus arriérés." He went on to enumerate the thousands of schools at all levels opened in the Central Asian republics, noting—correctly—that colonial France had not opened a single university in its West African colonies. ("Discours du 15 mars 1950." *Aimé Césaire. Ecrits Politiques: Discours à L'Assemblée Nationale, 1945–1983*. Edited by René Hénane. Paris: Jean-Michel Place, 2013, p. 78.)

5 See Véron, *Aimé Césaire*, pp. 329-333 and pp. 340-341.

6 It is unclear who translated Césaire's remarks to *Literaturnaya gazeta*, and it is possible that they may have been censored, altered, or even invented by Soviet authorities. Véron, *Aimé Césaire*, pp. 370-371.

7 Hénane, "Discours du 15 mars 1950."

8 For a discussion of the PCF's uneasy response to the XXth Party Congress and Khrushchev's speech, see Chapter 6 of Martelli, Roger et al. *Le Parti Rouge: Une histoire du PCF 1920-2020*. Paris: Armand Collin, 2020.

from Party loyalists such as Roger Garaudy. The speech act performed by the "Lettre à Maurice Thorez" has widely, and justly, been praised as both a brave denunciation of the PCF's collusion with Stalinism and a salutary decolonizing gesture: the chapter that Césaire biographer Romuald Fonkoua dedicates to the "Lettre à Maurice Thorez" and Césaire's political disalignment is entitled, fittingly, "To Finally Be Oneself," and Kora Véron's biography refers to Césaire's resignation from the PCF as an "ineluctable rupture."[9]

However, as I explore in this chapter, the aftermath of Césaire's demission was, in many ways, quite dissonant from the bold, even sanguine rhetorical tones of the "Lettre à Maurice Thorez." It should not be discounted just how disorienting and uprooting this split was for Césaire. Certainly, the "Lettre à Maurice Thorez" aired doubts and criticisms that he had long nurtured (we have already discussed one such disagreement, Césaire's objection to Aragon's PCF poetics, in the previous chapter). The demission came at great personal cost, however: as Fonkoua notes, it cost him several close friendships (including fellow Martinican communists René Ménil, Léopold Bissol and Georges Gratiant), as well as significant supplementary income and benefits tied to party membership, forcing his family to move from their Paris apartment near Odéon to the *banlieu* of Petit-Clamart.[10] It was also a significant factor in the decline of his marriage with Suzanne Césaire and their ultimate divorce.[11] Beyond these personal consequences, there was the fact of ideological isolation and disorientation in the wake of his demission, the lack of an ideological *point de capiton*; Césaire had indeed to invent his own route. To read Césaire's writings against the backdrop of the Césaire–Soviet split is to encounter a writer who finds himself "at the negative place of beginning," to recall Jodi Dean's phrase.[12]

In 1960, Césaire published *Ferrements*, a collection of poems he had written over the previous decade. For many critics, this text marks another radical break, this time a formal literary one, from another commitment that had been central to Césaire's thought: avant-garde poetic surrealism. Although Césaire never renounced surrealism,

---

9 For a discussion of the PCF's response to the events of 1956, see Chapter 6 of Véron, *Aimé Césaire*.
10 Fonkoua, *Aimé Césaire*, pp. 244–245.
11 Fonkoua, *Aimé Césaire*, pp. 287–289.
12 Dean, *Comrade*, p. 54.

scholars note a significant change in tone and style in *Ferrements*. Whereas Césaire's earlier poetry is characterized by linguistic "opacity,"[13] "hermetic" imagery, and a "cosmogonic"[14] heroism, *Ferrements* marks a shift to a new poetics marked by "literality and topical specificity,"[15] a "relative limpidity of style,"[16] and a tragic, melancholy emotional register.[17]

What is the relationship between these two splits? Scholarly accounts of how the changes in Césaire's poetics relate to his reconceived political commitments post-1956 vary significantly. Patrice Louis suggests that *Ferrements* performs Césaire's "farewell to poetry" in favor of theater, a genre ostensibly better suited to political interventions; he notes the collection's political topicality as a departure from the *Cahier*.[18] Nick Nesbitt groups *Ferrements* with the essay *Toussaint Louverture* (1960) and the play *Une Saison au Congo* (1966) as a sequence of texts where Césaire practices a new "anticolonialist socialist realism," his earlier left-libertarian surrealism having been "jettisoned."[19] Other scholars, however, take *Ferrements*'s introspective tone and its lack of the earlier poems' apocalyptic imagery as signs of Césaire's disillusionment with radical politics in the wake of his *désolidarisation*. Was not the reduction of poetry to political instrumentality—the "poésie nationale" Aragon had prescribed—just what Césaire denounced in his 1955 response to René Depestre, writing: "le poème n'est pas un moulin à passer de la canne à sucre"?[20] Had Césaire not insisted upon poetry's freedom from immediate political responsibility, the right of the poet to simply "look at springtime"? René Ménil even criticizes *Ferrements* for

---

13 Munro, Martin. *Shaping and Re-Shaping the Caribbean*. London: Modern Humanities Research Association, 2000, p. 64.
14 Nesbitt, *Caribbean Critique*, p. 117.
15 Nesbitt, *Caribbean Critique*, p. 117.
16 Davis, Gregson. Introduction. *Non-Vicious Circle: Twenty Poems of Aimé Césaire*. Stanford, CA: Stanford University Press, 1984, p. 8.
17 "Contexte historique et littéraire. Situation dans l'œuvre d'Aimé Césaire." *Du fond d'un pays de silence. Édition critique de* Ferrements, *d'Aimé* Césaire. Edited by Lilyan Kesteloot, René Hénane, and Mamadou Souley Ba. Paris: Orizons, 2012, p. 12 (all in-text citations refer to this edition of *Ferrements*).
18 Louis, Patrice. "Le temps de la poésie." In Arnold, *Aimé Césaire*, p. 59.
19 Nesbitt, *Caribbean Critique*, p. 117. Nesbitt writes convincingly of Césaire's political essays and of his 1960s dramatic writings, but mentions Césaire's poetry of the 1950s only in passing.
20 Césaire, "Réponse à Depestre," p. 114.

being *depoliticized* compared to the *Cahier*: "when, in certain poems in *Ferrements*, [Césaire] withdraws into the most futile within himself, when he flees reality (his own, as well as social reality), when he keeps mulling over unspeakable problems and indulges in mood swings [sautes d'humeur] and rancor—then, his poetic light is degraded, diminished, extinguished."[21] Part of what makes *Ferrements* such a fascinating collection to read—and commensurately challenging to analyze—is that its contents are varied enough to lend support to both readings. The collection is split between intervention and introspection; topical poems such as "Sur l'état de l'Union," "Salut à la Guinée," and "Pour saluer le Tiers Monde" present the image of a committed antiracist and *tiers-mondiste* Césaire, while hermetic poems of despair such as "Cadavre d'une frénésie" or "Beau sang giclé" suggest a disillusioned, inward-focused Césaire. These readings of *Ferrements* tend to make a few presuppositions about the relationship between poetry and politics. Ménil's critique seems to assume an incompatibility between lyrical introspection and political engagement. The critics who do see *Ferrements* as politically committed tend, on the other hand, to focus on the deployment in several of its poems of a sequence of referents to the decolonizing Third World.

I suggest in this chapter that the poems of *Ferrements* are engaged in a different way in the political currents of the period. In her pioneering book *The Emergence of Social Space*, Kristin Ross dismantles critical tendencies to "regard prose as the privileged vehicle for objective or political themes, and verse for subjective or individual ones,"[22] and argues convincingly that even the most apparently "hermetic" poetic language—her focus is on Arthur Rimbaud—can be "firmly anchored in society," and can pose "the problem of that society and especially of that society's future."[23] It is in this same spirit that I aim to recover elements of Césaire's political thought that lie unrecognized in his 1950s poetic writings. In fact, Césaire's own contemporaneous views on the relationship between aesthetic creation and political commitment

---

21 Ménil, *Tracées*, p. 177. By contrast, Ménil considered Césaire's *Cahier d'un retour au pays natal* a masterpiece of social realism. J Michael Dash, for his part, writes that heavily politicized readings of Césaire's poetry are "invariably centered" on the *Cahier* (Dash, "The Bearable Lightness of Becoming," p. 737).
22 Ross, Kristin. *The Emergence of Social Space: Rimbaud and the Paris Commune*. New York: Verso, 1988, p. 18.
23 Ross, *Social Space*, p. 129.

coincide with those of Ross's Rimbaud: "I find that there is no contradiction between what I write and what I do; it's simply a matter of two different levels of action," he says in a 1971 interview.[24] The poetics of *Ferrements*, which contrast so sharply with the audacity of the *Cahier* and other earlier poems, reflect Césaire's reevaluation of his politico-aesthetic vision in a moment defined by rupture, impasse, disappointment, and uncertainty.

My central claim in this chapter is that Césaire's poetry of the 1950s poses the problem of inhabiting the Cold War world-system at its contested peripheries. To reiterate a point I made in the Introduction, Césaire—along with Depestre and Alexis—viewed this world-system from a position that afforded him an exceptional critical purchase upon it. As a black Antillean who was simultaneously immersed in the politics of the French Fourth Republic; ambivalently aligned with international communism and also, less ambivalently, with myriad local antiimperialist struggles (including in the Eastern bloc); and fully committed to Third World liberation, Césaire is one among relatively few intellectual figures of the period whose lives and works cut transversally through all three "worlds" of the Cold War world (Depestre and Alexis are also among these few). Indeed, one advantage of privileging the Cold War as a historical context for Césaire is that the global political imaginary of Césaire's poetry becomes most clearly visible when these poems are read against the backdrop of the bipolar struggle.

My specific aim here is to demonstrate how Césaire uses the conceptual tools of lyrical poetry to think the complex geopolitical conjuncture of the 1950s: the discrediting of the Soviet Union, the emergence of the Third World and the birth of dozens of nations, the Cold War's overdetermination of local struggles across the planet (Fanon's "Suez and Budapest"), and the family resemblance between the insurrections against both superpowers that challenged this bipolar distribution. After Stalin's death, and especially after 1956, Soviet communism could no longer incarnate the alternative to imperialism and fascism that it did in 1945, when its victory over the Nazis was fresh. As Césaire recognized, this void could only be filled by conceiving a new paradigm of international solidarity, a geopolitical "universal" that remained "rich with all of the particular." While

---

24 Kesteloot, Lilyan and Kotchy, Barthélémy. *Comprendre Aimé Césaire. L'homme et l'œuvre*. Paris: Classiques africains/*Présence Africaine*, 2000. Quoted in Fonkoua, *Aimé Césaire*, pp. 315–316.

Césaire's prose and oratory engage with Cold War geopolitics on a tactical, pragmatic level, looking across the blocs to imagine possible new alignments, I contend that the formal and figurative qualities of the poems of *Ferrements* reflect Césaire's efforts to think through this impasse between particular and universal, local and global, subjective and structural, as only poetry allows him to do.

The chapter's first section traces how the Césairean geographical imaginary takes on a new purpose in *Ferrements* as a tool for the cognitive mapping of Cold War power relations. Second, I look at a sequence of elegiac poems in *Ferrements*, suggesting that this register of mourning is a key to understanding Césaire's changed attitude toward radical politics in the wake of 1956. In the chapter's third and final section, I consider several poems from *Ferrements* that are concerned with constellating an array of small and emergent nations—both satellites and colonies—situated between and beneath the two superpowers; I look especially to congruities between the poetics of *Ferrements* and the incipient idea of non-alignment.

Currents, Cataracts, and Deserts: Cold War Geopolitics and the Geographical Imaginary of *Ferrements*

Any reader of Césaire's poetry will note that geographical images and terms run throughout his entire oeuvre; indeed, it is perhaps the predominant lexical field in Césaire's poetic writings. As Eric Prieto argues, the *Cahier d'un retour au pays natal* is in large part a contestation of exoticized colonial depictions of Caribbean landscapes, the specificity of the poem's geographical imagery communicating a "powerfully localist message."[25] From the beginning, then, Césairean geography is about contesting the fantasies projected by colonial Europe upon the lands (and societies, though these are obscured by such exoticist representations) under its domination. This intention is best captured in a wonderful phrase from the *Cahier*: "And my original geography too, the map of the world made for my use, Not tinted with the arbitrary colors of the learned, but with the geometry of my far-flung blood."[26] Césaire not only rejects the abstract geography and arbitrary boundaries

---

25 Prieto, Eric. *Literature, Geography, and the Postmodern Poetics of Place.* London/New York: Palgrave Macmillan, 2012, p. 158.
26 *Cahier d'un retour au pays natal.* Arnold ed., *Césaire*, p. 208.

of the world maps produced by imperialist and colonialist Europe, but he also insists on imagining an alternative geography from below, one generated by his concrete inhabiting of the world and for his use.

I argue in this section that the poems that Césaire composed over the course of the 1950s reflect a radically different geographical imaginary from that of the *Cahier*, and I suggest that this new geography can be understood as Césaire's cognitive map of the Cold War world-system.[27] As I will show, Césaire uses geographic imagery in *Ferrements* not so much to ground a subjectivity as to schematize a global structure of power relations that circumscribe both the limits of subjectivity and the horizon of political action. In his 1944 essay "Poésie et Connaissance," Césaire holds up poetry as a way of writing "totality"; that is, poetry gives us a means of thinking beyond the alienating contradictions of modern experience, and thus of liberating consciousness from a Western capitalist positivism that "numbers, measures, classes, and kills."[28] In *Ferrements*, poetry remains a means of apprehending totality, but it has taken on a different and more concrete aim: the totality sought here is not the Surrealist "certain point de l'esprit" beyond the contradictions of colonial/capitalist modernity, but rather a total image of the contemporary world-system as one uneven structure of relations. Geographic imagery literally becomes a means of "world-writing" for Césaire in the poems of *Ferrements*, a tool for mapping the Cold War world-system, and for locating and orienting (i.e., aligning) himself within it.

The very first line of "Ferrements," the collection's opening poem, sets the scale of the spatial matrix that the poet will construct: "Le périple ligoté emporte tous les chemins."[29] In common usage, the French word *périple* simply denotes a long voyage, or a circumnavigation—the latter is its precise etymological meaning.[30] In its archaic meaning, however, the periplus is also a literary/cartographic genre, denoting a

---

27 A. James Arnold similarly notes a "cartographic vision" in several poems in *Ferrements*, though he connects this vision to the Third World independence and does not mention the global Cold War as a context for the collection. *Aimé Césaire. Genèse et transformations d'une poétique*. Würzburg: Königshausen & Neumann, 2020, p. 245.
28 "Poésie et connaissance." Arnold ed., *Aimé Césaire: Poésie, théâtre, essais et discours*, p. 1377.
29 Césaire, *Du fond*, p. 35.
30 "Périple au sens de Voyage." Académie française. Online. https://www.academie-francaise.fr/periple-au-sens-de-voyage.

written guide that prescribes a precise course along a shoreline and that contains details regarding ports, landmarks, distances, and dangers.[31] As a polysemic term meaning both an account of a voyage on a grand scale and a guide to maritime trade routes, therefore, the "periplus" in "Ferrements" that simultaneously binds and silences (*ligote*) clearly evokes the triangular Atlantic slave trade. The final stanza of the poem explicitly casts the poet and his beloved as slaves:

> l'eau des criques boueuse et cette douleur puis rien
> où nous deux dans le flanc de la nuit gluante aujourd'hui comme jadis
> esclaves arrimées de coeurs lourds
> tout de même ma chère tout de même nous cinglons
> à peine moins écoeurés aux tangages[32]

Like the slave in the hold of the *négrier*, the poet and his beloved are paradoxically both stuck in place and thrown helplessly into motion, transfixed by the "muddy creek water" and the "gluey night" and "stowed" (*arrimées*) as cargo, but also embarked on a trajectory over which they have no control.

In the simile "aujourd'hui comme jadis," the poet also explicitly connects this historical system of exploitation to the poem's present moment. Quite literally, the periplus is a "vieille route," precisely what Césaire says must be abandoned in the "Lettre à Maurice Thorez" in favor of charting autonomous "paths" towards emancipation. I am suggesting that the contemporary referent to which Césaire links the "jadis" of the slave trade is not just a dying colonialism, but rather the conjuncture of decolonization and the Cold War. The fixed courses of these two twentieth-century *periploi* run the gamut from Western neocolonial projects of uneven development (such as the French government's integration of Martinique into the European Common Market, which Césaire strongly opposed)[33] to the uniform Stalinist "path to socialism" predicated upon hypostatized notions of universal "stages of historical development."[34] Césaire himself cites this feeling

---

31 Kish, George. *A Source Book in Geography*. Cambridge, MA: Harvard University Press, 1978, pp. 21–28. Césaire, trained in classics, would likely have been aware of the *Periplus of Hanno,* the fifth century BCE voyage of Carthaginian explorer Hanno the Navigator along—not incidentally—the African coast.
32 Césaire, *Du fond*, p. 36.
33 "Discours du 6 juillet 1957." In Hénane ed., *Aimé Césaire. Écrits politiques I*.
34 Westad, *The Global Cold War*. See Ch. 2 of Westad for a thorough historical

of being embarked upon a course over which he has no control in his post-demission "Discours à la maison du sport": "So here is my situation: member of a party whose decisions bind me [*m'engagent*] to the entire world and on whose decisions I cannot weigh in."[35]

The periplus and the path, or paths, are thus introduced in the very first line of the collection as the two scalar poles of the spatial matrix Césaire constructs in *Ferrements*. These two levels correspond to the geopolitical and the local, or, as Fredric Jameson puts it, the structural and the phenomenological, world map and lifeworld.[36] Césaire's poetic map of the Cold War world is therefore also congruous with Fanon's "Budapest and Suez" model, discussed in this book's Introduction: the saturation of planetary space by an all-pervasive bipolar structure, and the consequent geopolitical significations imposed upon every local struggle. In "Ferrements," the amorous couple, perhaps the smallest and most localized unit of human relations, becomes similarly subsumed into an incommensurately vast global structure—*formerly* the triangular system of the slave trade, *now* the competing neocolonialisms of the Cold War—and, then as now, the lovers are violently disoriented by the pitching and tossing of the system's currents.[37]

If "Ferrements" opens the collection by establishing a geopolitical spatial matrix, the following poem, "Comptine," poses the problem of placement and location within geopolitical space. As its title suggests, the poem is structured like a nursery rhyme, with a sustained anaphora:

> C'est cette mince pellicule sur le remous du vin
> mal déposé de la mer
> C'est ce grand cabrement des chevaux de la terre
> Arretés à la derniere seconde sur un sursaut du gouffre

account of postwar Soviet anticolonial policy, especially Stalin's conception of the "non-skipping of stages" in Third World countries' development towards socialism. Westad explains that this ideology of History led to the Soviet Union supporting bourgeois nationalists in countries that were deemed not yet "ready" for socialism, often to the ruination of local communist parties.

35 "Discours à la maison du sport." Arnold ed., *Aimé Césaire*, p. 1518.
36 Jameson, Fredric. "Cognitive Mapping." p. 351. In Nelson, Cary and Lawrence Grossberg eds., *Marxism and the Interpretation of Culture*. Urbana and Chicago, IL: University of Illinois Press, 1988, pp. 347–360.
37 The poet's seasickness in "Ferrements" is also analogous to Jameson's description of the experience of late capitalist "saturated space" as a "peculiar disorientation." Jameson, "Cognitive Mapping," p. 351.

> C'est ce sable noir qui se saboule au hoquet de l'abîme
> C'est du serpent têtu ce rampement hors naufrage
> Cette gorgée d'astre revomie en gateau de lucioles
> Cette pierre sur l'océan élochant de sa bave
> Une main tremblante pour oiseaux de passage[38]

Gregson Davis notes that the poem mimics a children's game, the repetition of the demonstrative pronoun *ce* evoking the "pointing finger of the player who performs the ditty."[39] While Davis reads these lines as a sequence of metaphors for "life in colonial Martinique," the poem's use of deixis and linguistic shifters—that is, its organization around the gesture of indicating or pointing out, as on a map—suggests that the poem is more centrally about Antillean space.

Unlike "Ferrements," which opens at the global scale of the periplus and then zooms in to the poet and his lover's location, "Comptine" is more localized, beginning with a demonstrative instead of a definite article. Two details from the poem's first lines allow us to identify the poem's geographical referent as the Antilles archipelago. First, the "sable noir" mentioned in line 5 is a geological feature found in several Antillean islands, including Martinique. Second, the denigrating tone of the poem's description is the same language that Césaire uses elsewhere, in both poetry and prose, to portray the Antillean archipelago as atomized and particulate.

Although scholars tend to read "Comptine" as a deeply negative, almost masochistic poem, it reveals itself to be more detached and analytical if we look at it formally, as a poem that schematizes the historical forces that produced the Antilles. In short, "Comptine" can be read as a map, a spatial representation of Antillean history and geography. The counting game that opens the poem is interrupted by an aside that breaks the anaphora:

> ici Soleil et Lune
> font les deux roués dentées
> savamment engrenées
> d'un Temps à nous moudre féroce[40]

With the deictic *ici*, the poetic voice shifts from indicating different points in a given field and points instead to its own position—not

---

38 Césaire, *Du fond*, p. 41.
39 Davis, *Non-Vicious Circle*, p. 62.
40 Césaire, *Du fond*, p. 44.

only *its* own, but "ours" as well, that of the poetic "nous"—as if to say, "You are here." The poet locates the "nous" of the poem in a non-place between the mechanized Sun and Moon, which have become "toothed wheels," the "skillfully meshed" gears in "a Time to grind us up ferocious." Time—as Davis rightly suggests, a "gnomic" or generic Time[41]—is represented schematically here: a mechanical system in which the "nous" are placed and which acts upon them, grinding them into something else.

In the final lines of "Comptine" the counting game becomes scatological: "c'est ce mal être/ cette fiente/ ce sanglot de coraux." The Antilles are recast as not simply as dust, but rather as excremental; a waste product of history, specifically of the slave trade. Finally, the last four lines bring the game to its climax:

> ce rapt
> ce sac
> ce vrac
> cette terre[42]

We may note first that the language of the poem, its very lexical substance, undergoes a process of syntactic and typographical transformation: the longer, complex phrases of earlier stanzas are broken down by the end into monosyllabic, staccato utterances, as if the lines of the first stanza had themselves passed through the "roues dentées" machine and emerged in a refined form. Note also that from the poem's beginning to its end the predicates of the demonstrative *ce* shift from specific to generic, from complex to simple. The historical forces that have produced the Antilles reduce them to three words: *rapt* ("abduction" or "kidnapping," i.e., the slave trade), *sac* ("sack," industrialized sugar production), *vrac* ("bulk," as in a product sold "in bulk," but also "jumble," signifying the archipelago's social, cultural, and political fragmentation).

In the poem's final line, the substance that began as complex, multiple, and contingent has been shed of all its particular content and condensed into a generic *subject*: what emerges from this process is "cette terre," a linguistic shifter, no more or less a "terre" than any other "terre." Doris Garraway argues perceptively of Césairean Negritude that "it is only when the black condition is embraced and understood as an effect of history rather than essence that the irreducible humanity of blacks

---

41 Davis, *Non-Vicious Circle*, p. 63.
42 Césaire, *Du fond*, p. 46.

comes into full view."[43] In precisely the same way, "cette terre" is the effect of every line that has come before it, not simply canceling this determinate content but sublating it.[44] Above all, the emergent subject in the last line is not an individual, psychological subject, a *moi*, but rather a political collectivity, a *terre*. "Comptine" thus inscribes the Antilles into the world map as a location that—though a product of a particular historical development—is nonetheless placed within a situation of universal global connectivity. The poem presents this situation in all its ambiguity, poses this situation as pregnant with both potential and danger.

Together, these opening poems lay out the two poles of particular and universal, structural and phenomenological. Although this dialectic is ever present throughout Césaire's writings, here it is explicitly framed specifically in terms of geopolitics. "Ferrements" poses this problem from the top down, showing how global economic and political relations circumscribe the lives of individuals in a given location. "Comptine," moving in the other direction, demonstrates how a specific collectivity determined by particular circumstances comes to exist nonetheless in relation to the global totality. This negotiation between the local and the global, this question of locating—and perhaps, of contesting—one's place within a world, is the main political problem that Césaire poses through his use of geographical imagery.

The periplus of "Ferrements" and the gear mechanism of "Comptine" also suggest another important facet of Césaire's geopolitical vision: a lexical field of courses and trajectories, centripetal and centrifugal forces, telluric flows and currents, together posing the problem of motion, displacement, inertia, and velocity—in short, the poems schematize the *dynamics* of the world system as well as its scale and dimensions. The poetics of motion and velocity in Césaire's oeuvre is a vast question, and would merit a study in its own right. For our purposes, though, we may say broadly that Césaire's early poetry is greatly preoccupied

---

43 Garraway, Doris. "What is Mine: Césairean Negritude Between the Particular and the Universal." *Research in African Literatures*, Vol. 41, No. 1 (Spring 2010), p. 79. Garraway goes on to argue that "to speak the universal from the colonial periphery" is a contestation of "a racially exclusive notion of liberty, sovereignty, or human rights" (p. 84).

44 For a philosophical discussion of the dialectical process of sublation as a passage from the "immediacy" of particularity to the universal "conceptual structure," see the Preface to Žižek, *Sublime Object*.

with speed. The poetic voice of the *Cahier*, for example, moves like a shark in water, constantly spiraling through its dialectic of subjectivation and finally soaring upwards towards the sun. In the poems of *Les armes miraculeuses*, things tend to move at a similarly frenetic pace. The collection is strewn with "cannonballs" and "brushfires of fraternity" ("Avis de tirs"), "rockets" and "whinnying thoroughbreds" ("Les Purs-Sang"), and "buffaloes of irrepressible angers" ("Visitation"); its signature gesture is the "great machete blow of red pleasure" ("Les armes miraculeuses"). Such violent, phallic thrusts are associated in the collection with the spontaneous creation–destruction of revolutionary change, a burst of uncontainable energy as seminal and generative as a volcanic eruption.

Motion is much more difficult in *Ferrements*, as if "all the paths" had literally been taken away. Indeed, in a 1960 interview, Césaire describes his melancholy turn in *Ferrements* precisely as a change of pace: "Aujourd'hui je suis peut-etre un peu moins optimiste, un peu plus amer. La révolution n'avance pas vite."[45] Another facet of Césaire's geographical imaginary, then, is the concern to map ideological landscapes. It is the slowed advance of revolution that sets the overall velocity of *Ferrements*, a hindered pace reflected in the clogged-up and stagnant poetic landscapes to be found throughout the collection.

One region where this slowed pace manifests is in the proliferation of swamps and quagmires in the poems of *Ferrements*. Towards the end of "Comptine," for example, the poem moves from relatively fast-paced anaphora to a typographical bottleneck:

> cage
>
>   et
>
> marécage[46]

This condensed image is set off from the lines above it, a typographical mirroring of the lexical field of confinement signified by "cage" and "fen." Throughout *Ferrements*, there accumulates a pattern of frankly gross images of blocked flows and stagnant waters: "... l'eau des flaques/ l'eau des fièvres se déconcerte aux yeux," "une sanie de coquillages sévères" ("Royaumes")[47]; "Les rêves échoués desséchés font au ras de

---

45 Césaire, "Interview," p. 35.
46 Césaire, *Du fond*, p. 45.
47 Césaire, *Du fond*, p. 61.

la gueule des rivières/ de formidables tas d'ossements muets" ("C'est moi-même Terreur")[48]; "la noire eau bien empuantie des mangles" ("Fantômes").[49] While these images resemble the imagery of disease and putrefaction in the *Cahier*'s descriptions of Fort-de-France, the "ville inerte" where the poem opens, they are drawn differently and they serve a different function here. In the *Cahier*, the putrid zones mark the poet's point of departure—they are mostly localized at the beginning of the poem and associated with the misery and economic stagnation of the island, a Martinican landscape stripped of its exoticist camouflage.[50] The fetid swamps and marshlands of *Ferrements*, however, function as spatial metaphors for political and economic dynamics on an international scale.

I would like to suggest two specific and concrete ideological impasses of the 1950s as the principal referents of this imagery of blockage and stagnation. The first referent is local, concerning Martinique's postwar incorporation as a French overseas department. While Césaire had championed departmentalization in 1946 precisely as a path towards Martinicans' political and civil equality as French citizens, it quickly became clear to him that this permanent tethering of Martinique to the French republic artificially foreclosed potential connections with the rest of the world, especially from the other Antillean islands and from what appeared from the vantage point of the late 1950s to be a resurgent Africa. *Ferrements*' unsanitary "puddles" of "fever water" represent precisely the stagnation and festering—economic, cultural, and political—that result from this blockage, the unwholesome *ferment* that results from Martinique being bound by irons (the direct meaning of the archaic French word *ferrements*) to metropolitan France.

The second "impasse" to which this swamp imagery refers, I would suggest, is a broader ideological deadlock: what Césaire, like many of his Western and Third World Marxist contemporaries, viewed as the generalized impasse of the international Left in 1956. In his political rhetoric of the preceding decade, Césaire had frequently used the metaphor of putrefaction to denounce Europe's moribund colonialism, which he saw as a symptom of "capitalism in its rotting state."[51] The exordium of Césaire's *Discours sur le colonialisme*, similarly, describes

---

48   Césaire, *Du fond*, p. 98.
49   Césaire, *Du fond*, p. 121.
50   See Suzanne Césaire, "Le grand camouflage."
51   Hénane, "Discours du 15 mars 1950," p. 79.

Europe as "a decadent," "stricken," and "moribund" civilization.[52] In the "Lettre à Maurice Thorez," however, Césaire applies this same language of putrefaction and stagnation to describe the PCF, which he castigates for having refused to reform in the wake of the Khrushchev report's revelations. Césaire now writes of the "malaise" into which this stagnation has plunged the international Left; instead of wielding the language of putrefaction as a rhetorical weapon against colonialism and capitalism, in *Ferrements* he uses the fetid swamp as an image of the ideological stagnant waters where leftists in the francophone world and across the globe find themselves stuck.

Where the waters are not stagnant in *Ferrements*, they are treacherous. The imagery of swamps and festering puddles coexists with an isotopy of violent undertows and backwashes: "nous montons/ nous descendons/ [...] les ressacs abyssaux nous ramènent..." ("Spirales")[53]; "nuit sac et ressac," "le courant ramène sommaire/ toujours/ et très violent" ("Nocturne d'une nostalgie"[54]), "lasso des courants des plus perfides" ("Grand sang sans merci").[55] This tidal ebbing and flowing recalls the spiral-like trajectory of the *Cahier*, structured as a dialectic of expansion and contraction of the poet's consciousness.[56] In *Ferrements*, however, the referent once again shifts to the geopolitical. It is not so much a question of the filling and emptying of the poet's consciousness, but rather of a powerful and deadly centripetal force: the "backwash," the inertial "lasso," the violent current that pulls in Martinique and other peripheral localities in defiance of their own initiative. The "undertow" ("ressac") is not the same dialectical negation represented by the moments of "contraction" in the *Cahier*'s spiral structure, but rather a "bad" infinity (in the "sable noir qui se saboule," for example), a system that can only reproduce more of the same and that makes any dialectical advancement impossible.

It is a very similar inertial force that Césaire denounces when he criticizes the PCF's refusal to change course despite the revelations of Khrushchev's report: "What! All the Communist parties are stirring: Italy, Poland, Hungary, China. And the French party, in the middle of the whirlwind, examines itself and claims to be satisfied. Never before have I

---

52 Arnold ed., *Césaire: Poésie, théâtre, essais, discours*, p. 1448.
53 Césaire, *Du fond*, p. 52.
54 Césaire, *Du fond*, p. 73.
55 Césaire, *Du fond*, p. 79.
56 Davis, *Aimé Césaire*. Cambridge: Cambridge University Press, 1997, p. 32.

been so conscious of so great a historical lag afflicting a great people ...."[57] At a moment when the global communist movement rippled with the clamor for reform, when figures like Palmiro Togliatti condemned the "bureaucratic degeneration" of Stalinism;[58] when, as Wladyslaw Gomulka noted, the insurgent working class of Poznan has taught Polish Communist Party leadership a "painful lesson";[59] and when even the Soviet Union was moving towards reform under Khrushchev, the PCF seemed, maddeningly, to be among the few national parties to remain stagnant. What the recalcitrant PCF lacked here was the old Marxist practice of ruthless self-criticism needed to maintain itself as a vital, dynamic, self-correcting political force. The imagery of stagnation in *Ferrements* is a figuration of this resultant political and intellectual inertia.

Besides swamps and violent undertows, another terrain carrying great symbolic significance throughout *Ferrements* is the desert, which seems always to appear in *Ferrements* at the most desperate moments. The first appearance of the desert is in "Grand sang sans merci," where the poet speaks "du fond d'un pays de silence" and "du fond d'un pays de soif":

> Défaite Défaite désert grand
> où plus sévère que le Kamsin d'Egypte
> siffle le vent d'Asshume[60]

This passage, in its heightened register and in its specific geographical markers, is unmistakably a reference to the biblical Exodus of the Israelites. More specifically, it refers to the period of wandering in the wilderness. Crucially, this moment in the biblical narrative of the Israelites is an interregnum, a period of uncertainty falling between bondage and receiving the Covenant, a moment when the people's chains are broken but when the path to redemption seems distant and uncertain.

Martin Munro gives an astute reading of Césaire's desert imagery, linking it to Maurice's Blanchot's troping of the desert in "La parole prophétique." Here, the desert is figured as a primordial "dehors," an "espace sans lieu, et un temps sans engendrement," linked to an "interruption momentanée de l'histoire, vide où le catastrophe hésite à se renverser en salut, où dans la chute déjà commencent la remontée et le

---

57 Césaire, "Lettre à Maurice Thorez." Arnold ed., *Aimé Césaire*, p. 1501.
58 Césaire, "Lettre à Maurice Thorez."
59 Césaire, "Lettre à Maurice Thorez."
60 Césaire, *Du fond*, p. 79.

retour."⁶¹ Munro associates the aporetic space of the Blanchotian desert with the ambiguous figure in Césaire's poetry of "mythical Africa," dispossessed of its history and made a non-place by colonialism. Citing the poem "Prophétie" from *Les armes miraculeuses*, Munro associates Césaire's "prophetic voice," through which "the moment of failure is transformed into a vision of future harmony," with Blanchot's notion of prophecy as a "'pourtant' qui brise l'impossible et restaure le temps."⁶²

Though Munro is right to link the Césairean desert to the Blanchotian desert, there is a different desert image in Blanchot that captures more precisely what I think is at stake in *Ferrements*. In "L'infini littéraire: L'Aleph," Blanchot casts the desert as a Borgesian "labyrinth" where "there are no more markers of reference. The world and the book send back eternally and infinitely their reflected images. This indefinite power of shimmering, this scintillating and limitless multiplication [...] will be all that we find, vertiginously, at the depths of our desire to understand."⁶³ This is not quite the same desert. Rather than a momentary interruption of history within which a prophecy of redemption is generated, this desert of endless mirrors and mirages is a spatialization of Hegel's "bad infinity," one from which there is no exit, no guarantee of meaning, identity, or origin, no future or past. This "literary infinity" is an endless proliferation of signifiers without signified. It is the lack of any stable reference point, the absence of a "borne de reference," that makes it impossible to string together a determinate meaning in such a semiotic desert, and that thus radically disorients the subject who can only maintain a vain "desire to understand."⁶⁴

Note the similarities between this "infinite" desert and the Césairean desert in "Va-t-en chien des nuits":

>   dans le paysage qui se défait toujours à reprendre je cherche
>   un souvenir de marée une fleur d'eau un rumeur de fureur
>   mais trop de pistes brouillent leurs caravanes
>   trop de mauvais soleils empalent aux arbres leur rancoeur
>   trop de menteurs portulans s'enlisent
>   aux lignes de faîte toujours divergentes

---

61 Quoted in Munro, *Shaping and Re-Shaping*, pp. 18–20 (Blanchot, Maurice. *Le Livre à venir*. Paris: Gallimard, 1959, p. 110).
62 Quoted in Munro, *Shaping and Re-Shaping*, p. 19 (Blanchot, *Livre à venir*, p. 112).
63 Blanchot, *Livre à venir*, p. 119.
64 Blanchot, *Livre à venir*, pp. 219–220.

> des hautes fourmis polisseuses de squelettes
> de ce fougueux silence de la bouche de ce sable
> surgira-t-il rien sinon les pointes cariées de la futaie sechée[65]

Producing an intensifying sense of panicked disorientation, this passage finds the poet lost in a constantly fluctuating landscape, a formless space that, just like Blanchot's desert, contains a proliferation of signifiers but has no stable, anchoring point of reference. The poet can neither locate himself within this spatial field nor properly orient himself towards the object of his desire—indeed, he cannot name this object without falling into metonymic slippage ("un souvenir ... une fleur ... un rumeur ..."). This desert is indeed a space without stable place, but it is not an empty space; to the contrary, it is an oversaturated one. The anaphora "trop de," repeated three times, generates a rhizomatic tangle of paths, caravans, ridgelines, and ant columns, in further metonymic displacement. Crucially, all signposts are deceptive, the "bad suns" as well as the "lying portolans." There is no stable point by which to find one's bearings, no transcendental signifier, no sun to light the way, and the map is a lie, inaccurately reflecting the terrain to be traversed.

I would argue that the nightmarish desert of "Va-t'en chien des nuits" is a spatial representation of specifically *ideological* disorientation in the wake of Césaire's desolidarization from communism. In Lacanian terms, what is missing in the poem is a *point de capiton*, a master-signifier that anchors meaning and stops the metonymic slippage of the signifying chain, thereby allowing subjects to experience social reality as a coherent whole.[66] The poet's nightmare in the passage above portrays precisely the loss of such a symbolic anchor: the illusion of coherence breaks down, and the imaginary picture of the whole is revealed as a lie. Consequent to this unhinging of the symbolic order, the traumatic Real, the "chien des nuits," resurges in the poem's last lines: "inattendu et majeur à mes tempes/ tu tiens entre tes crocs saignante/ une chair qu'il m'est par trop facile de reconnaître."[67] The "chien des nuits" appears when the symbolic order fails, the master-signifier that had held it together having been tainted, rendered inoperative. Thus, the vicious

---

65 Césaire, *Du fond*, p. 85.
66 Slavoj Žižek applies the Lacanian concept of the *point de capiton* to the analysis of ideological fields: floating signifiers in the political lexicon such as "freedom" and "democracy" require ideological *points de capitons*, such as "communism" or "God," to ground their meaning. *Sublime Object*, p. 112.
67 Césaire, *Du fond*, p. 86.

dog rending the flesh of the poet's kin, a clear reference to the founding historical trauma of slavery, resurges.

We know that the Communist Party as embodied in the figure of Stalin was precisely the master-signifier that Césaire renounced in 1956. The deserts of *Ferrements*—these "great desert[s]" of defeat—mourn this loss and map the shattered ideological terrain left in its wake. It is with this disalignment in mind that we must read Césaire's insistence in the "Lettre à Maurice Thorez" upon summoning the "force d'inventer notre route": such invention entails daring to act from within this abyss, without symbolic guarantee, navigating point-to-point.

Elegies for the Vanquished: Left-Wing Melancholia in Césaire's Poetic Tombeaux

The nightmarish Cold War landscapes of *Ferrements*, in which Césaire maps both geopolitical relations of domination and the ideological impasses of the postwar Left, constitute only one aspect of a broader shift in Césaire's poetics from sanguinity to melancholia, from major to minor key. To develop this contrast, we may recall Sartre's description in "Orphée noir" of the Césairean poem as explosive "like a rocket [...] a perpetual overtaking," the poem's words "thrown into the air like rocks by a volcano."[68] This sanguine, virile, expansive voice could not be more different from the melancholy notes of *Ferrements*. Although seven poems in the collection are relatively hopeful odes to the emergent Third World, we have already seen enough of *Ferrements* to note that most of its poems convey a strong feeling of despair. As Lilyan Kesteloot and René Hénane correctly note, *Ferrements* seems to have been composed under the sign of "souffrance."[69]

In this section I would like to complicate the too easy separation made in much criticism between *Ferrements*' melancholic, introverted poems of "suffering" on the one hand and its more sanguine *tiers-mondiste* poems on the other. It is certainly true, as A. James Arnold claims, that *Ferrements* represents the most "stylistically diverse" collection in Césaire's poetic oeuvre, alternating between hope and despair, heroic ode and elegy. We may also accept Arnold's schema of the "three voices" of *Ferrements*: a "virile voice" hailing the Third World, a "tragic" voice

---

68 Sartre, "Orphée noir," pp. xxvi–xxvii.
69 Kesteloot, Hénane and Ba, Préface, *Du fond*, p. 12.

of the suffering, sacrificial hero; and an "elegiac" voice. What I would like to challenge, however, is the implicit ascription of political positions to these voices: the virile voice as the die-hard radical channeling his militancy into Third Worldism, as opposed to the disillusioned "elegiac" and "tragic" voices of a wiser, ex-revolutionary Césaire. For Arnold, "the last word" in Césaire's poetics here "is elegiac," the "mature" Césaire taking solace in a "poetic flight" from the contradictions of the real world once he has realized that revolution is "an unacceptable alternative."[70] Commitment, following this logic, is implicitly tied to naivete and youthful libido, while to be wise is to be in some sense deradicalized.

While Arnold's study of Césaire's poetics remains in many ways definitive, I do not see disillusioned detachment from radical political commitments as the "last word" of Césaire's poetics, and certainly not in *Ferrements*. Commitment to a politics of emancipation, after all, does not dictate an axiomatic belief that the volcano of revolution is just about to erupt. The styles, modalities, and strategies of a serious political commitment will certainly adapt according to changes in material conditions. The shift that is apparent in *Ferrements* is not that of an ex-radical who now knows better, but rather a shift in focus from action to analysis, from romantic fervor to sober critique—or, to borrow from Milton, from the mode of *L'allegro* to that of *Il penseroso*. If Césaire's poetry turns inward in *Ferrements*, as I agree it does, this is not in order to renounce commitment to emancipatory politics as such but rather in order to regroup and *think*, to take the measure of an emergent situation that neither he nor anyone else fully understands.

We have seen an aspect of this melancholic turn above, in Césaire's mapping of geopolitical relations and ideological topologies. This section considers another crucial facet of this turn in the elegiac poems of *Ferrements*, which I suggest reflects what Marxist intellectual historian Enzo Traverso calls "left-wing melancholia." Traverso defines left-wing melancholia as an "identification with a *lack* rather than with a *loss*"; its mourned lost object, and what Césaire mourns in these elegies, is "communism as it was dreamed and expected, not as it was realized (state socialism)."[71] What Traverso emphasizes, and what I think describes Césaire's attitude towards revolution in the *Ferrements* elegies, is that left melancholy, though "born from defeat," nonetheless

---

70 Arnold, *Modernism and Negritude*, pp. 278–279.
71 Traverso, *Left-Wing Melancholia*, p. 52.

maintains a "fidelity to the emancipatory promises of revolution."[72] If Césaire gives lyrical expression in *Ferrements* to a political imaginary thrown catastrophically out of alignment, the poet's fidelity to such emancipatory promise nonetheless remains intact, though it must now take different forms.

On the occasion of the 1948 World Congress of Intellectuals for Peace in Wroclaw, Poland, Césaire composed the poem "Varsovie," one of his most powerful elegies and a precursor to the elegies of *Ferrements*. The poem is a lament for a city that has been unmade, disintegrated into bricks:

> Ici la brique est le ricanement du mal
> briques sur les rues dispersées
> briques sur les juifs massacrés
> briques briques briques
> fers tordus moignons nus rats sas tas sac tas
>
> ici la brique est la syllabe la plus simple du cauchemar
> ici la brique s'emmêle à la brique comme le corps du cadavre
> ici la brique est l'accumulation des jours frappés en plein soleil
> et des lettres sans réponse[73]

The lexical and semantic fragmentation in the poem reproduces the physical disarticulation of Warsaw as well as that of the Jews of the Warsaw ghetto. The poem is a heap of rubble: bits of language ("rats sas tas sac tas"), buildings ("fers tordus"), human bodies ("moignons nus"), time ("l'accumulation des jours frappés en plein soleil"), and human relationships ("lettres sans réponse") are all heaped together with bricks ("briques briques briques") in a lexical field of ruination and disintegration. Not unlike the deserts discussed above, the "ici" of "Varsovie" is a space without place, a heap of debris from a disarticulated lifeworld.[74]

In the poem's second movement, however, Césaire gestures towards the possibility of new life emerging from the ruins of the poem's first half: the "brique" becomes "le pas premier du monde," the "poussée de

---

72 Traverso, *Left-Wing Melancholia*, p. 52.
73 Reproduced in Alliot, *Le Communisme est à l'ordre du jour*, p. 264.
74 See also Marla Zubel's insightful analysis of "Varsovie" in "From Decolonization to Destalinization: Aimé Césaire and the 'Polish Question.'" *Journal of Postcolonial Writing*, Vol. 59, No. 2, pp. 157–171.

l'enfant en avance sur l'encoche," "l'aile feu de l'oiseau feu." The poem's final lines are optimistic, even triumphant:

> L'ESPOIR
> notre ESPOIR
> moins fort seulement
> que les prairies bleues où se balancent les yeux de tes enfants
> POLOGNE
>
> et l'insolence tranquille des vastes tournesols[75]

The poet subordinates the universal (the generic *nous*) to the particular (the Polish nation) in this last movement: "notre ESPOIR," the fraternal goodwill of the outside observer, is explicitly less strong than the strength that the Polish people, rooted in their own terroir, draw from their struggle to rebuild. This deference to the specificities of the Polish nation—its blue prairies and blue-eyed children, its sunflowers that still blossom in "tranquil insolence"—intensifies the climactic effect of proclaiming the name "POLOGNE." We can see that Césaire's "powerfully localist" stance is an internationalist localism—it applies not just to his own defense of Martinique or the Caribbean but universally, to every locality resisting domination. Like Edouard Glissant, the Césaire of "Varsovie" believes in the future of small countries.[76]

Despite its staccato rhythm and its fragmented syntax and lexicality, "Varsovie" proves a rather traditional elegy in thematic terms. Jahan Ramazani notes of the poetic elegy that it is often structured as a therapeutic process of mourning, the grief being expurgated and the trauma of the loss being sublimated by the creation of the poem itself as a compensatory emblem of the deceased.[77] Though Césaire does not spare us the horror of Warsaw's destruction by fascism, the poem's first stanzas are nonetheless "hitches along the way to recovery,"[78] their horror redeemed—and the mourning process consummated—by the final promise of regeneration. In finally apostrophizing "POLOGNE" in the penultimate line, the poet performs a sort of resurrection, a joyous

---

75 Arnold ed., *Aimé Césaire*, p. 1506.
76 Glissant, Edouard. *Le discours antillais*. Paris: Gallimard, 1981, p. 12 and *passim*.
77 Ramazani, Jahan. *Poetry of Mourning: The Modern Elegy from Hardy to Heaney*. Chicago, IL and London: University of Chicago Press, 1994, p. xi.
78 Ramazani, *Poetry of Mourning*, p. 3.

salutation to the Polish nation reborn—reborn, and oriented towards a redemptive (socialist) future.[79]

In *Ferrements*, Césaire radically revises the elegiac voice of "Varsovie" in a sequence of four poems: "Tombeau de Paul Eluard," "Mémorial à Louis Delgrès," "À la mémoire d'un syndicaliste noir," and "Sur L'État de l'Union." Each poem is a song of praise or mourning for a deceased person, the poet directly apostrophizing the honored dead. There is also an ideological coherence to these four poems, as each honoree is in some sense a figure of resistance to domination: Eluard, Resistance poet and communist peace activist; Delgrès, Guadeloupean free man of color who led an 1802 rebellion against the Napoleonic army come to reenslave the population; Albert Crétinoir, Martinican communist union organizer and mayor of Basse-Pointe, dead in 1952 at age 47; and Emmett Till, African-American boy of 14 tortured and murdered in 1955 for allegedly speaking to a white woman in Mississippi.

Gary Wilder makes a crucial observation about the political vision of *Ferrements*, claiming that its poems seek both to "reestablish spatial solidarities by aligning with popular rebellions and radical actors" and to "restore temporal solidarities by calling upon past spirits and reclaiming historical legacies."[80] Building upon this general observation, I would like to argue that the elegiac sequence in *Ferrements* offers a key to understanding the development of Césaire's political thought over the course of his 1950s Cold War engagements. These poems do not resolve into the sanguine, socialist realist optimism of the last movement of "Varsovie"; however, in no sense does their tragic tone suggest political resignation. Their melancholy radicalism, I suggest, consists of two related operations that each poem performs upon the figure being eulogized. First, the poet inscribes the figure he is commemorating into a global history of vanquished insurrections, making visible the connections between the contemporary hero or martyr and distant moments (temporally and geographically) of emancipatory promise. Second, each elegy distills and preserves the emancipatory promise that the life (or death) of

---

79 This thematic treatment of Poland as a nation reborn and, thanks to socialism, full of the promises of youth is consistent with Dominique Desanti's representation of socialist Poland in *Nous avons choisi la paix* (Paris: Seghers, 1949), a short volume of reportage from the Wroclaw conference (see "Wroclaw: Ville témoin de la guerre et de la paix," p. 9).
80 Wilder, *Freedom Time*, p. 183.

the deceased figure represents, offering this suspended promise as an unfinished project to be taken up again.

The titles of these elegies announce Césaire's interest in the politics of commemoration. The "tombeau" and the "mémorial" are architectural terms that connect the poetic elegy to the public monument; the "State of the Union," similarly, suggests an address to the people by an orator speaking from the national *tribune*, an official snapshot of the nation at a moment in history.[81] Césaire offers these poetic memorials as radical alternatives to the figures commemorated by official monuments and discourses. Symbolically interring Eluard, Delgrès, Crétinoir, and Till side by side, Césaire creates a kind of alternative Panthéon of radical insurrectionary figures and martyrs.

"Tombeau de Paul Eluard" accomplishes this task of reestablishing spatiotemporal solidarities with particular efficacy. To begin with, the poem's title anchors the poem to a precise time and place: the crucial referent for this poem, I contend, is Eluard's actual burial place in Père Lachaise cemetery, where he was interred in 1952 after a funeral organized and paid for by the PCF (the French government did not grant him the honor of a state funeral).[82] Most importantly, Eluard's grave is located along the *mur des fédérés*, the site where Republican soldiers massacred 147 Communards during the repression of the 1871 Paris Commune (roughly 5 percent of all the Communards executed) and the site of the mass grave where these revolutionaries are buried. The *mur des fédérés* soon became a pilgrimage site for the French left, and was famously the site of a 1936 Front Populaire rally that drew a crowd of 600,000.[83] The title of Césaire's poem thus not only refers to Eluard's tomb but also invokes a memory site of capital importance to the French and international left. We may indeed read this sequence of elegies as a *mur des fédérés* of Césaire's creation.

It is not only the poem's title that connects Eluard to the Communards—this link is developed throughout the poem, and in quite a surprising way. To get to this surprise, we must first note that the poem depicts Eluard as a traveler above all else. Eluard does not rest in peace ("ni tu

---

81 Rumeau, Delphine. "Du monument au rituel, les poèmes funéraires d'Aimé Césaire." *Présence Africaine*, No. 189 (2014), pp. 27–38.
82 See "Obsèques de Paul Eluard." Online video clip. Institut National de l'Audiovisuel. ina.fr.
83 See Rebérioux, Madeleine. "Le Mur des Fédérés." *Les Lieux de Mémoire*, Vol. 1. Edited by Pierre Nora. Paris: Gallimard, 1984, pp. 619–649.

ne gis"), nor does he join some otherworldly paradise ("ni tu n'accèdes à terre plus pure")—rather, he travels across horizons:

> tu te promènes très clair
> ressoudant les mains
> croisant des routes
> recusant la parole violette des naufrageurs de l'aube[84]

In a later stanza, the poet expands Eluard's global promenade to the broadest scale:

> Arpenteur mesureur du plus large horizon
> Guetteur sous les caves d'un feu sous les évents
> Sur les mers salueur des plus subtils flocons[85]

This set of images, I argue, indexes two specific referents from Eluard's life: the first is Eluard's well-known seven-month world tour by steamer in 1924, apparently triggered by a bout of depression. Secondly, the mention of Eluard's "resoldering [of] hands," beyond signifying a broad communist fraternity, may refer specifically to Eluard's involvement in the postwar international peace movement.[86] Eluard's connection to the earth is telluric in the poem—his fraternal reach extends to the furthest ends of the globe, and even underground as he takes root and makes surprising new connections: "quelles surprises de racines/t'enlaceront ce soir?"[87] The poet's mourning is sublimated into a renewed commitment to the socialist virtues of internationalism and solidarity of which Éluard becomes an immortalized paragon in the poem.

The last lines of the Eluard tombeau complete the crucial, if encoded, connection to the Commune:

> sur le jade de tes propres mots que l'on t'étende simple
>
> conjuré par la chaleur de la vie triomphante
> selon la bouche operculée de ton silence
> et la haute amnistie des coquillages[88]

To explain this final line, Hénane, Kesteloot and Ba posit what they consider to be a "fragile hypothesis" that the "haute amnistie des

---

84 Césaire, *Du fond*, p. 188.
85 Césaire, *Du fond*, p. 191.
86 Césaire, *Du fond*, footnote, p. 195.
87 Césaire, *Du fond*, p. 191.
88 Césaire, *Du fond*, p. 192.

coquillages" may be an oblique reference to the thousands of Communards deported to the Île des Pins penal colony in New Caledonia, an island that, they note, is called "le coquillage" because of its shape.[89] This hypothesis becomes less weak when one considers the place referent of the poem's title, and is stronger still if one looks at the penultimate stanza:

> ô meute capricorne
> les mots leurs pouls battent on les sait fabuleux
> allaités hors temps par une main volière les paroles tombées
> ramassées les saisons pliées arrondies comme des portes
> saisons
> saisons pour lui cochères[90]

This "Capricorn horde" is a much clearer reference to the deported Communards: New Caledonia and the island prison of Île des Pins (perhaps the "aviary/zoo" [*volière*] of the poem) is located almost exactly on the Tropic of Capricorn. What is perhaps most remarkable about this poem is the sheer span of the metonymic sequence that Césaire manages to embed within it. The tombeau of the title is not at all a static monument meant to encase and freeze in time—it is neither tower nor cathedral, to refer to a famous line from the *Cahier*. Éluard's tombeau is rather a "rendez-vous de la conquête," a nodal point where progressive paths intersect and reunite across vast stretches of space and time, a universal truly "riche de tout le particulier."

There is one further point about spatiotemporal solidarities to be made in connection with this poem. J. Michael Dash holds up Édouard Glissant's figuration in *Sartorius* (1999) of the Anse Caffard monument in Martinique as exemplary of a "new world space of memory" in Glissant's thought; this relational spatial matrix indicates a "poetics of displacement" in which "wind and sea ultimately turn location into relation and link this hemispheric *lieu commun* on a tiny French Overseas Department" to distant points on the globe.[91] Furthermore,

---

89 Over 4,000 Communards were exiled to the penal colony on the Ile des Pins in New Caledonia, starting in 1872, and amnesties allowing their reinsertion into France were granted beginning in 1879. See Godineau, Laure. "Le retour d'exil, un nouveau exil? Le cas des communards." *Matériaux pour l'histoire de notre temps*, Vol. 67, No. 7 (2002), pp. 11–16.

90 Césaire, *Du fond*, p. 191. The editors of this edition, whose annotations are otherwise exhaustive, do not gloss these last lines of the poem.

91 Dash, Michael. "Martinique Is (Not) a Polynesian Island: Detours of French

the Anse Caffard monument, according to Dash, "is not a sacred site but always subject to the play of secular, mirroring images."[92] Similarly, Wilder notes of Césaire that the latter conceives of the poetic image as "both embodied and self-surpassing, able to condense within itself more than it appears to be."[93] I would argue that Eluard's "tombeau"—a vehicle from the *mur des fédérés* to Polynesia to the "widest horizon," from the time of the Commune to the time of Cold War and decolonization—is precisely the same kind of non-sacred relational site and self-surpassing image that Dash and Wilder, in different contexts, indicate.[94] For Césaire, this poetic device of condensation is also a geopolitical statement: the promise of the Commune, like that of Eluard, does not belong (only) to one nation, or even to a single place, but travels in unpredictable ways, a cause that crosses oceans and is picked up again on distant shores, that survives defeat to be regenerated elsewhere and in different times.

The "Mémorial de Louis Delgrès," similarly, seeks to recuperate and memorialize an occluded moment of emancipatory promise. The title refers to a monument that does not exist, the monument that should have been built—perhaps instead of the statues of creole slaveholder Joséphine de Beauharnais and the conquistador d'Esnambuc, really existing monuments to slavery and colonialism that stand in the main public square of Martinique's capital, Fort-de-France.[95] As in "Tombeau de Paul Eluard," the singular figure that the poem commemorates is a portal to myriad moments of emancipatory promise. The two epigraphs to this encomium—a Larousse encyclopedia entry on Delgrès and a quote by Haitian revolutionary leader Dessalines praising Delgrès—effectively plug Delgrès into a broader historical constellation of insurrectionary moments.[96] I would argue that this effect is intensified by the sequence

---

West Indian Identity." *International Journal of Francophone Studies*, Vol. 11, Nos 1–2 (2008), p. 123.
92 Dash, "Martinique Is (Not) a Polynesian Island," p. 124.
93 Wilder, *Freedom Time*, p. 35.
94 Dash also notes Césaire's reference to the Caribbean archipelago in the *Cahier* as "cette Polynésie," and explains helpfully that the Polynesian islands were a privileged site in the imaginary geography of the Surrealists. "Martinique Is (Not) a Polynesian Island," p. 124.
95 Césaire, *Du fond*, footnote, p. 206.
96 Wilder notes this briefly, arguing that the epigraphs trace "geographical connections among Martinique, Guadeloupe, and Haiti and historical continuity among Delgrès, Dessalines, and Césaire." Wilder, *Freedom Time*, p. 183.

of dates listed in the epigraphs. Four dates are mentioned: "1772" and "28 mai 1802," the dates of Delgrès' birth and death; "(1870)," the publication date of the quoted Larousse encyclopedia; and "28 avril 1804," the date of Dessalines' "Proclamation aux Haitiens." Just as "26 julio" was emblazoned upon the flag of the Castroite revolution, these dates are themselves commemorative symbols. I would suggest—speculatively, admittedly—that Césaire's mention of the date "1870" may also be understood as an oblique reference to the September 1870 Insurrection du Sud in Martinique. Like Delgrès' rebellion, this short-lived and brutally repressed revolt of sharecroppers was a refusal to be reenslaved.[97] If we do accept this interpretation—indeed, it is difficult to think of another reason why Césaire would cite this date—then we are able to note an additional stratum in Césaire's elegiac political vision. Embedded within the relatively occluded history of Delgrès, then, is yet another insurrectionary moment, as if suggesting that the trail keeps going further and further.

There is a shift in tone in Césaire's third elegy, "À la mémoire d'un syndicaliste noir," which celebrates the Martinican communist organizer and political leader Albert Crétinoir, who died of natural causes in 1952. The poet's attitude toward the deceased is at once intimate and solemn. On the one hand, the poet notes small details of Crétinoir's appearance and mannerisms—his kind smile, the warmth in his eyes, his strong peasant features—with palpable affection. As Delphine Rumeau notes, however, it is the deceased's political commitment that the poet inscribes for commemoration: Crétinoir is the only one of the four commemorated dead to remain unnamed, referred to only by his function.[98] Crétinoir thus has two bodies: the cheerful, simple man (there are at least seven references to his smile), and the unbreakable labor militant ("toi le refus de la sombre défaite/chef dur soutien des cases").[99] It is the latter whom the poet inscribes "in imputrescible fern" to be revered, as a positive hero of the Martinican laboring classes ("la lumière tu la redistribues toute").[100]

Two bloody events that occurred in 1948, the centenary of abolition in Martinique, haunt this elegy to Crétinoir. First, at Le Carbet in March,

---

97 Landi, E. "Insurrection du Sud de Septembre 1870." Serge Letchimy personal website. Published Sep. 28, 2009. Internet.
98 Rumeau, Delphine. "Du monument au rituel, les poèmes funéraires d'Aimé Césaire." *Présence Africaine*, No. 189, 2014, p. 29.
99 Césaire, *Du fond*, p. 212.
100 Césaire, *Du fond*, p. 212.

a group of gendarmes shot and killed three workers protesting for higher wages, a police killing that Prefect Pierre Trouillé defended. Months later, Guy de Fabrique, a member of the white *béké* planter class, was hacked to death by machetes after a confrontation with workers on a sugar cane plantation near Basse-Pointe, where Crétinoir was mayor. Sixteen workers were arrested, held without trial in Martinique for three years, and finally tried in metropolitan France, where they were acquitted for lack of proof.[101] The poet memorializes this atmosphere of popular unrest in the face of domination:

> un vent mauvais souffle des bagasses pourries
> ton peuple a faim a soif trébuche ton peuple
> est un cabrouet qui s'arrache de la boue toujours
> plein de jurons et cinglé au fil sourd de la nuit noire des cannes
> d'un sentiment de sabres[102]

The Martinican people's anger is the product of hunger, thirst, and exploitation, a violent unrest born of desperation that contrasts sharply with Crétinoir's easy confidence; the popular rage is cathected into Crétinoir's happy communist militancy: "tu marches pèlerin tu marches et tu souris."[103] Clearly written before the split, this poem strikes a rare note of sanguinity in the collection, yet it does not paper over the real conditions of the Martinican people to whom the poet offers Crétinoir as a symbol of hope for future redemption.

The reader finds Césaire's poetic voice at the nadir of outrage and despair in "… sur l'état de l'Union," his lament for Emmett Till. In sharp contrast to the heroes of the first three elegies, the young Till is a pure martyr. Just as the brick was the motif regulating the space-time of "Varsovie," here the entire poem is bathed in Till's blood: "tes yeux étaient une conque marine où pétillait la bataille/ de vin/ de ton sang de quinze ans";[104] "de sang pas une goutte/et pour le tien qu'il me cache le Soleil, qu'à mon pain il se mêle."[105] Although Césaire mentions the bread and wine of the eucharist, implying that Till is a symbolic sacrifice, there is no redemptive transubstantiation here—Till's blood blocks

---

101 Kristen Stromberg Childers gives a thorough and well-narrated account of Martinique's year of unrest and struggle in 1948 in *Seeking Imperialism's Embrace*, pp. 108–114.
102 Césaire, *Du fond*, p. 212.
103 Césaire, *Du fond*, p. 212.
104 Césaire, *Du fond*, p. 215.
105 Césaire, *Du fond*, p. 216.

out the sun, as if running down a camera lens, and is soaked up in his bread. Emmett Till's blood becomes the blood of the United States itself, consubstantial with the nation, and the nation is drained dry by Till's lynching. The final stanza is implicitly written in Till's blood, "letters of rust" splattered on the wall by Till's murderers:

> 20 ans de zinc
> 15 ans de cuivre
> 15 ans de pétrole
> et 180 ans de ces états
> mais au coeur indolore horlogerie
> quoi, rien, zero,
> de sang pas une goutte
> au carne blanc coeur désinfecté?[106]

The question mark that ends "sur l'état de l'Union" caps off a general sense of impotent outrage, a sense that there is nothing to be done, no possibility for redemption. There are no firebirds, defiant flora, fraternal underground networks, or positive heroes in "sur l'Etat de la union." There is only the repetition of the horrific event itself: "GARCON de CHICAGO," the epithet that Till's murderer used, is repeated twice, and the repetition of "15 ans" in the survey of natural resources echoes Till's "15-year-old blood" (the "180" years of the United States is a multiple of 15, repeating the number yet again). The poet is caught in what Jahan Ramazani calls, after Freud, "melancholic mourning": a poetic depiction of grief that is meant "not to achieve but to resist consolation, not to override but to sustain anger, not to heal but to reopen the wounds of loss."[107] The sustainment of anger, the need to mark and immortalize outrage at an injustice, is indeed the principal function of this poem: the last stanza of "Sur l'état de l'union," quoted above, is not only an assessment of the current "state" of the United States, but a judgment that the poet pronounces upon it. Césaire is recording this injustice for a future time when this sentence can be carried out, preserving in poetic form the "lieu et la formule" (to recall Rimbaud) of this political anger and outrage.

Overall, Césaire's concern in this sequence of elegies is to serve as a sort of custodian of moments of insurrectionary promise, distilling the "lieu et la formule" of these moments and offering them as memory

---

106 Césaire, *Du fond*, p. 217.
107 Ramazani, *Poetry of Mourning*, p. xi.

sites for current and future generations of progressives. It is to this end that the first three elegies confer epithets upon the deceased by virtue of their deeds (Eluard: "déchiffreur," "[a]rpenteur mesureur du plus large horizon";[108] Delgrès: "O Briseur Déconcerteur Violent";[109] Crétinoir: "Maître maronneur des clartés.")[110] The predominant affect of suffering in *Ferrements* is not, *pace* Ménil, merely a withdrawal into the poet's internal anguish; rather, it denotes a disciplined political reflection in the wake of ideological defeat and at a moment of impasse.

Three Worlds, Two Codes: *Ferrements* and Non-aligned Vernacular

Thus far, we have seen the melancholy radicalism of *Ferrements* in the collection's devastated landscapes and in the specters of lost futures conjured in its elegiac poems. In this final section, we turn to a third facet of Césaire's Cold War poetics: the ways in which the poems of *Ferrements* figure the inner psychic and affective dimensions of the subjects who must live between and beneath the superpowers within the Cold War world-system. To repurpose a term from Sartre's "Orphée noir," Césaire's poetics in *Ferrements* portray the *être-dans-le-monde* of the Third World subject; this subject is defined by its precariousness, its vulnerability to forces outside and above it—or, as he puts it in "Salut à la Guinée," a "liberté fragile."

Geographer Alfred Sauvy had the French Third Estate explicitly in mind when he coined the term "tiers monde" in a 1952 article for *L'Observateur*: for Sauvy, the population of Europe's former African and Asian colonies were the "nothing [...] that wants to be something" of the contemporary world order. The Third World in Sauvy's view is also something like the wide geographical expanse constantly fought over by the superstates in George Orwell's *Nineteen Eighty-Four*: "What matters to each of the two worlds," writes Sauvy, "Is to conquer the third or at least have it on its side. And from there come all the troubles of coexistence."[111]

---

108 Césaire, *Du fond*, p. 191.
109 Césaire, *Du fond*, p. 203.
110 Césaire, *Du fond*, p. 210.
111 Sauvy, Alfred. "Trois mondes, une planète." *L'Observateur*, Aug. 14, 1952, p. 14.

This vision of the Third World as global proletariat is one that seems to preoccupy Césaire beginning in the 1950s. Staying true to his notion from the *Cahier* of a geography traced "on the compass of suffering," Césaire denounces with great rhetorical force the predatory interventions of both Cold War superpowers in his 1950s political writings. The US invasion of Guatemala and its systematic brutalization of African-Americans, the Soviet Union's repressions of Polish and German workers and of the Hungarian Revolution, Stalin's campaigns against ethnic minorities in the Soviet Union, and French colonial massacres from Madagascar to Côte d'Ivoire to Vietnam all bore a family resemblance in Césaire's estimation.

If Césaire explicitly denounced such predatory interventions in his political discourse, he used poetry to give voice to the ways in which that domination was lived. He does this most explicitly in "Vampire liminaire," perhaps his most obviously Cold War-themed poem.

> Il se fait une lumière atroce
> de l'Occident à l'Orient à contre courant
> le hurlement des molosses du brouillard y répond
> de la Ville selon la Peur plenière agitant à foison de drapeaux
> dix milliers de langues gluantes et la parade visqueuse entre deux nuits
>
> reniflant au pied de l'arbre de vie
> les rats noirs cardinaux du mensonge mêlés à
> l'unicorne de la haine raciale
> au bout du fil l'oreille de l'inquisiteur[112]

The poem opens with a reversal of Hegel's famous statement that world history travels from East to West: the atrocious "lumière," which in this context should be read both as light and enlightenment, moves "against the current" from West to East. The "watchdogs of the fog" are the obverse of this atrocious light/enlightenment, their response closing the trap upon the poet who stands between them, "between two nights." The "Ville" here is the global city, the world stage of the postwar era, represented in an image of the United Nations as a grotesque cavalcade of flags convened by a "plenary Fear," trudging in a "viscous parade" between the two antipodes—the atrocious light and the night hounds—who bark across the globe to one another. This dyad that seems to divide

---

112 Césaire, *Du fond*, p. 105.

all the poem's space between the "two nights" is reiterated in the second stanza, as two predatory figures sniff around the tree of life.

Echoing the symmetry between light and night in the first stanza, the "unicorn of race hatred" (the United States) and the "black rats cardinals of lies" (the Soviet Union) converge into a single, complex entity dominating the whole space. In an interview for the documentary *Aimé Césaire, une voix pour l'histoire*, Césaire similarly connects the Soviet Communist Party to the hierarchy of the Catholic Church. He cites what he says is an old adage repeated to Catholic priests who doubt their faith: "Above all, don't go to Rome. If one goes to Rome, one comes back as Luther. Well, I've been to Rome—my Rome was Moscow."[113] Césaire did, in fact, visit Moscow on the occasion of Stalin's funeral in 1953. Though one hesitates to read too much into a facetious remark, it is nonetheless interesting that Césaire positions himself in relation to Moscow as Martin Luther vis-à-vis Rome, i.e., as a *protestant*, one who does not lose his faith, but who contests the hierarchical organization of the institution that claims the right to speak for his faith, and seeks to reform it from the ground up.

In "Clair passage de ma journée profonde" the poet is also stuck between two monstrous entities, except that here he is also positioned beneath them:

> il y a cette verticale terrible dont le nom fidélité me fixe
> à vif
> au pommeau tournoyant du glaive à double tranchant
> dont je ne suis que la garde affable dans le temps et que
> chaque goutte de mon sang en vain s'efforce de diviser
>
> il n'est pas pour autant facile de dessiner la carte du champ
> de bataille clairière chaque fois mouvante dont le remords
> m'essaime à tout coup plus sauvage vers la face
> loyale des constellations[114]

This positioning of the poetic voice between and beneath is for Césaire the quintessential location of the Third World subject, both individual and collective. It is echoed by the image in the poem's first stanza of a "tour véneneuse qu'on finit par ne plus entendre" and, in the penultimate stanza, of waking up "en torpeur au pied peremptoire des palmiers/ femmes frigides étroitement gainées et qui toujours et de/ très haut/

---

113 *Aimé Césaire, une voix pour l'histoire* (dir. Euzhan Palcy, 1994).
114 Césaire, *Du fond*, p. 110.

s'éventent."[115] Fidelity, the name of the "vertical terrible" that pins the poet down, lies at the source of the poet's suffering here. The object of the poet's fidelity is on another plane entirely, somewhere on the other end of the "vertical terrible" that has run him through, and imperceptible from within the time-space of the poem. The poet remains an "affable guard" nonetheless, and spills his blood in vain out of fidelity to this absent figure, though he does not even know the terrain of the battlefield. Alignment, I would argue, is the sign tying this set of images together: the poet is being constantly pinned down and turned over without any control over his own orientation, forced into an alignment by telluric forces. Whereas the poet wandered without direction in the deserts discussed in this chapter's first section, here the poet knows where he is being led, but not why he is being forced to go there.

A key scene in Césaire's Cold War play *Une Saison au Congo* (1966) dramatizes the Third World's "in-betweenness" in a similar way. The protagonist, Congolese prime minister Patrice Lumumba, is in a plane flying to Elisabethville, capital of the Belgian-backed Katangese rebels, with the plane's pilot and Congo's president, Joseph Kasa-Vubu. The plane is caught in a storm, which Lumumba says—lest we miss the metaphor—is "just as bad as the situation in Congo." When he orders the pilot to land, Lumumba learns that separatist leaders have refused to allow him to land in Elisabethville. Lumumba, defiant, insists they land nonetheless, but the pilot says that the plane must remain in the air, explaining, "The weather is terrible!" As the plane must keep moving, the pilot asks Lumumba, "Which direction, sir?" Kasa suggests they return to the capital, Léopoldville (now Kinshasa), but Lumumba chooses another direction, the only one that will allow him to keep fighting: "No! Arms! Arms! To Moscow! To Moscow!"[116] The metaphor is extremely clear and instructive: Lumumba, finally seeing his country's independence struggle from a macrocosmic, geopolitical perspective—from a bird's eye view rather than from the viewpoint of one fighting it out on the ground—realizes that he must align his particular cause within the planetary contest between superpowers. The Third World nationalist in the Cold War world-system is flying a plane in a storm—there is no going back, no stopping, and one can only go in certain circumscribed directions.

This scene is reinterpreted for the audience in a monologue that closes

---

115 Césaire, *Du fond*, p. 108.
116 *Une saison au Congo* [1966] In Arnold ed., *Césaire*, pp. 1130–1136.

the first act, by a previously unseen "Ambassadeur Grand Occidental" who stands downstage from a muted Congolese crowd dancing the "independence cha-cha" and cheering Lumumba. The Ambassadeur gives his interpretation of the earlier scene:

> I'm well aware that as a Nation, we have a bad reputation. We're accused of having an itchy trigger finger, but can you do politics in a rocking chair while the world goes crazy over nothing, and the people start to boil over! And then, you heard him, how in the plane, he shouted 'To Moscow! To Moscow!' Well, people should know that we're not just the policemen, we're also the firefighters of the world! The firefighters appointed to contain everywhere the fires lit by the communist pyromania! And I mean "everywhere!" In Congo, as elsewhere!
> A word to the wise!"[117]

We never see this Ambassador again, yet his interpretation of Lumumba's earlier dialogue determines the rest of the plot—the civil war, Lumumba's assassination, and the disarticulation of his emancipatory project. Césaire translates this geopolitical disparity, brilliantly, into its dramatic analog: the Third World nationalist is to the US superpower precisely as the classical tragic hero is to the *deus ex machina*—or, to recall *King Lear*, "as flies to wanton boys are we to the gods."

William Pietz writes of "Cold War discourse" as constituting an ideological "master code" in the mid-twentieth-century United States. Cold War discourse forcibly reinterprets all anticolonial struggles in the Third World "in terms of the geopolitical contest for zones of power" between the "free world" of Western civilization and a "totalitarian" non-Western enemy.[118] Césaire dramatizes precisely this overdetermination of the Third World by the "Grand Occidental"—i.e., US–European (neo)colonialist—master code in the above scenes, and demonstrates that the violence inherent in such acts of interpretation is not merely discursive, but directly a matter of life and death.

Before 1956, Césaire thought of the Soviet Union as possessing the antidote to such colonial domination, this fearsome surveillance from above and outside. He said as much in the Chambre des Députés in 1950:

---

117 "Une saison au Congo." [1966] In Arnold ed., *Césaire*, p. 1141.
118 Pietz, William. "The 'Postcolonialism' of Cold War Discourse." *Social Text*, Vol. 19/20 (Autumn 1988), pp. 55–75.

Are you unaware of what the Soviet Union represents for us, Antilleans, for us, the victims of a colonialism [...] that has authored the long calvary that slavery has been for us, to which has succeeded, since 1848, a colonialism barely more human? Think, ladies and gentleman. For us, Antilleans, [...] the Soviet Union is the country that, in an historic gesture, has destroyed precisely that which weighs upon us, that which oppresses us, that which prostrates us, that which humiliates us, colonialism.[119]

The Soviet Union thus represented a key to cracking the European colonialist master code for Césaire: it was an example of a country that had successfully thrown off the yoke of capitalism and instituted programs to rapidly develop its former colonial empire, putting the formerly colonized (so Césaire believed) on an equal material footing with the metropolitan center.[120] If it represented a menace to bourgeois Europe, it looked to Antilleans like a way out of colonialism.

After 1956, as we have seen, the Soviet Union no longer looked like this universalist anticolonial "contre-poison" from Césaire's vantage point. In the "Lettre à Maurice Thorez," Césaire takes care to separate the Cold War from the colonial question: "the colonial question cannot be treated as a part of a more important whole, a part over which others can make deals or pass such compromises as seem just to them in the context of a general situation that only they can appraise."[121]

The verb *transiger* is especially evocative here, an indictment of both the capitalist West and the Soviet Union at once. This image of peripheral countries being treated as geopolitical currency is Césaire's assessment of the effects upon the rest of the world of the zero-sum game between the two Cold War camps. The PCF's May 1956 endorsement of the Mollet government's military interventions in Algeria crystallized this subordination of anticolonial struggles to metropolitan political calculation by the party's Central Committee:

---

119 Hénane, "Discours du 15 mars 1950," pp. 76–77.
120 See also Padmore, George. *How Russia Transformed Her Colonial Empire: A Challenge to the Imperialist Powers*. London: Dennis Dobson, 1946.
121 "Lettre à Maurice Thorez." In Arnold ed., *Césaire*, p. 1502. Tito made a very similar statement in 1945 after the Soviet Union failed to support Yugoslavia during the US–UK invasion of Trieste: "We have no wish to be dependent on anyone. We do not want to be small change. We do not want to be involved in any policy of spheres of influence." Quoted in Prashad, *The Darker Nations*, p. 97. The similarity between Césaire's statement and that of the cofounder of the Non-Aligned Movement is fortuitous.

not only was the colonial question deprioritized in favor of Eurocentric foreign policies, but the specific content of the Algerian struggle was evacuated, reduced to exchange value. Césaire in fact denounces Moscow for this same kind of superpower overdetermination, recounting in an interview his bemusement at the Soviets' kneejerk condemnation of jazz music as decadent and bourgeois, presumably because this music originated in the United States: "c'est la musique populaire de ma race!" he counters.[122]

In *Ferrements*, Césaire contests this forcing of local content through a falsely universal master-code at several points. For example, in "Salut à la Guinée"—a 1958 poem written on the occasion of Guinea's "No" vote in the referendum to join the Union Française—the poet brings the question of translation and (un)translatability to the fore:

> Dalaba Pita Labé Mali Timbé
>   puissantes falaises
>   Tinkisso Tinkisso
> eaux belles[123]

Note in these opening lines the exaggerated imprecision and generality of the French translations compared to the hieratic sonority of the Guinean place names, an effect heightened by their typographical misalignment. The French "decoding" of the vernacular can only provide generic approximations that denude these proper names of their specificity and force, the typography also suggesting the disjuncture between translation and original.

In addition to the above lines from "Salut à la Guinée," there are a number of lines in *Ferrements* that have to do with untranslatability and indecipherability:

>   nous savoir qui rêvames
> là
> *sans chiffre ni rune*
> l'indicible musique retenue prisonnière
> d'une mélodie quand même à sauver du Désastre" ("Nous savoir...")[124]
>
> alors vent âpre et des jours blancs seul juge
> au noir roc intime sans strie et sans noyau
> jugeant selon l'ongle de l'éclair en ma poitrine profonde

---

122 Alliot, *Le communisme est à l'ordre du jour*, p. 145.
123 Césaire, *Du fond*, p. 56.
124 Césaire, *Du fond*, p. 77. Emphasis mine.

tu me pèseras gardien du mot cloué par le précepte" ("Saison âpre")[125]

There is in these lines what we might call a proto-Glissantian desire for opacity, for a vernacular language with no "code" [chiffre], no Rosetta Stone through which its meaning can be decrypted, as the Ambassadeur Grand Occidental does, to the ruination of Lumumba's promise of liberation.

It is perhaps out of this desire not to be translated, for the local content not to be "weighed" and "judged" from above, that some the most joyous moments of *Ferrements* consist of the enunciation of names. We have already seen such effusive declamation of the name in "Salut à la Guinée." In "Seisme," a poem that is otherwise classifiable as one of *Ferrements*' many nightmare visions, the final stanza offers a faint glimmer of the possibility for redemption:

> pris pris pris
> rôles précipités
> selon rien
>
> sinon l'abrupte persistance mal lue
> de nos vrais noms, nos noms miraculeux
> jusqu'ici dans la réserve d'un oubli
> gîtant[126]

The "abrupt misread persistence" of the name is, I claim, precisely what Césaire—dubbed "Der Schwarzer Tito," "the Black Tito," by the German daily *Die Zeit*[127]—sees as the hope of non-alignment: the option to refuse the offered choice between two, to subtract oneself from the bloc and opt to remain in the vernacular. As Kristin Ross writes, "The vernacular is that which must be uplifted, swept up into the universal language and the forward momentum of progress. But it resists."[128]

---

125 Césaire, *Du fond*, p. 127.
126 Césaire, *Du fond*, p. 35.
127 Bächler, Wolfgang. "Der Schwarzer Tito." *Die Zeit*, Nov. 8, 1956. For a discussion of Césaire's interest in connections between black and Balkan Slavic cultures, see Humphrey, Anna Jovic. "Aimé Césaire and 'Another Face of Europe.'" *MLN*, Vol. 129, No. 5 (Dec. 2014), pp. 1117–1148.
128 Ross, *Emergence of Social Space*, p. 27.

Conclusion

In "L'homme de culture et ses responsabilités," an address delivered at the 1959 Second Congress of Black Writers and Artists in Rome, Césaire argues that anticolonial intellectuals must be "propagators of souls, even inventors of souls."[129] This phrase directly contests Stalin's definition of writers as "engineers of the human soul": Césaire wants to scrap the existing blueprints for the human soul and work towards the discovery of altogether new relations and processes. He views the work of the left intellectual (antiimperialist and anticapitalist) not as an engineer, simply executing the plans contained in preexisting blueprints, but as a propagator (which we can read here both as germinator and evangelist) and as an inventor of new paradigms of solidarity. He indeed committed himself to just such an endeavor in his political career immediately upon his demission from the PCF, building the Parti Progressiste Martiniquais as a non-aligned, localist Marxist tendency, and committing himself thereafter to a democratic socialist program of development in Martinique.[130]

To conclude this chapter, I recall Enzo Traverso's comment on the potential productivity of melancholia for a defeated left. Writing about a post-Cold War present moment defined by neoliberalism, Traverso claims the need for a left melancholia that "does not mean lamenting a lost utopia, but rather rethinking a revolutionary project in a nonrevolutionary age."[131] The poetry of Césaire's *Ferrements* is dedicated, *mutatis mutandis*, to exactly this ideological project of rethinking, motivated by the feeling of a lack: the need for a left that *is* not, and the urgent task of rebuilding one.

---

129 In Arnold ed., *Césaire*, p. 1557.
130 Nesbitt, *The Price of Slavery*, p. 162.
131 Traverso, *Left-Wing Melancholia*, p. 20.

CHAPTER FOUR

Engineer of the Haitian Soul
Jacques Stephen Alexis' Experiments in Socialist Realism

"It was by virtue of Marxism, Your Honor, and by virtue of dialectical materialism, its beating heart, that we succeeded in narrating our story."

(Abdel Khadiq Mahgoub, "By Virtue of Marxism, Your Honor..."[1])

"Nous faisons partie d'une grande phalange, l'armée internationale des combattants d'un nouveau humanisme, mais nous restons ce que nous sommes, un bataillon haïtien; nous n'oublions pas le passé des luttes propres à notre peuple."

(Jacques Stephen Alexis[2])

"Socialist realism is a possibility rather than an actuality; and the effective realization of the possibility is a complex affair."

(Gyorgy Lukács[3])

---

1   Quoted in Hassan, Salah D. *How to Liberate Marx from His Eurocentrism*. Ostfildern, Germany: DOCUMENTA (13), Hatje Cantz Verlag, 2013, p. 22.
2   "Lettre ouverte au poète Jacques Lenoir." Quoted in Séonnet, Michel. *Jacques Stephen Alexis ou le voyage vers la lune de la belle amour humaine*. Paris: Lamourier, p. 93.
3   "Critical Realism and Socialist Realism." *The Meaning of Contemproary Realism*. Translated by John and Necke Mander. London: Merlin Press, 1963 p. 96.

Of the authors studied in *Cold War Negritude*, Jacques Stephen Alexis is the only direct casualty of the Cold War. Alexis, only four years older than his comrade René Depestre, also led the Haitian Revolution of 1946 and was exiled for doing so, and also remained a committed communist throughout his 1950s Parisian exile. Flush with enthusiasm at Fidel Castro's victory in 1959, and by some accounts encouraged by Nikita Khrushchev himself, Alexis landed at the Haitian port of Bombardopolis on April 22, 1961 with five comrades, intending to infiltrate the country and organize a political resistance to the right-wing *noiriste* dictatorship of François Duvalier.[4] Alexis was almost immediately captured by Haitian authorities and disappeared. In response to his inquiry into Alexis' whereabouts, Louis Aragon—a friend and patron who had promoted Alexis' writings both in France and in the Eastern bloc—was told flippantly by a representative of the Duvalier regime to "go and ask Peking."[5] Alexis' brutal torture and murder by the regime were confirmed in 1965. An obituary essay by Aragon published in *Les lettres françaises* also features a communiqué from Alexis' surviving comrades of the Parti d'Entente Populaire, who represent Alexis as a martyr to the cause of Haitian liberation, and a victim of Cold War intervention: they allege that Alexis' landing was spotted by a US navy ship, which communicated this intelligence to the Haitian authorities.[6] We may appreciate the tragic irony of the fact that the global conflict that so greatly influenced the trajectory of Alexis' intellectual and literary development also created the conditions for his murder.

Like Aimé Césaire and other global Marxist intellectuals of color active in the 1950s, Alexis recognized a tectonic shift in the world order as the US–Soviet ideological struggle and the growing clamor to end a moribund European colonialism formed what Jini Kim Watson calls a "Cold War-decolonising matrix."[7] Alexis also shared with Césaire

---

4 Depestre speculates that Alexis had obtained the direct support of Nikita Khrushchev, including funding, for his expedition. *Bonsoir tendresse*, Ch. 8. Florence Alexis explains that her father sought material support for his political projects from the PCF, the Soviet Union, and the People's Republic of China. "Jacques Stephen Alexis n'a jamais été à Fort Dimanche—Florence Alexis." *YouTube*, uploaded by AyiboPost, Apr. 22, 2022. https://www.youtube.com/watch?v=etNX8oB1Oss.

5 Aragon, Louis. "Le poète assassiné." *Les lettres françaises*, No. 1110 (Dec 16–23, 1965), p. 16.

6 "Les faits." *Les lettres françaises*, p. 16.

7 Watson, *Cold War Reckonings*, p. 3.

and Depestre a formation in Marxist philosophy and politics and, like both of them, he viewed literature as a specific mode of critical thought and sought accordingly to work out literary forms that would be most adequate to the needs of the moment. However, unlike Césaire—who, as we saw in Chapter 3, attempted to take the measure of the Cold War order through a revised poetic writing—Alexis expressly viewed the realist novel as the literary form best suited to this new conjuncture.

Alexis opted for the realist novel as the privileged literary vehicle for progressive politics, a conclusion that was certainly determined by Alexis' political alignment with the Soviet bloc. The main concern of this chapter is to delineate precisely how Alexis' theory of the novel and practice of novelistic writing are informed by the global Marxist political and literary thought in which he was immersed. I am interested primarily in teasing out from Alexis' novelistic, literary theoretical, and political writings the author's specific "politics of prose,"[8] one that emerges from the author's attempt to square his commitment to an axiomatically universalist communism with his dogged defense of Haitian cultural and political autonomy.

As many who knew him have attested, Alexis was a remarkable polymath. In addition to his literary career, he practiced medicine as a neurologist and studied a broad range of subjects, from botany to Haitian folklore, from Italian Renaissance architecture to urban planning. Depestre remembers Alexis' intellectual breadth with something approaching awe: "He wanted to know everything, to have read and deciphered everything, in all disciplines of thought [...] He didn't conceive that a human being ever finished studying and appropriating with rage the thousand new directions of universal knowledge."[9] Like El Caucho, the socialist-realist positive hero of his novel *L'Espace d'un cillement* (1959), Alexis appears to have striven to conduct himself as an "hombre total," a revolutionary subject whose every effort would fully integrate theory and practice, action and contemplation, harmonizing the human faculties of "reason, affectivity, and sensibility."[10] Alexis sought always to articulate his literary practice—as he did his practice

---

8 Here I refer to the title of Denis Hollier's book on Jean-Paul Sartre's politics and aesthetics, *The Politics of Prose: Essay on Sartre*. Minneapolis: University of Minnesota Press, 1987.

9 Depestre, *Bonjour et adieu à la négritude*, pp. 224–225.

10 "... l'intellectuel est celui qui a pris l'engagement envers lui-même de porter au plus haut point l'harmonie de ces trois facultés qui réagissent l'une sur l'autre."

in any specific field of intellectual inquiry—with the Marxist-Leninist theory of dialectical materialism, which he considered to be a general theory explaining natural processes as well as the laws of historical development.

It is quite easy to view Alexis' ideological commitment as more rigid than rigorous, as a slippage into dogmatism unworthy of his exceptional capacities. Haitian intellectual Georges Anglade indeed views his commitment to communism in this way—as the party apparatchik's "catechism" that Alexis sometimes tries to force upon his otherwise vital and uninhibited literary creativity.[11] Several other critics agree, and not entirely without justification. In this chapter, however, I argue for a far-reaching continuity between Alexis' communism and his creativity rather than what Anglade sees as a "dissociation totale."[12] Without wishing to belabor the religious metaphor, I would suggest that Alexis' Marxist alignment is, rather than a "catechism," something more closely resembling what Marxist literary critic Lucien Goldmann—another contemporary of Alexis—calls a "wager," after Pascal: it is a faith "in the future that we must make for ourselves by what we do, so that this faith becomes a 'wager' which we make that our actions will, in fact, be successful."[13] For better and for worse, Alexis saw Marxism-Leninism as the best hope for humanity's universal emancipation and enlightenment, including Haiti's. Alexis' comrade and patron Louis Aragon wrote of the Soviet Union in the postwar decade as the "seat not of a Renaissance, but of a birth, which is that of the new man."[14] Alexis, who fully endorsed this quasi-messianic view, created his own name for this universal Renaissance to come: "la Belle Amour Humaine."[15] If certain literary, creative, or intellectual constraints were consequent to this commitment, they were constraints that Alexis chose. However they may have hindered him, these constraints also enabled him in

---

Alexis,, Jacques Stephen. "La Belle Amour Humaine 1957." *Europe*, Vol. 49, No. 501 (1971) p. 23.

11 Anglade, Georges. "Le dernier codicille d'Alexis. Sur le parcours de Jacques Stéphen Alexis dans la théorie littéraire." *Présence Africaine*, Nos 175–176–177 (2008), p. 562.

12 Anglade, "Le dernier codicille," p. 562.

13 Goldmann, Lucien, *The Hidden God: A Study of Tragic Vision in the Pensées of Pascal and the Tragedies of Racine*. 1956. Translated by Philip Thody. London: Verso, 2016, p. 90.

14 Aragon, *Littératures soviétiques*. Paris: Denoël, 1955, p. 14.

15 Alexis, "La Belle Amour Humaine 1957," p. 21.

other ways. This chapter focuses not on what his political commitments blinded him to, but upon what and how they helped him to see.

Alexis' alignment with the Soviet project brings up a second point of contrast with Césaire and Depestre, this time a political one: while Depestre maintained his commitment to communism through comrades who kept alive the promise that really existing communism had broken, and Césaire split entirely with the communist bloc to seek out new dissident left solidarities, Alexis remained aligned with what he saw as the best chance at emancipation and material development for the majority of the world's population. Maintaining a united front among the global Marxist left seems indeed to have been an ideological priority for Alexis. Alexis traveled extensively throughout the entire socialist bloc; one notable excursion with his comrades in the Parti d'Entente Populaire, travelling from a writers' conference in Moscow to Irkutsk and then to Beijing, where he met personally with Mao Zedong. According to one of these comrades, the poet Rassoul Labuchin, Alexis personally urged Mao to reconcile with the Soviet Union and end the Sino-Soviet split.[16] René Depestre, for his part, remembers a conversation with Ho Chi Minh in which the Vietnamese leader spoke in "laudatory terms" of Alexis' intervention at the 1960 International Meeting of Communist and Workers' Parties in Moscow, where Alexis made an "vibrant appeal for the unity of international Communism."[17] Whereas Césaire warned in his "Lettre à Maurice Thorez" against an overbearing and crypto-colonialist Soviet "fraternalisme," Alexis viewed international communist fraternity as the only possible path towards maintaining a winning coalition in the struggle against capitalism and imperialism. Alexis thus definitively chose a side in the Cold War: for Alexis, the Soviet Union remained "a citadel of hope and promise [espérance]" for all nations of the world, including Haiti.[18]

Alexis' commitment to global communism was a central influence upon his literary aesthetics as well as his political thought. Alexis viewed the question of literary aesthetics through the lens of a fundamental political choice between (socialist) realism and (imperial capitalist)

---

16 Labuchin, Rassoul. Interview with Schallum Pierre. YouTube. 2014.
17 Depestre, *Bonjour et adieu à la négritude*, p. 223.
18 The full passage reads as follows: "Après avoir construit, grâce aux efforts héroïques de son peuple et à l'appui de toute l'humanité progressive, au milieu d'un monde d'exploitation, d'oppression et de rapines, une citadelle de l'espérance, les plus vieux rêves des hommes ont enfin un visage." ("Où va le roman?" p. 93).

modernism. Just as he aligned with global communism as decolonizing peoples' best chance at emancipation and development, Alexis chose realism, and he thus attempted in his writings to work creatively within the constraints of this choice. His theory of "marvelous realism"—no doubt his best-known theoretical intervention—was, in the author's own words, directly inspired by the Soviet literary doctrine of socialist realism. In his "Manifeste du réalisme merveilleux des haïtiens," Alexis states this unequivocally:

> Social realism, conscious of the imperatives of history, promotes an art human in its content but resolutely national in its form [...] Haitian artists have made use of the Marvelous in a dynamic sense before they realized what they were doing was Marvelous Realism. Little by little, we have become conscious of this fact. Engaging in realism corresponds for Haitian artists to setting out to speak the same lanuage as their people. The Marvelous Realism of the Haitian people is thus the integral part of Social Realism—in its Haitian form it obeys the same preoccupations.[19]

This passage makes clear that Alexis promoted the "marvelous" precisely in so far as it constituted an integral part of how Haitians experienced their social reality. Alexis is also quite explicit about his preference for specifically Soviet realism over the literary modernism prevalent in the West: "in its fundamental content we consider the contemporary Soviet novel as considerably more promising than the novel of constipated aesthetes, the falsely intellectualist, anemic and decadent invert novel that constitutes the greater part of novelistic production in the bourgeois West."[20] For Alexis, then, marvelous realism was nothing more or less than socialist realism with Haitian characteristics. As Maximilien Laroche insightfully notes, for Alexis, the substitution of the word "marvelous" for "socialist" as a modifier of "realism" is not a replacement or rejection of socialist realism;

---

19 Alexis, Jacques Stephen. "Du réalisme merveilleux des haitiens." *Présence Africaine*, Nos 8–10 (Jun.–Nov. 1956), p. 267. Although many critics draw a clear distinction between social realism and socialist realism proper, Alexis does not appear to have drawn such a sharp distinction—he is clearly using "social realism" to refer to Soviet literary aesthetics here.

20 "Où va le roman?" p. 90. One must also note a strain of homophobia in Alexis' characterization of Western literature as the product of decadent "inverts," a common misapprehension of same-sex love among communists of the period, though the misclassification of homosexuality as pathological was a matter of broad consensus in the 1950s.

rather, the latter term connotes the former, a metonym that completes and supplements it.[21]

Despite Alexis' own pronouncements endorsing socialist literary aesthetics, many critics and admirers of his work have tended—especially since the end of the Cold War—to qualify, minimize, or even disregard these communist influences in his writing.[22] A 1993 book review encapsulates this tendency rather succinctly: "Now that the Cold War is over, interpreters have moved beyond seeing Alexis as another 'Marxist' writer to appreciate the marvelous realism [...] that reverse[s] exoticism to show how the world looks from the standpoint of the 'wretched of the earth.'"[23] Martin Munro explains the "calls for justice, proletarian solidarity, and cultural nationalism" in Alexis' writing as orthodox dogma that dates his works, "faint echoes of a Marxist indigenist past, drowned out by the clamor of history";[24] more relevant to us in the twenty-first century, he argues, is Alexis' status as an exiled, diasporic writer. Anglade suggests that Alexis' final writings before his death constitute a "codicil," an incipient turn away from Marxist dogmatism and towards an exploration of properly Haitian national literary forms, especially the *lodyans*.[25] Alexis' own daughter Florence imagines that her father, had he lived longer, would have eventually outgrown his *esprit de parti*: "your honesty and your rigor would have led you to face Stalinism with wide-open eyes, the 'good' as well as the 'bad' imperialism, under the harsh light of evidence."[26] Just as communism was consigned to the dustbin of history after 1989, Alexis' communist politics and unapologetically socialist realist literary aesthetics are often

---

21 Laroche, Maximilien. *Contribution à l'étude du réalisme merveilleux*. Québec: Université Laval, GRELCA, 1987, p. 25.

22 Two notable exceptions are Claude Souffrant's *Une Négritude socialiste* (1978) and Jean-Jacques Cadet's excellent recent study *Le marxisme haïtien* (2020). While Souffrant focuses on Alexis' attitude towards religion and development and Cadet concentrates on Alexis' Marxist philosophy, my focus in this chapter is on Alexis' communist literary aesthetics.

23 Wylie, Hal. "Elisabeth Mudimbe-Boyi, *L'Œuvre Romanesque de Jacques Stephen Alexis*." Book review. *World Literature Today*, Vol. 67, No. 2 (Spring 1993), p. 46.

24 Munro, Martin. *Exile and Post-1946 Haitian Literature: Alexis, Depestre, Ollivier, Laferrière, Danticat*. Liverpool: Liverpool University Press, 2007, p. 39.

25 Anglade, "Le dernier codicille," pp. 564–565.

26 "Lettre à Jacques Soleil." Preface to *L'Espace d'un cillement*, p. xvii.

dismissed as anachronisms or embarrassing intellectual dead ends that we are well rid of today.

When critics do engage with Alexis' communist alignment, it is most often viewed negatively, either as an ideological handicap, an impediment to authentic aesthetic vision, or even as a symptom of a dangerous authoritarian streak.[27] In a 1957 review, Edouard Glissant reproaches Alexisian socialist realism for forcing Antillean reality through an "a priori" Marxist ideological prism.[28] Among twenty-first-century critics, Margaret Heady—who goes farther than most in acknowledging the influence of orthodox Marxist thought upon Alexis' writing—nonetheless concludes that Alexis' aesthetics are guilty of "essentialism and universalism" and are thus ultimately self-undermining.[29] Haitian writer Jean-Claude Fignolé stops just short of accusing Alexis of latent totalitarianism, expressing his hesitancy to "call up the ghosts of the Red Guard and Pol Pot" when talking about Alexis but nonetheless effectively insinuating the connection by preterition.[30]

I would argue that Alexis' literary aesthetics are best understood as a series of experiments within socialist realism, and, furthermore, that Alexis' adoption of the constraints of this aesthetic was in fact generative in crucial ways. Rather than searching for an implicit way out of socialist realism within Alexis' writings, I focus on how he thought with and through it. Unlike so many writers who did live under state socialism—and we may certainly appreciate the irony in this distinction—Alexis was not coerced by any state apparatus into following the constraints of socialist realism, nor was his relatively free formal experimentation within this aesthetic punished by party censors.[31] For Alexis, the socialist

---

27 Alexis' predecessor and mentor Jacques Roumain, the founder of the Haitian Communist Party, also received harsher criticism for his socialist realist aesthetics. Edmund Wilson panned *Gouverneurs de la rosée* (1944) as "the inevitable Communist novel that is turned out in every country in compliance with the Kremlin's prescription." Wilson, Edmund. *Red, Black, Blond, and Olive*. New York: Oxford University Press, 1956, p. 116.

28 "Note sur une 'poésie nationale' chez les peuples noirs." *Les Lettres Nouvelles*, No. 4 (1956), p. 394.

29 Heady, Margaret. *Marvelous Journeys: Routes of Identity in the Caribbean Novel*. New York: Peter Lang, 2008, p. 3.

30 Fignolé, Jean-Claude. "Marvelous Realism! Metamorphosis of the Real?" *Journal of Haitian Studies*, Vol. 16, No. 1 (2010), p. 49.

31 Alexis' works were censored for years by the Duvalier government, however, due to Alexis' communist affiliation, as Dany Laferrière attests in a 2012 panel

realist mode was not an arbitrary set of rules imposed from outside and above but a genuine source of inspiration.[32] Writing within socialist realism was a considered aesthetic decision. To fully understand Alexis' literary aesthetics, then, we must take the measure of his engagement with writings on literature emanating from the international communist movement with which Alexis remained aligned for all of his unjustly short life. This includes the officially sanctioned socialist realism of the Soviet bloc, formulated by figures such as Maxim Gorky and practiced by figures such as Mikhail Sholokhov and Alexander Fadeyev. It includes the Marxist humanism theorized by Western Marxist intellectuals such as Lucien Goldmann and Gyorgy Lukács. It includes—importantly, as we shall see—the Soviet socialist realist aesthetics translated into French and propagated in the 1950s by PCF ideologue Louis Aragon. Finally, it also includes Third World socialist aesthetics such as Mao Zedong's reflections upon literature in the 1942 Yenan Forum. I show in this chapter that these chosen influences go significantly further and are more systematic in Alexis' writings than critics have hitherto appreciated.

Alexis does indeed adopt socialist realist aesthetics as his own, but he does not do so uncritically or mechanistically; it is indeed a commonplace of what Bhakti Shringarpure calls the "Cold War paradigm" of literary criticism to assume that the former necessarily implies the latter.[33] Alexis in fact acknowledges—while praising Soviet writers like Sholokhov, Feodor Gladkov, Ilya Ehrenbourg, and Alexei Tolstoy—that some socialist pronouncements on art and literature are limited by "a certain rigidity, a certain intolerance, and a certain dogmatism."[34] These errors are nonetheless based upon premises that, for Alexis, are true: "We still await the refutation of the fundamental theses of socialist realism, if they ever manage to be, for their time. Completed, developed, enriched, shed of their slag, yes, they certainly will be."[35] Like the author's broader

---

discussion with Florence Alexis. (Littafcar. "Quand des écrivains belges prennent Jacques Stephen Alexis au pied de la lettre – 24/05/12 – CEC." *YouTube*, Apr. 28, 2016.

32 As Edmund Wilson states of 1950s Caribbean Marxism, "The Kremlin has its agents in the Caribbean, but these little island countries are remote from Moscow and not just now of any importance to it. It is still possible here for persons of sincere democratic sympathies to be sold on the Communist party through the idealism of Marx and Lenin." *Red, Black, Blonde, and Olive*, p. 88.
33 Shringarpure, Bhakti, *Cold War Assemblages*, Ch. 4.
34 Alexis, "Où va le roman?" p. 91.
35 Alexis, "Ou va le roman?" p. 91.

approach to Marxist thought, Alexisian socialist realism is plural and internationalist in its chosen influences, syncretic and experimental in its practice. I will show that, just as he argued for unity between the Soviet Union and China, Alexis' literary aesthetics evinces a unique syncretism between Soviet, Western Marxist, and Maoist theories of literature.

My analysis will consider, in succession, the entirety of Alexis' oeuvre published during his lifetime: the novels *Compère Général Soleil* (1955), *Les arbres musiciens* (1957) and *L'Espace d'un cillement* (1959) and the frame narrative *Romancéro aux étoiles* (1961). I treat these texts as successive steps in an iterative process of literary experimentation whose aim was to ground a new Haitian national literature, the formal qualities of which would reflect the values of the revolutionary Haitian society that Alexis sought to bring about.

The Socialist Realist Structures of *Compère Général Soleil*

Alexis' first and best-known novel, *Compère Général Soleil* (1955), bears the most obvious resemblance to standard socialist realist novelistic conventions. As Evgeny Dobrenko explains, Soviet socialist realism stressed "'ideological commitment' (ideinost'), 'party-mindedness' (partiinost'), 'popular spirit' (narodnost'), 'historicism', and 'typicality.'"[36] Briefly summarized, socialist realist guidelines stipulated that the novel should be structured according to a clear understanding of dialectical materialism; that its narration should not pretend to be neutral but should be openly partisan; that it should be for a popular audience, in understandable rather than rarefied language; that it should depict the past in its unfolding towards socialism, and that it should portray scenes of everyday social life.[37] The content of *Compère Général Soleil* certainly goes beyond these criteria—it is a rich, complex novel that does

---

36 Dobrenko, Evgeny. "Socialist Realism." *The Cambridge Companion to Twentieth-Century Russian Literature*. Edited by Evgeny Dobrenko and Marina Balina. Cambridge: Cambridge University Press, 2011, p. 100. See also Dobrenko, Evgeny. *The Political Economy of Socialist Realism*. New Haven, CT and London: Yale University Press, 2007.

37 Rossen Djagalov explains helpfully that socialist realism in the Eastern bloc was a "short-lived phenomenon," strictly imposed only for a short period between roughly 1948 and 1956. ("The Zone of Freedom? Differential Censorship in the Post-Stalin-Era People's Republic of Letters." *The Slavonic and East European Review*, Vol. 98, No. 4 (Oct. 2020), p. 602). Alexis was involved in what Djagalov

many other things besides satisfy them—but the novel does also satisfy them rather neatly.

As many critics have noted, Alexis' adherence to socialist literary aesthetics is due in significant part to the influence of Jacques Roumain, poet, novelist, ethnologist, and founder of the Haitian Communist Party. Indeed, Alexis' formation in Marxism is due in significant part to Roumain's mentorship. Roumain's great peasant novel, *Gouverneurs de la rosée* (1944), is a crucial intertext for Alexis' first novel.[38] It narrates the efforts of Manuel, a Haitian migrant worker (*viejo*) come home after years working in the sugar cane fields of Cuba (during which he acquired a Marxist class consciousness) to redeem his native village. Returning to a land suffering from a devastating drought caused by industrial deforestation, Manuel wakes his peasant comrades from their resignation, discovers a source of water that the villagers had lost hope of finding, and unites the entire population in a collective effort to build a canal connecting this source to the village. Manuel must die for this last feat to succeed: stabbed by a member of a rival family, he survives long enough to ask his comrades not to seek vengeance and to complete the canal, a project that will require the cooperative labor of both feuding factions.

Hilarion Hilarius, the protagonist of *Compère Général Soleil*, closely resembles Roumain's protagonist Manuel. Both are migrants uprooted from their rural homes by global market forces, though Hilarion's itinerary is almost exclusively within Haiti and largely within the city of Port-au-Prince. Whereas *Gouverneurs de la rosée* is confined to an archetypical rural village and its environs, Hilarion appears to traverse nearly all of Haiti in *Compère Général Soleil*. Here, Haiti is a social field composed of a multitude of distinct milieux. Hilarion is the central mechanism by which this social field is catalogued in the novel, a listening device that grants the reader access to a wide array of social tableaux: bourgeois interiors, secret prisons, Port-au-Prince neighborhoods of all strata, peasant villages, and the contested Dominican borderlands.[39] If Manuel's is a narrative of return, Hilarion's is a narrative of displacement.

---

calls the People's Republic of Letters (see Introduction), had read extensively in Soviet literature, and would certainly have been familiar with its prescriptions.

38 For a perceptive and convincing comparative analysis of these two novels, see Kaussen, Valerie, *Migrant Revolutions: Haitian Literature, Globalization, and US Imperialism*. Lanham, MD: Lexington Books, 2008, Ch. 3.

39 For a discussion of the "tableau" as narrative device in Alexis' writing, see

Hilarion does not possess a Marxist class consciousness *tout fait* at the novel's opening as Manuel does. Rather, Alexis' protagonist develops this consciousness through a material struggle that forms the novel's core. Hilarion is almost literally homeless in his first appearance in the novel's prologue, his only shelter a rotting shack in a Port-au-Prince *bidonville* with holes in its roof. He is barefoot and starving in the novel's prologue, his mind emptied by hunger: "The void. Was there yesterday? Will there be tomorrow? Hell no! The body alone exists and trembles ...."[40] Hilarion is instinctively hostile to what the narrator calls the "Established Order" when he sees its signs—he is enraged, for example, at the riches contained in an elite mansion he wanders into.[41] But Hilarion will only develop an understanding of the class structure and a commitment to emancipation over the course of his travels, struggles, and experiences of solidarity.

The space where Hilarion's *prise de conscience* is born is not the sugar plantation, as is the case for Roumain's Manuel, but the prison. In the first chapter, Hilarion is incarcerated for trespassing in the mansion mentioned above. This opening section sets up Hilarion's class consciousness in at least three ways. First, it portrays the brutality of Haiti's repressive state apparatus: inmates are beaten, tortured, and forced to stand in their own excrement, while the guards, coerced into their jobs out of need, are themselves made into brutes. Second, the inmates develop a sense of solidarity, forged by suffering: their "collective outcry" becomes "a powerful toccata of desperation [...] from a race of pariahs, this desperation that must be destroyed to the last stone in order for life to triumph over resignation."[42] Finally, Hilarion meets Pierre Roumel, a bourgeois Haitian communist and obvious fictionalization of Roumain, who first tells Hilarion, "have confidence in yourself," thus planting the seed of his eventual Marxist awakening. This opening scene establishes the Haitian state as predatory and in thrall to global capital, its

---

Mudimbe-Boyi, Elisabeth. *L'œuvre romanesque de Jacques Stephen Alexis.* Kinshasa: Editions du Mont Noir, 1974, p. 29–34.

40 Alexis, *Compère Général Soleil*, p. 12.

41 The Established Order here is the Haitian ruling class and the US corporate interests that dominate it. As Cedric Tolliver notes, the novel depicts "the racialized hierarchies structuring the region's economy, which the novel describes as dominated by American capital." *Of Vagabonds and Fellow Travellers*, p. 81.

42 Alexis, *Compère*, pp. 46–47.

victims as a revolutionary community in the making, and the path towards emancipation as the oppressed subject's defiant assertion of self-respect. Like Manuel's displacement to Cuba, Hilarion's time in prison also grants him critical distance from his given situation, a gap out of which a critical consciousness can develop.

This, however, is merely the first of many displacements that push and pull Hilarion across Haiti, each stop on his itinerary adding another facet to the panorama of Haitian society that accrues over the course of the novel. Hilarion serves as an unwitting ethnographer throughout. A prime example of this quasi-ethnographic technique is the scene of Hilarion's visit to his peasant family in the village of Ça-Ira. His encounter with a beautiful peasant woman named Zurenne occasions a commentary on the plight of all Haitian peasant women: "Ah! Haitian girls are beautiful! Shame she has to stay here ... She'll suffer the same fate as all country women...handle the hoe, the axe, the machete, and get old! Unless some young buck coming from the city on vacation debauches them."[43] On the other end of the social hierarchy, a comment by Hilarion's employer Mrs Borkmann yields insight into bourgeois women's class hatred:

> When she said "my dog" or "my rug," the words sang in her mouth like a caress ... but when she addressed these individuals, disgust marked her immobile mouth like a light rictus. She hated them, she spat upon them... This hate was hereditary, it would last as long as their strength lasted. But could this power last, since they acted as if it was eternal?[44]

Again, the specific case is a synecdoche of a social type. Such vignettes litter the narrative, the characters' attitudes and affects determined by their material conditions of existence. Hilarion's homelessness grants him unique efficacy as a cataloguer of social types: Hilarion must go wherever there is work. Mobile and equipped with eyes and ears, Hilarion is the mechanism that allows Alexis to chart the class antagonisms that structure Haitian society over the course of the novel.

Hilarion and his wife are displaced in turn by flood, famine, and fire; they finally migrate to the town of Macoris across the Dominican border, where Hilarion finds work cutting cane. There is, however, one final and fatal displacement. Hilarion becomes a victim of the 1937 "Dominican Vespers," a massacre of thousands of Haitian migrants in

---

43 Alexis, *Compère*, p. 188.
44 Alexis, *Compère*, p. 188.

an ethnic cleansing authorized by Dominican president Rafael Trujillo, a client of the United States.[45] Hilarion is killed just as he crosses the border back into Haiti, the closing scene of the novel.

Hilarion's return to Haiti to die is a thoroughly ambiguous scene. Hilarion's last request is as follows: "You tell Jean-Michel that I have clearly seen the day when, in front of my eyes, a great red sun lit up the chest of a worker called Paco Torres [...] you tell him to follow the path that he wanted to show me, he's got to follow that sun!"[46] Hilarion dies smiling, finally seeing "Compère Général Soleil," the red sun of Haitian proverbs who watches over Haitians. The novel's final words, however, shift to Claire-Heureuse: "She was alone." Here is the final scene of the *Gouverneurs de la rosée* rewritten as tragedy. Claire-Heureuse is alone, their newborn daughter Désiré killed, Hilarion and his comrades dead and unburied. There is the uncertainty of the road to be followed and the weakly perceptible promise of a future deliverance, but no "immanence of meaning," as early Lukács argues about the novel form. The only guarantee here is that the struggle will carry on. Hilarion's hope for a socialist future did nothing to keep him alive. The novel's ending gestures forward to the road that must be travelled towards socialism, but does not offer a guarantee of future redemption, only a horizon of possibility that is visible to the reader but almost impossibly distant to the characters.

Cedric Tolliver offers an insightful reading of *Compère*'s portrayal of the US occupation and Trujillo's massacre, suggesting that Alexis brings this dark history of the 1930s to bear against the "triumphant Cold War discourse" of the postwar United States. He argues that the novel "excavat[es] the history of American intervention in the Caribbean as a precursor to its conduct as a global power," and that Alexis "places the massacre squarely within the context of continued American domination in the region."[47] To Tolliver's persuasive analysis of the novel's Cold War geopolitical claims, I would add that Alexis performs the anti-US imperialist critique that Tolliver prescribes precisely through the novelistic protocols of socialist realism. In this sense, Alexis' choice to follow these guidelines is perhaps as much a repudiation of the cultural and aesthetic standards aligned with US imperialism as it is a preference for socialist realism as such.

45 Kaussen, *Migrant Revolutions*, Ch. 3.
46 Alexis, *Compère*, p. 350.
47 Tolliver, *Of Vagabonds*, pp. 75 and 82.

Les Arbres musiciens: A Prehistory of the Haitian Present

Les arbres musiciens is a historical novel depicting the violent uprooting of the Haitian peasantry in the 1940s under the presidency of Elie Lescot. Set against the geopolitical backdrop of the Second World War, the novel focuses upon two specific events that more directly affected the Haitian peasantry: first, the Catholic Church's *Campagne antisuperstitieuse*, a crusade against the popular *vodou* religion; second, the expansion of the American SHADA[48] corporation into the Haitian countryside. Both campaigns converge into a *de facto* war upon the Haitian peasants; indeed, the novel portrays them as two coordinated prongs of the same offensive. The result of this campaign—which the novel gestures towards in its final chapters but does not depict—will be the enclosure of the rural Haitian commons and the destruction of the Haitian peasants' lifeworld, leading to their brutal proletarianization over the course of the 1950s.

In terms of narrative structure, *Les arbres musiciens* resembles *Compère Général Soleil* in several ways. Both novels are world-historical in scope, aiming to articulate a total portrait of the forces determining Haitian society at a specific historical conjuncture.[49] *Compère Genéral Soleil*, as we have just seen, achieves this total coverage through its migrant worker protagonist Hilarion Hilarius: constantly displaced, Hilarion observes social structures and behaviors as he is pushed and pulled through Haiti and across the Dominican border, and the partisan narrator gives a materialist analysis of the raw data generated by Hilarion's observations.

Les arbres musiciens also aims for a total portrait of Haitian society, but its focus is at once narrower and more varied than that of *Compère*. First, the cast of characters is significantly expanded and the narrative points of view multiplied. There is no single Hilarion figure observing the various social tableaux; instead, there are a number of point-of-view characters whose perspectives are related by the narrator in free

---

48 Société Haïtiano-Americaine de Développement Agricole.
49 As Robert Bird explains, "articulation" (*Gliederung*) held a specific and important meaning for Lukács: the function of narrative that "reveal[s] details to be the limbs or members of an organism," that is, how narrative shows the historical necessity uniting seemingly disparate and even incidental details. Bird, Robert. "Articulations of (Socialist) Realism: Lukács, Platonov, Shklovsky." *e-flux Journal*, Vol. 91 (May 2018). Online.

indirect discourse. The novel's focus is narrower than that of *Compère Général Soleil* in that it highlights one particular class antagonism as definitive of the era: that between the embattled peasants and the bourgeois elite seeking to profit from their expropriation. The bourgeoisie is represented principally by the three Osmin brothers: Edgard, an army officer; Diogène, a Catholic priest; and Carles, a failed poet and bohemian. The Osmin family is thus a neat synecdoche for the Haitian state apparatus, each brother representing one branch of this apparatus that maintains the Haitian ruling class's hegemony: the army, the clergy, and the intelligentsia.[50] The much more numerous and diverse peasantry is represented by a wider cast of characters, including the virtuous *houngan* Bois-d'Orme Létiro; his double, the nefarious sorcerer Danger Dossous; and Gonaïbo, an *enfant sauvage* descended from the long-extinct indigenous Tainos. As conflicts arise both within and between classes, the novel aims to depict the totality of Haitian society as it is reproduced and transformed by the playing out of its internal social contradictions.

For Alexis, plot is the key element of the novel genre that gives it political purchase. He states in "Où va le roman?" that, contrary to contemporary "scholastic conceptions," the novel's power derives "as much from the chosen plot [*affabulation*] of the recounted story as from the manner of the narration."[51] At a moment when the protocols of the *nouveau roman* are dominant within the Parisian literary scene, Alexis takes a resolutely realist and antimodernist approach towards novelistic writing, arguing that the *affabulation* of the story itself— the *affabulation*, which can mean the plot or moral—is as important as the style through which it is told.[52] The novelist works upon the story like a worker tempering steel: "he imposes upon the fabulation [affabulation] a definitive mold, he pours it into rigid bronze, drapes it upon a skeleton, imprints a contour upon it, a movement that have an importance equal [...] to the subject."[53] Plotting is thus primarily

---

50 For a thorough Gramscian reading of *Les arbres musiciens*, see Heady, Margaret, *Marvelous Journeys*, Ch. 3.
51 "Où va le roman?" p. 84.
52 The choice of what—and whose—story to tell is a *political* choice for Alexis: "Si l'artiste est libre de son choix, son choix n'implique pas moins une prise de position qui le situe par rapport au reel, sur le plan du fond comme sur celui de la forme." Alexis, "Où va le roman?" p. 84.
53 "Où va le roman?" p. 84.

a rhetorical consideration for Alexis, a way to "enhance, beautifully" a content that is "realist, dynamic, and humanist."[54] In *Les arbres musiciens*, we can see the narrative *praxis* that Alexis extrapolates from his theory of the novel.

Katerina Clark explains that Soviet novels from the 1930s onward were often "written to a single master plot," one that "shapes the novel as a sort of parable for the working out of Marxism-Leninism in history."[55] *Les arbres musiciens*, I would argue, is similarly plotted as a parable for the working out of Marxism-Leninism in Haitian history. Alexis' aim is to portray Haitian society in movement between successive economic modes of production, with socialism as the projected final stage. This movement of history is the novel's principal structuring force; referred to by the narrator as an "immobile and indefatigable tortoise,"[56] history advances "lazily as always, but inexorably."[57]

This representation of Haiti at a given point on its road to socialism is not as reductive or deterministic as it may appear. Alexis does not simply force the facts of Haitian existence to fit into an abstract Marxian phase of history. Instead, he shows a keen awareness of what Ernst Bloch calls the "simultaneity of the nonsimultaneous"—that is, the complex co-presence of several modes of production, some emergent and some residual, within the same historical moment.[58] Nor does the novel betray a vulgar Marxist understanding of cultural forms as mere illusory reflections of schematic economic categories; instead, he shows how the economic relations at the "tréfonds" of Haitian society are lived as, in Lukács' words, "immediate forms of existence of human life [...] within which the metabolism of every individual person with nature and society takes place."[59]

Overall, *Les arbres musiciens* is the story of Haiti's period of primitive accumulation. Marx provides the *ur*-text for this historical turning

---

54 "Où va le roman?" p. 85.
55 Clark, *The Soviet Novel*, p. 9.
56 Alexis, Jacques Stephen. *Les arbres musiciens*. Paris: Gallimard, 1957, p. 157.
57 Alexis, *Les Arbres musiciens*, p. 298.
58 Quoted in Lazarus, *The Postcolonial Unconsciousness*, p. 109.
59 Lukács, *The Historical Novel*, p. 294. Lukács thus differentiates the task of the progressive artist as from that of the historian. The historian must "examine concretely the varied and differing effects of the economic situation of the classes" and especially discover "the most varied, complex and very indirect connections in order to really explain the ideological problems of a past epoch." The novelist, however, "can only disclose these connections if he is able to see in economic problems the concrete problems of existence of concrete men," p. 294.

point in *Capital*, taking early modern Britain as a paradigmatic case: "when great masses of men are suddenly and forcibly torn from their means of subsistence, and hurled as free and "unattached" proletarians on the labour-market. The expropriation of the agricultural producer, of the peasant, from the soil, is the basis of the whole process."[60] The bourgeoisie is the ascendant revolutionary class in this period, but the proletariat is simultaneously constituted from the expropriated peasants who, separated from their traditional means of subsistence, are forced to migrate towards the towns with nothing to sell but their labor. *Les arbres musiciens* locates the initial stages of this movement in Haiti from feudalism to capitalism in the 1940s, fixing the *Campagne antisuperstitieuse* and the SHADA land grab as events analogous to the enclosures discussed by Marx.[61]

Alexis designs the plot of *Les Arbres musiciens* in such a way as to show, in all its complexity, the specific manner in which this *fabula* of primitive accumulation unfolded in Haiti. Like light shone through a prism, the story is refracted through the various class perspectives of its characters. The reader thus sees how the SHADA/Anti-superstitious campaign is experienced by the imperialists who plan it, the haute bourgeoisie who profit from it, the petite bourgeoisie who carry it out, and the various strata of the peasantry whose lives it disrupts. The total social portrait that is the novel's overall aim thus emerges from the juxtaposition of the various individual class perspectives.

This narrative strategy is evident in the early scene introducing the peasant milieu of Fonds-Parisien. This "land of lakes," the narrator relates, "always sings an immense aspiration to joy." The narrative voice then mimics this popular singing:

---

60 Marx, Karl. *Capital*, Vol. 1, Ch 26. Although Marx sees primitive capitalist accumulation as an inevitable step in the progression of history, he lays out in full detail the human misery wrought by this shift from feudalism to merchant capitalism: "The spoliation of the church's property, the fraudulent alienation of the State domains, the robbery of the common lands, the usurpation of feudal and clan property, and its transformation into modern private property under circumstances of reckless terrorism, were just so many idyllic methods of primitive accumulation. They conquered the field for capitalistic agriculture, made the soil part and parcel of capital, and created for the town industries the necessary supply of a 'free' and outlawed proletariat." Marx, *Capital,* Vol. 1, Ch. 27

61 Tolliver also refers to the Marxian account of primitive accumulation in his compelling discussion of the African diaspora "vagabonds" created by Cold War repressions. *Of Vagabonds*, pp. 16–17.

Joie des flamants roses et rouges qui s'élèvent sur les eaux vertes.
Joie gourmande du *hutia* qui bondit dans les fourrés.
Joie [...] pour tous les fruits lacustres et les fleurs des savanes! Eblouissante joie du Bahoruco!"[62]

The narrator quickly moves on from such lyricism, however, to show the relations of production that produce this form of cultural expression. In free indirect style that seems to relate the perspective of the entire class, the narrator shows how the nature of the peasants' labor determines their worldview. Their sense of time follows the rhythm of the seasons and the harvest, and they repeat the same year-long cycle all their lives: "What would merchants from the neighboring towns have to say this year? How much would *indienne* cost, enamelware [...] *This year*, what would life have to say?"[63] They make offerings to the *lwa* of the waters, Agouet Arroyo, "to calm his thirst." The "grands dons," or landowners, or are a tolerable nuisance: though they always send their agents "at the moment when they are least expected [...] to demand something" they remain distant, external.[64] The lands of Fonds-Parisien are held in common and "without limits," without linguistic or territorial boundaries: "No one can say where the agglomeration begins and ends." [65] Finally, news of SHADA's expansion does not disturb their leaders, as the village always pays its share of the crops on time: "Nope! No SHADA in these parts [...] Let us drink our clairin and let things go on like before!"[66] This rendering of the semi-feudal situation of the Haitian peasantry borrows these pastoral tropes, including imitations of popular oral forms of literary expression, from the Haitian peasant novel tradition.[67]

If the peasants of Fonds-Parisien are portrayed using conventions borrowed from the Haitian peasant novel, the bourgeois Osmins are constructed as characters in a nineteenth-century *bildungsroman*. Each brother's narrative arc focuses upon his formation in a profession and the conflicts surrounding his initiation into bourgeois society. Lieutenant Edgard Osmin is a *parvenu* eager to improve his station

---

62 Alexis, *Arbres musiciens*, p. 70.
63 Alexis, *Arbres musiciens*, p. 71. Emphasis mine.
64 Alexis, *Arbres musiciens*, p. 72.
65 Alexis, *Arbres musiciens*, p. 73.
66 Alexis, *Arbres musiciens*, p. 73.
67 For a discussion of *Les Arbres musiciens* within the tradition of the Haitian peasant novel, see Dayan, Joan. *Haiti, History, and the Gods*. Berkeley: University of California Press, 1999, Ch. 4.

but blocked by the old élite's "apartheid according to the nuances of the skin."[68] A combination of Rastignac and Julien Sorel, Edgard chooses to conspire with the *yankees* for the dual purpose of making his fortune and "revolutionizing the country." Diogène, the priest, seeks truth rather than social advancement. Although beset by doubt and a Kierkegaardian "trembling" at the prospect of leading a crusade against *vodou*, he resigns himself to his duty and chooses to become the sword of his faith. (Diogène is unaware that, in doing so, he has in fact become the instrument of *yankee* imperialism.) Finally, Carles' arc unfolds as a *künstlerroman*: viewing the world in abstract, purely aesthetic terms, Carles finds the trappings of bourgeois life ugly and boring, and shows his contempt by playing the "sarcastic bohemian, cynical and believing in nothing."[69] Unlike the scenes set in the peasant communities, all three brothers' narratives are internally focused: they are each given complex individual psychologies and they are (unconsciously) motivated by conflicting desires and repressed libidinal energy. It is strongly implied, for example, that Edgard is latently homosexual (he keeps a letter from a long-dead "ami," Perrot, the "only being in the world" that he had ever loved). Diogène, for his part, canalizes his repressed sexual drive into the antisuperstitious campaign: "He would be the fist, spearhead, and the rod of his cross would hide the blade of a brilliant sword!"[70] Carles is sexually promiscuous and incapable of commitment. All three brothers, then, show what Alexis would have seen as typically bourgeois pathologies. For all three of these monadic bourgeois subjects, social realities are mere background to their own inner psychological dramas.

Gonaibo, the *enfant sauvage*, is a different kind of literary protagonist. His worldview is tied to his material existence, but he is in a class all his own: Gonaïbo starts out in a sort of Rousseauian, pre-social state of self-sufficiency, living alone in a hinterland that is taboo to other peasants. Unlike the Osmin brothers who seek to define themselves by what they do, Gonaibo simply *is*: "a child-king, wild king of the limitless savannah." As a residual trace of Taino culture, his scenes take on the dimensions of myth—he communicates, for example, with the animals of the forest. This wholeness is undone when Gonaibo espies a "cavalry of white men [...] galloping on strange iron horses, at a mad speed, like a

---

68 Alexis, *Arbres musiciens*, p. 23.
69 Alexis, *Arbres musiciens*, p. 99.
70 Alexis, *Arbres musiciens*, p. 63.

cloud of destroying archangels";[71] the reader knows that this is scouting party of SHADA motorbikes. This intrusion signals "the end of his uninterrupted dream [...] the devouring of a past that had not stopped lasting, the negation of the perennity sung by each blade of grass."[72] The SHADA convoy carries history in its wake, piercing the self-sameness of Gonaïbo's pre-Oedipal world; crucially, it causes him to question his own destiny for the first time: "What was he, after all? What were the works to which his existence was destined? What to do to reach supreme joy, satisfaction of existence?"[73] Commensurate with this movement from prehistory into history, then, is a shift in literary genre: Gonaïbo is wrenched from the world of the epic (spontaneity, circularity) and forced into the world of the novel (consciousness, development).[74]

The American imperialists themselves are the class to which the reader has the least access. Aside from one scene written from the point of view of the American ambassador to Port-au-Prince—the scene where he coordinates the SHADA/anti-*vodou* campaign with the archbishop—their presence is almost always felt at several layers of mediation and the full scope of its influence on the plot is never perceived. To the novel's main characters, the *blanc 'mericains* are unknown and unknowable: none of the main characters interacts directly with a *yankee*, and their presence is at first a mere rumor, only later a visible but still mysterious presence.

As no single class perspective is able to grasp the entire picture, it falls to the Marxist-Leninist narrator to fill in the gaps between the characters' consciousness and the objective movement of history. Making ample use of what Gérard Genette calls the "ideological function" of the narrator,[75] Alexis' narrator at several points stops narrating and leaves the diegetic world to one side in order to explain to the reader the objective relations that make groups of characters see their reality as they do. In a long expository interlude, for example, Alexis' narrator gives an analysis of the "furious social typhoon" brewing in Haiti under Lescot, including what could be a stand-alone essay on the Americanization of the Haitian elite and the stirrings of proto-fascist ressentiment among the black petit

---

71 Alexis, *Arbres musiciens*, p. 87.
72 Alexis, *Arbres musiciens*, p. 99.
73 Alexis, *Arbres musiciens*, p. 92.
74 Lukács, Gyorgy. *Theory of the Novel*. Translated by Anna Bostock. Cambridge, MA: MIT Press, 1971, p. 88.
75 Genette, Gérard. *Figures III*. Paris: Seuil, 1971, p. 273.

bourgeoisie. In so doing, Alexis has recourse to a writerly strategy that is very similar to one Lukács notes in Tolstoy's *War and Peace*. Lukács notes that, for the most part, Tolstoy does not depict the Napoleonic Wars "in extenso," but instead "take an episode from the war [...] of particular importance and significance" for the development of the novel's characters and "portray[s] these episodes so that the entire mood of the Russian army and through them of the Russian people gains expression."[76] However, when Tolstoy "attempts to deal with comprehensive and strategic problems of the war [...] he abandons himself to historico-philosophical effusions."[77] Alexis has recourse to the same strategy. Alexis is perhaps cheating in these expository excursuses, but is careful not to violate the realist rule of vraisemblance: the *narrative* stops at the limits of what its characters can possibly comprehend from their class positions.

There is one character, however, who comes close to this objective perspective. At the novel's end, Carméleau Melon, a former peasant who has joined the proletariat, foretells a parallel future for the peasants of Nan-Rémembrance to *houngan* Bois d'Orme, their spiritual leader. He tells Bois d'Orme that his people will have to leave their homes behind—the Americans who have now acquired the land would certainly not have jobs for everyone—and that their only hope was to migrate to the city, "vers la misère, la prostitution pour les filles, le désespoir pour les vieux et le vagabondage pour les gosses" (pp. 350–351). Carméleau, the novel's avatar of the socialist realist positive hero, thus prophesies the violent upheaval that took take place in fact over the course of the 1950s.

We may therefore conclude that *Les arbres musiciens* is plotted as what Lukács calls a "concrete prehistory of the present," portraying "the evolution of the people through the crises of the past up to the present."[78] Indeed, there are many moments within this novel set in 1942 that suggest the seeds of what will develop by Alexis' present moment of 1957. Perhaps the darkest of these, especially given Alexis' torture and death, is the figure of Danger Dossous, the obverse of the virtuous (if naïve) *houngan* Bois d'Orme. If Bois d'Orme is an idealized, tragic version of Haitian peasant culture, Dossous is the grotesque, obscene inversion: secretly collaborating with the invaders, Dossous's plan was

---

76 Lukács, Gyorgy. *The Historical Novel*. Translated by Hannah and Stanley Mitchell. London: Merlin Press, 1962, p. 43.
77 Lukács, *Historical Novel*, p. 43.
78 Lukács, *Historical Novel*, p. 296.

to insinuate himself into political power: "he would establish his law upon the region. He would reign over all, rich, powerful, sovereign master, he would exert his influence in the high political spheres of the capital itself."[79] Referred to as "le terrible gangan-macoute," Dossous is a clear figuration of François Duvalier, who, before his rise to power in 1957, was part of the reactionary cultural nationalist Griot movement that extolled Haitian peasant culture along racialist lines. Paired with the death of Bois d'Orme, Dossous' defeat at the novel's end symbolically lays to rest the legacy of indigenisme (and noirisme, its fascist perversion) and clears the way for the proletarian movement, embodied by Carméleau (and Gonaibo, who is proletarianized by the novel's end), to rise as the subject of history.[80]

In addition to reflecting Alexis' vision of historical development, *Les arbres musiciens* also dramatizes his view of literature's social responsibility—and especially the responsibility of the literary author—in a specifically Haitian context. Here, I aim to explain the reasons why Alexis' vision of literature's social function privileges narrative prose and leaves little room for lyricism.

From very early on, the novel presents lyrical abstraction negatively. This is sharpest in an early scene, in which the American ambassador is receiving the French archbishop at his Port-au-Prince villa to coordinate their war on the peasantry over a lavish dinner. The ambassador looks eagerly and admiringly upon the traditional creole meal prepared by his Haitian chef, Victor. "Vraiment," he thinks, "Victor était une perle, *un poète* sans aucun doute."[81] The narrator continues: "The pork leg grilled with parsley, the 'Three Thieves' sauce, the boneless stuffed chicken, the croquettes à 'l'arbre véritable,' the tam-tam purée, and other fine pleasures, one could put these to the Negroes' credit, like jazz, rumba, primitive art and Bantu philosophy. That didn't cost anything."[82] This scene offers a clear, and quite ungenerous, caricature of the modernist and surrealist tendencies associated with literary Negritude. The white imperialists are literally eating up the reified products of black culture, "primitive" art placed on the same plane as their grilled pork as commodities to be

---

79 Alexis, *Arbres musiciens*, p. 124.
80 There is a haunting irony in the fact that Alexis represents Dossous so apparently lightly, as a buffoonish cartoon villain easily defeated, when seen in light of the later struggle against the Duvalier regime that would take Alexis' life.
81 Emphasis mine.
82 Alexis, *Arbres musiciens*, pp. 80–81.

consumed and forgotten before dessert. Alexis even inserts a jab against Father Placide Tempels' landmark text *La Philosophie bantoue* (1945), published by *Présence Africaine* and admired by Léopold Sédar Senghor, among others.[83] The ambassador and his fellow imperialists are not wrong to praise such cultural treasures, but their praise contrasts with their contempt for the living people who have produced them: "This menu that translated all the warmth, the innocence, the blaring taste of a fiery people, into consummate western bourgeois, they took it in a concupiscent, lascivious sense."[84] As Alexis argued at the First Congress of Black Writers in 1956, simply making "declarations of love to black culture"[85] does nothing to advance subjected peoples' concrete struggle for liberation, and it costs the imperialists nothing to recognize a black cultural genius for poetry and rhythm. Alexis does not dispute lyrical poetry's undeniable aesthetic merit, but as it does not make one *commit* to anything, he rejects it for being too easily recuperated by the enemy.

Modernist poetry—or rather, a certain image of the poet—is further critiqued in the character of *poète maudit* Carles Osmin. Indeed, I would suggest that the character of Carles is a vehicle that Alexis uses to embody everything that is wrong with the prevailing Western literary movements of his time. We can see this from the novel's beginning, when the narrator establishes a connection between Carles and his brother, Diogène. The poet and the priest are

> the doubling, the Dr. Jekyll and Mr. Hyde of one same body [...] To tell the truth, they were both in search of holiness. One, conscious of his limits, patient, bet his life on a celestial, eternal holiness, through virtue and prayer, the other, incorrigible eater of the absolute, impetuous, played the terrestrial beatitude card, artistic to the point of immorality, through experimentation in the greatest number of sensations, plainsong, good skeptical and negligent works.[86]

Even in this early expository scene, it is not difficult to discern the narrator's preference for Dr Jekyll over Mr Hyde. Though an adversary of the people, Diogène is—like his namesake—an ascetic, his every action governed by his fidelity to a (false) truth. Carles, by contrast,

---

83 In his contribution to the First Congress, Senghor quotes Tempels approvingly, emphasizing the African mind's understanding of being as a "force vitale." *Ier Congrès*, p. 53.
84 Alexis, *Arbres musiciens*, pp. 80–81.
85 *Ier Congres*, p. 71.
86 Alexis, *Arbres musiciens*, pp. 33–34.

shows the same symptoms of petty bourgeois idealism that contemporary Marxist critics regularly diagnosed in the aesthetics of the surrealist movement: Roger Garaudy, for example, accuses Breton and the surrealists of valorizing "the infantile and mythological demand of the immediate realization of desire."[87]

Carles seems fully to incarnate this stereotype of the onanistic *poète maudit* throughout the novel. When he and his brothers attend an elite social gathering held by the powerful mulatto Desoiseaux family, Carles runs straight to the piano. Defiantly, he chooses to play *La Valse aux Etoiles*, a composition by Haitian composer Ludovic Lamothe, and loses himself in the melody: "Carles saw through this audience of puppets, he frolicked in midair, snatching the stars away from the tropical night. He rode the wind, he floated over a sea woven from small lights and milky surf."[88] Paying no attention to his audience—he ignores one light-skinned mulatto who mocks him as a possessed "nègre bossale," for example—Carles continues to play, this time choosing Justin Elie's *Hymne au Soleil*: "Then arose the rhythms of beautiful Ahiti that the musician faithful to the past, had recreated based upon the drunken choreographies of king Ostro and his princes [...] There arose abrupt rara melodies, wild arpeggios from distant sources and the riotous *Zanmi man-manman* of his youth."[89] The mulatto host then stops Carles, giving polite praise but suggesting that the guests would have preferred to listen to "more of a Regency bacchanale ....or else some good dance music ...."[90] The music Carles plays in this scene is reified in the same way as the creole meal at the ambassador's villa: like the "poet" chef, Carles' function as artist is nothing more than to provide light entertainment for the ruling class, his art reduced to a luxury commodity alienated from the cultural practices of the great majority of Haitian people. The only difference here is that the Haitian mulatto elite, anxious to "whiten their lineage," does not share the white American ambassador's appetites for "primitive" or "black" cultural commodities. Carles' response to his bourgeois audience's contempt for his talent is that of the *poète maudit*'s artistic revolt. Adopting the position of the "sarcastic bohemian" who wishes to "repay contempt with contempt for

---

87 Garaudy, Roger. *L'itinéraire d'Aragon. Du surréalisme au monde reel*. Paris: Gallimard, 1961.
88 Alexis, *Arbres musiciens*, p. 96
89 Alexis, *Arbres musiciens*, pp. 96–97.
90 Alexis, *Arbres musiciens*, p. 97.

this 'society,'" he thinks to himself: "I dominate you and I defy you [...] I defy you the gift of my heart! [...] You are nothing!"[91] Carles' revolt is self-regarding, purely negative, antisocial and apolitical, his "politics" intended merely to *épater les bourgeois*.

Carles' political awakening later in the novel is depicted as similarly solipsistic. Sitting at the dinner table with his brother Edgard, he reads of the return to Haiti of Pierre Roumel, the novelized version of Jacques Roumain who appeared in the prison scene in *Compère Général Soleil* and radicalized Hilarion. When Edgard denounces Roumel as an extremist, claiming that the old era of indigenist resistance is dead, Carles responds with a *cri de coeur*:

> I feel within me the ardors of the time of the *Revue indigène*! [...] I'm just a bohemian, I know, I will only produce some mediocre verse at most, I will be but a minor poet, I concede it—action gives me vertigo!—but believe me, Edgard, my life will be worth even more than yours! At least I will keep my purity of heart![92]

The sincerity of Carles' professed political awakening here is immediately undermined by the many repetitions of the first-person "je" and "moi," a consistent feature of Carles' enunciations. The above passage also hints at a wider critique of the contemporary Haitian intelligentsia by imbuing Carles with the "ardors" of *la Revue indigène*, a 1928–1929 literary review that sought to reclaim Haitian cultural authenticity during the US occupation through the incorporation of indigenous cultural forms into literary writing. Carles' romanticized nostalgia for this *indigeniste* review does not stir him to act but rather provides him with an alibi for his disengagement. Poetry for Carles is not a means of contributing to the transformation of society, nor a medium for thinking through its contradictions; rather, it is a privileged refuge from the ugliness of real social antagonisms, a means of assuaging his bad conscience without ceding his class resources.

Ultimately, Carles lacks the courage of his indigenist convictions. His final scene in the novel takes place in the peasant hinterlands. Here, Carles encounters an old man who leads him into the nearby forest. As they penetrate deeper into the woods, Carles is transported by the beauty of the ethereal "song of the anolis," its harmonies recalling

---

91 Alexis, *Arbres musiciens*, p. 100.
92 Alexis, *Arbres musiciens*, p. 153.

an "angelic orchestra."[93] When they arrive at their destination, a hut near the forest's center, Carles learns that he has been led to the home of a peasant girl he had seduced weeks earlier, and that the old man—the girl's father—expects him to marry the girl, whom he has impregnated. Feeling trapped, Carles immediately panics: he escapes by threatening the peasant girl until she agrees to let him go, bursts out of the hut, and flees the scene on horseback. In art as in love, Carles relishes the ecstatic moment but simply will not commit. The scene of his abandonment of the Princieuse shack and the peasant girl he has impregnated is very similar to a recognition scene in the genre of melodrama: Carles' betrayal reveals his true position as an enemy of the peasant class.[94] By the novel's end, Carles has married a respectable bourgeois woman and joined the Lescot regime as a diplomatic attaché to Washington.

Carles thus fails to do what Mao Zedong, in his Yenan talks on literature, sets out as the principal task of the revolutionary writer:

> revolutionary writers and artists, writers and artists of promise, must go *among the masses*; they must for a long period of time unreservedly and whole-heartedly [...] go into the heat of the struggle, go to the only source, the broadest and richest source, in order to observe, experience, study and analyse all the different kinds of people, all the classes, all the masses, all the vivid patterns of life and struggle, all the raw materials of literature and art.[95]

Alexis endorses precisely this understanding of the writer's political responsibility in "Où va le roman?," wherein he also castigates the petit-bourgeois "jeunesse intellectuelle" in the capitalist West for its disconnection from the masses:

> Verbally this petite bourgeoisie rejects the values of the decadent bourgeoisie, but in practice it refuses equally the companionship of the popular masses whom capitalism has disfigured and alienated on the intellectual and artistic level [...] most often, despite their sayings, they do not blend in with the people, they do not fight artistically from the

---

93 Alexis, *Arbres musiciens*, p. 306.
94 On scenes of recognition in melodrama, see Brooks, Peter, *The Melodramatic Imagination: Balzac, Henry James, Melodrama, and the Mode of Excess*, New Haven, CT and London: Yale University Press, 1995, Ch. 2.
95 Mao Zedong. "Talks at the Yenan Forum on Literature and Art." 1942. Marxists Internet Archive.

positions of the people, they do not try to become of one flesh with the people.[96]

Alexis literalizes this image of becoming "of one flesh" with the people by having Carles first take sexual advantage of the peasant girl, impregnating her, and then refuse to marry her. Thus for Alexis, as for Sartre in "Orphée noir," the *poète maudit* comes to be associated with treason (as discussed in the Introduction).

Alexis' critique of avant-garde poetry is also achieved by contrasting the character of Carles, in two crucial scenes, with proletarian Carméleau. These two opposite figures never meet, but are triangulated through Gonaibo, the *enfant sauvage*, who for much of the novel is engaged in futile spontaneous revolt against the invading *blancs* and is badly in need of guidance. In parallel scenes—their structures are nearly identical—Carles and Carméleau both speak to Gonaibo about his and Haiti's situation, and both give more or less the same message: he must stop his vain revolt and move to the cities, become initiated into the working class, and join the revolution when the time is right. In a pair of scenes that seem to dramatize the literary debates between Alexis and Léopold Senghor at the First Congress of Black Writers and Artists (discussed in Chapter 1), both characters visit Gonaibo and try, through different rhetorical modes of address, to persuade him to flee the countryside for the city.

Carles is the first would-be tribune. Carles' speech is presented through Gonaibo's point of view, in indirect discourse, and the reader therefore has access only to Gonaibo's reception of it. The boy listens, but his curiosity about the message is quickly overtaken by his growing distrust of the messenger. The following quote is what Gonaïbo is able to understand from Carles' verbose speech:

> Poverty was the soil of all religious aberrations, that was true, but one didn't thus uproot a faith amalgamated into the hearts of men by their primitive living and working conditions [...] However the temples would be destroyed and the lands were lost! He, Gonaibo, he was condemned, even more than the peasants...The life he had made for himself out in the moors was an anachronism, his domain was a little island that contradicted the overall reality of the country [...] He had to emigrate towards the cities where a new grain was rising, a grain that that promised a new flour of tomorrow, a sweet flour of

---

96 "Où va le roman?" p. 87.

liberty [...] If Gonaïbo wanted to preserve his eternal dream, he would have to sacrifice his bucolic life his big spaces and the intoxicated cry he let out each morning in the moor. Oh, he, Carles Osmin, was not very qualified to teach him this lesson, but his friendship commanded him to communicate what he knew ....[97]

The choice of internal narrative focalization in this passage makes the reader see Carles through Gonaïbo's eyes—Gonaibo and the reader see through Carles' words not unlike the way schoolchildren see through an inept teacher. Carles speaks in an elevated register completely out of tune with his addressee, and his speech is overstuffed with florid images and abstract jargon that the boy could not possibly understand. He disparages the lifeworld that Gonaïbo has been fighting to protect—the only one the boy knows—as primitive and anachronistic, and his religious beliefs as mere superstitions. Urging Gonaibo to abandon his home, he can give nothing but a lame poetic flourish ("the sweet flour of liberty") as encouragement. Finally, his false humility bespeaks a capacious narcissism and self-regard. Unsurprisingly, the scene ends with the boy banishing Carles from his lands.

Every aspect of the dynamic between Gonaibo and Carles is inverted in the later scene where the boy encounters Carméleau Melon. The narrative structure of this scene is indeed a direct and symmetrical inversion of the earlier scene with Carles. Here, Gonaïbo is the one to approach the outsider, curious about this "big reddish Black man with a mobile and prepossessing face" who has entered his domain. Unlike Carles, who rides in awkwardly on horseback and seems badly out of place, Carméleau seems intimately familiar with the lands, "caressing the grassy expanses with an emotional eye, as if rediscovering them."[98] Watching this stranger from a distance, Gonaïbo notices "an intense internal joy" in the man as he catches his reflection in the lake's surface and observes that he is acting "as if he were at home." Once he notices that Gonaïbo has been observing him, Carmeleau reacts forcefully but tactically: with an "iron hand" he catches Gonaïbo by the ankle, and immediately interpellates him, demanding to know who he is and why the boy was "spying" on him. The physical strength of this stranger awes Gonaïbo: "For the first time, he was experiencing the strength of another."[99] Gonaibo bites the man's hand, a desperate *passage à*

---

97 Alexis, *Arbres musiciens*, p. 220.
98 Alexis, *Arbres musiciens*, p. 337.
99 Alexis, *Arbres musiciens*, p. 337.

l'acte that emphasizes both his relative weakness and his distrust of outsiders. The man finally identifies himself as a "worker from over yonder, the Fôret des Pins," returned after years of labor in a lumber camp to see his home one last time before it is destroyed by the white industrialists.

Whereas Carles has only an abstract (pseudo-)understanding of class relations, for Carméleau class consciousness is the result of years of labor, struggle, and study, the sense that he has *made* of his concrete experience. As Carméleau later relates to Bois d'Orme:

> If you knew what I've had to suffer in the cities to learn it, to understand it, papa Bois d'Orme! I gorged myself with life [...] I toiled, I cried, I suffered to learn a trade, to lean to read, to become a true worker. I sought out and found men who explained to me ... I know now that a day will come when this will no longer be, but how we'll need to fight before that day arrives![100]

The Carles scenes also contrast with the Carmeleau scenes narratologically. Whereas Carles' lecture is rendered in the text as a long block of free indirect discourse from Gonaibo's point of view, the encounter with Carméleau is a dialogue, an authentic exchange rather than a patronizing lecture. Carméleau delivers a Marxist message that is not so different from Carles', but its rhetorical efficacy lies in its being delivered simply, directly and in terms the boy understands. A true dialectician, Carméleau even takes into account what the boy cannot yet understand: "You can't understand now ... Later you'll surely remember our encounter, everything ... It will be after a long absence, then, when you've come back to these lands ...."[101] Rather than expel Carméleau as he did Carles, this time Gonaibo accepts the difficult truth that he must accept the sweep of history. The scene ends as Carméleau, his arm wrapped fatherlike around the boy's shoulder, begins to tell the boy a story: "You see the big *icaco* over there? Right! Listen ...."[102] Like a Haitian analog of Chapaev, the eponymous positive hero of the Soviet film who, in a famous scene, explains military tactics to his peasant comrades using a handful of potatoes, Carméleau instructs Gonaibo in

---

100 Alexis, *Arbres musiciens*, p. 352.
101 Alexis, *Arbres musiciens*, p. 338.
102 Alexis, *Arbres musiciens*, p. 338.

the laws of historical development using concrete images from his own lifeworld that he can easily relate to and understand.[103]

Carméleau thus emerges as an avatar of a figure that Lukács calls, after Lenin, a "tribune of the people."[104] In order to have a chance of changing an oppressive system "in deed, and not only in intent," Lukács argues, popular rebellions must "make [their] way into consciousness"; the tribune of the people is the evangelist of this consciousness, helping it take root in the popular imagination. The popular tribunes of history were not "dazzling orators" like Mirabeau, Vergniaud, or Danton, Lukács argues, but "the simple Marat and the dry Robespierre." Simplicity, directness, and conviction, combined with an awareness of the "social totality in its movement," are the requirements for such a figure. The *poète maudit* Carles proves himself to be a mere "bureaucrat," a symptom of a dying bourgeois literature rife with the "sparse, thin and problematic poetry of despair, which only manages to create a subjective authenticity out of the depths, cannot find tones for celebrating the rebirth of humanity and humankind."[105] Carméleau possesses every one of these qualities, however, and, as such, embodies precisely the kind of engaged writing that Alexis sees as the kind of literary production that the moment called for.

The Science of the Marvelous in *L'Espace d'un Cillement*

Alexis' third novel is in many ways a significant departure from his earlier writing. While *Les Arbres musiciens* and *Compère Général Soleil* are plotted on a world-historical scale and contain grand ensemble casts, *L'Espace d'un cillement* takes place almost entirely within a single neighborhood of postwar Port-au-Prince: La Frontière, the red-light district where prostitutes entertain US marines and the popular *rara* festival takes over the streets after nightfall. Nor is this novel the story

---

103 *Chapaev*. Directed by Georgi and Andrei Vasilyev. Lenfilm, 1934.
104 "As the principal hero of our books we should choose labour, i.e., a person, organized by the processes of labour, who in our country is armed with the full might of modern technique, a person who, in his turn,. so organizes labour that it becomes easier and more productive, raising it to the level of an art. We must learn to understand labour as creation." Gorki, Maxim. "Soviet Literature." 1934. Marxists Internet Archive.
105 Lukács, Gyorgy. "Tribune or Bureaucrat?" *Essays on Realism*. Edited by Rodney Livingstone. Cambridge, MA: MIT Press, 1981, p. 213.

of a struggle between social groups—or, it is, but much less explicitly so. Centrally, it is a love story. The two protagonists, emancipated proletarian worker El Caucho and prostitute La Niña Estrellita, encounter one another and fall in love as they investigate and explore each other through their five senses, becoming physically closer and more intimate with each encounter: they first see each other, then come close enough to be able to smell one another, then speak to one another, and finally consummate their desire through touch.

The novel also contains some of Alexis' most lyrical prose. As its title suggests, *L'Espace d'un cillement* is more concerned with the moment than with sweeping historical panorama. The entire plot takes place in the recent past over the course of a single week—Holy Week, or the week leading up to Easter[106]—and the narrator focuses on the two main characters' immediate sensory experience from moment to moment, long descriptive passages relating the train of sensory details perceived by the two protagonists. J. Michael Dash, an incisive reader of Alexis, points to the "dense, poetic prose" of *Espace d'un cillement* as evidence that Alexis' connection to socialist realism is less far-reaching than the author himself claims.[107]

And yet, for all its focus on subjective experience, for all the sensual richness of its descriptive passages, *L'Espace d'un cillement* remains a novel engineered according to socialist realist guidelines. Whereas Alexis' concern in *Les arbres musiciens* was to show the totality of class relations, *L'Espace d'un cillement* is devoted to tracing the material process of how individuals develop into class-conscious subjects. The central love story is an allegory for the development of revolutionary consciousness. Just as philosopher Alain Badiou connects love to political revolution by treating both as events that can occasion the articulation of a truth, El Caucho and La Niña's process of falling in love is—like revolution—an ongoing project to which they commit, their encounter a marvelous event that "initiat[es] a shared investigation of the Universe."[108]

---

106 Louis Aragon's novel *La Semaine sainte*, published in 1958, relates the political dilemmas of painter Theodore Géricault during Holy Week (March 19–26) in the year 1815. Given the close timing of the two novels' release and the close ideological, professional, and personal affinities between the two authors, it is most tempting to link *La Semaine Sainte* with l'*Espace d'un cillement*.
107 Dash, *Literature and Ideology in Haiti*, p. 194.
108 Quoted in Hallward, Peter. *Badiou: A Subject to Truth*. Minneapolis: University of Minnesota Press, 2003, p. 6.

It is this logic of investigation in the wake of an event, this attempt to rationalize the marvelous, that governs the structure of *L'Espace d'un cillement*.

We first notice Alexis' concern to rationalize the marvelous in the architecture of *L'Espace d'un cillement*. The novel is divided into six chapters called *mansions*, each concentrating on one of the senses (the sixth *mansion* corresponding to the "sixth sense"). The archaism *mansion* connotes several things at once: first, the stations of a ritual or ritualized journey, as in the Stations of the Cross; second, in astrology, the 12 houses of the zodiac; finally, in medieval theater, mansion stages were small, booth-like scenic structures that symbolized specific Biblical settings (Heaven, Hell, Eden, and so on) and were generally juxtaposed, so that spectators would move from one mansion to another.[109] Similarly to these medieval mansion stages, those of Alexis' novel present a number of different tableaux or scenes that throw one another into relief.

However, the mansions of *Espace d'un cillement* are structured so as to be almost exactly alike, but for a single modification. Each mansion takes place over the course of a single day and night, and begins with a character waking up, so that we can closely track changes and developments from section to section. In each mansion, Alexis isolates one aspect of the narrative situation and examines it closely, as one controls in scientific experiments for different variables. Each mansion isolates one of the five senses, and the "sixth sense" of the sixth mansion is an emergent sense, a synthesis of the previous five. Here we may note a similarity to the structure of *Compère* and *Les arbres musiciens*: Alexis refracts the set of relations he wants to examine into its constituent elements and then reassembles them, thus showing how each determinate element relates to the totality.

The novel opens in a symbolic haze, however, a state of almost total indistinction that recalls Césaire's poems of ideological impasse discussed in Chapter 3. La Nina, who is just waking up, is having a difficult time finding her bearings: "Nine! ... Nine or ten? No, she must have made a mistake. It must have just struck ten o'clock. [...] They haven't heard [the clocks] of the Hospice Saint-François and the Asile Français ...."[110] Given the din of the Rara bands, the traffic, the rowdy marines, and the roaring

---

109 Aune, M.G. "The Medieval Stage." California University of Pennsylvania. Online.
110 Alexis, *Espace*, p. 16.

of the sea, "on n'arrive pas à distinguer grand-chose."[111] All of this is exacerbated by her grinding hangover, the effect of too much (American) Pabst beer from the previous evening. Like Hilarion in *Compère General Soleil*, La Nina is completely spontaneous and reactive at first, a jumble of impulses and fragments. While Hilarion's first sensations are hunger pangs in his stomach, the first thing La Nina feels is pain, in the part of her body most connected to her labor: "La Nina Estrellita perceived her sex like an open wound whose lips were being spread, a tear [...] a flayed heel, on fire, in a too-wide shoe."[112]

It is not only La Nina's body that is enflamed, blurred, and fragmented. Her other faculties—her "reason" and her "affectivity," to recall Alexis' understanding of the faculties of human consciousness—are hardly in better shape. Paralyzed by anxiety and depression—"the gaping black hole, in the depths of which she's been struggling close to eight days"[113]—she relies on the Maxiton amphetamines prescribed to her by La Frontière's resident doctor, Chalbert, to make it through the day; in spite of (or due to) the stimulants, La Nina is prone to violent mood swings. Her cognition is also badly addled, as evidenced by her various superstitions; a believer in numerology, she turns to religion for solace, praying to the "Virgen del Pilar," and she saves money in the hope of someday breaking out on her own, "sans *chulo*." None of her faculties is attuned to the material world around her. When we first encounter her, then, La Nina is shackled by what Lukács calls the "stupefaction" of habit that sets the pace of life under capitalism, a mechanistic relationship to "living events"[114]: her "lower abdomen is a sweaty, desensitized plaque that palpitates, palpitates mechanically, that palpitates professionally, palpitates in spite of everything, palpitates always underneath the paunch imprinted upon it."[115]

Her exploited sex work is what sets this mechanical rhythm to her life, as suggested by the imagery of "palpitation" quoted above. Time for La Nina is measured in busloads of American marines who come to patronize her brothel, the Sensation Bar (the name is in English). Not unlike Sartre's *garçon de café* who dissolves into his role as waiter, La Nina plays the role of *putain* a bit too well, blowing kisses and flirting

---

111   Alexis, *Espace*, p. 16.
112   Alexis, *Espace*, p. 16.
113   Alexis, *Espace*, p. 14.
114   Lukács, "Tribune or Bureaucrat?" p. 212.
115   Alexis, *Espace*, p. 16.

as if she were a programmed automaton: "... Mwah ... mwah ... mwah! ... Thanks, my coco!"; "There you go, pigeon! You're cute!"; "Paws off, my gringos!"[116]

La Nina's encounter with El Caucho, a "man in blue overalls" who fixes her in his gaze, is the first time in the novel when she actually looks and *sees*: "La Nina opens her eyes. The man has walked away. He's no longer visible ... Yes, he is ... he's retracing his steps ... La Nina recloses her eyes ... He passes by her again ... Then she reopens her eyelids, looks at his swaying neck ...."[117] The unknown man returns her gaze, but does not approach or solicit her. This was simply not done: "You don't just look at La Nina Estrellita for over a minute! You don't undress her with your eyes, you take her in your paws!"[118] Unable to account for this man, she scans him with her eyes, part by part, systematically: his legs, then his thighs, the silhouette of his penis, his buttocks, and so on. She notices that he favors one leg, and that he must be very strong. Her visual scan of this mysterious man is interrupted by firecrackers going off outside (marines, again) and she returns to her station, but she continues thinking about the man, generating hypotheses about who he is and where he has come from.

In short, La Nina embarks upon an *investigation* in this scene, one that she will pursue throughout the novel. As Bruno Bosteels explains, the investigation is a central principle of the philosophy of Mao Zedong: it denotes "a form of concrete analysis of a concrete situation," a gathering of the concrete facts of a given situation conceived in fidelity to a truth and oriented towards bringing reality into closer alignment with this truth.[119] La Nina follows the logic of the Maoist investigation in her scanning of El Caucho with her five senses: there is something that she cannot account for and that may change everything, and she must collect more information. The initial sensory haze gives way to sharp focus, and—until the inertia of her situation pulls her back in—there appears to be an opening, the glimmer of something new.

This scene, which we might call a scene of investigation, is repeated exactly in each mansion. In each successive scene, La Nina exercises one of her sensory faculties as if for the first time, generating each time

---

116 Alexis, *Espace*, pp. 18–20.
117 Alexis, *Espace*, p. 25.
118 Alexis, *Espace*, p. 28.
119 Bosteels, Bruno. "Post-Maoism: Badiou and Politics." *Positions: East Asia Culture Critique*, Vol. 13, No. 3 (2005), p. 579.

a long list of sensory details from which she draws new conclusions about El Caucho. In one remarkable passage, La Nina reconstructs the itinerary of El Caucho's journey through the Caribbean by smelling him: "That smell of tobacco! It's ... But it's ... Cuba! Yes, Cuba ... La Nina gives herself over again to her sensibility [...] Papaya leaves a resin, a kind of persistent, captious, heavy turpentine ... Yes, he has lived in Mexico ...."[120] La Nina quite literally sniffs out the truth in this scene, rigorously following her nose, abandoning herself to her investigation and following it through to the end: "La Nina is no longer anything but the fraternal stacking of all these bouquets she smells around the silent and prostrate unknown man." As La Nina falls deeper in love, she hones her senses even further, and also begins to think more clearly. Her amorous project anchors her, allowing her to begin to reflect more generally on her situation: "She rewatches backwards the film of these last three days [...] She had lived until then like a postulate, the preconceived idea that her entire life would always unfold in linear fashion, in the same direction, according to a scheme concocted by some mad god."[121] In the remaining mansions, La Nina questions her superstitions, gains confidence, stands up for herself against another prostitute's sexual advances, and finally—in her moment of *jouissance* the first time she and El Caucho have sex—remembers her true name, Eglantina. Even here, however, her path towards consciousness is not finished, as she embarks upon her own journey around the Caribbean, continuing the perpetual struggle towards consciousness. To recall Lacan's ethical maxim, La Nina/Eglantina's imperative appears to be not to give up on her desire.

In his essay "La Belle Amour Humaine 1957," Alexis similarly discusses human subjectivity as an ongoing struggle, a dynamic process of investigation: "it is struggle, continuous improvement, and the essential thing is that we be always in movement towards it."[122] This description bears close resemblance to Lukács' desire for a socialist realism that would develop new forms that make visible tendential movements in the present moment:

> On the one hand, reality is forever throwing up new material, permitting older material to disappear from view. But the investigating subject, caught in its flux, is yet able to discover tendencies whose significance

---

120 Alexis, *Espace*, p. 121.
121 Alexis, *Espace*, p. 217.
122 Alexis, "La Belle Amour Humaine 1957," p. 25.

had not previously been understood. The development of new forms is intimately related to this active, unceasing exploration of reality.[123]

In *Espace d'un cillement*, Alexis tracks in minute sensory detail precisely this struggle of El Caucho and La Nina/Eglantina, two such "investigating subjects," towards emancipation. Motivated by love, and through rigorous investigation that makes use of their senses, reason, and emotions, they take the measure of their situation, draw hypotheses to which they remain true, and consequently produce new forms: the transformed patterns of Eglantina's daily existence, the couple's amorous relation, and new revolutionary subjectivities.

Similarly, in an article titled "Jdanov et Nous," Louis Aragon describes socialist realism as literary art produced according to scientific principles: "socialist realism is the organizational conception of facts in literature, of detail in art; it interprets this detail, gives it meaning [*sens*] and force, integrates it in the movement of humanity, beyond individualism[.]"[124] I would argue that this quote from Aragon describes the structure of *L'Espace d'un cillement* more or less precisely. It is through this very process of organizing and interpreting empirical fact and detail, of finding the thread that La Nina and El Caucho are able to come together, and that La Nina/Eglantina emancipates herself from her original state of alienation.

The "Time of Anthologies": *Romancéro aux étoiles* and Haitian Book Culture

> "The October Revolution has almost everywhere, among peoples where oral literature reigned, transformed these bards who have become their propagandists. Lyricism has everywhere found its object."
>
> (Louis Aragon, *Littératures Soviétiques*[125])

The final text that Alexis published before his disappearance, the *Romancéro aux étoiles*, represents another formal departure from his previous narrative texts. Most obviously, the *Romancéro* is a

---

123 Lukács, "Critical Realism and Socialist Realism," pp. 97–98.
124 Quoted in Garaudy, *L'itineraire d'Aragon*, p. 261.
125 Aragon, *Littératures soviétiques*, p. 82.

collection of short stories rather than a novel. Most of the stories collected in the *Romancéro* are retellings of stories from the Haitian narrative tradition: the tale of Bouqui and Malice, the legendary Taino queen Anacaona in "Dit de la Fleur d'Or," a modernized version of the *zombi* trope in "Chronique d'un faux amour," and so on. These tales are anthologized with others whose settings are more contemporary: "Le sous-lieutenant enchanté," in which a racist US marine "goes native" in the Haitian countryside during the occupation; and "Le Roi des Songes," a whimsical, quasi-surrealist story that takes place aboard a jet airliner where the passengers enter a fantastical realm of dreams. The collection thus weaves together various tropes from the Haitian *lodyans* storytelling tradition while adding modern and contemporary settings, forms, and tropes.

The frame narrative uniting these short stories is that of the narrator's encounter with Vieux Vent Caraïbe, "that old catchpole [*recors*], the oldest witness of our ancient ages, of the dreams, the struggles and the marvels of all the Haitian peoples, our ancestors the Ciboneys, our ancestors the Xemes and the Caribs, our Negro and Zambo fathers, this old fogey, this toothless minstrel ...."[126] Alexis acknowledges drawing from the Haitian storytelling tradition, especially from the figures of the "conteur," the "simidor," and the "samba"; Vieux Vent Caraïbe is a condensation of these popular storyteller figures. Vieux Vent Caraïbe and the narrator take turns telling each other stories, and thus collectively produce the text of the *Romancéro* between them.

This section investigates how Alexis' retelling of popular Haitian legends fits into the Alexisian socialist realist aesthetic whose development I have been tracing across his oeuvre in this chapter. Georges Anglade, a theorist and master artist of the *lodyans* genre, views the *Romancéro* as Alexis' "final codicil," a hint that Alexis was tending away from the "dogma" of marvelous realism that "sticks [*plaquer*] a politically acceptable theory on top of a novelistic practice that spills out of this narrow theory" and towards a more natural and liberated style based upon the *lodyans* form.[127] I do not contest Alexis' interest in *lodyans*, but again I see more continuity between this interest in national forms and the Marxist aesthetics that Alexis worked through over the course of his three previous novels. I argue that the *Romancéro* is a text that Alexis

---

126 Aléxis, *Romancéro*, p. 12.
127 Anglade, "Le dernier codicille," p. 564.

conceives in alignment with his understanding of Haitian political economy and with his project for a Haitian cultural revolution.

We have already established that Alexis believed Haitian society to be in a semi-feudal mode of production, with other modes of production simultaneously co-present.[128] Perhaps for this reason, an idiosyncratic thread of medievalism, related to the author's understanding of political economy in Haiti, runs throughout Alexis' writings. In his manifesto of marvelous realism, for example, Alexis locates the Haitian Creole language "at the stage where French was in relation to Latin throughout the Middle Ages," with Creole as the vulgate "language of the people" and French, like medieval Latin, as the "language of the literate and the learned."[129] In *Les Arbres musiciens*, notes Claude Souffrant, the peasant milieu of Nan-Remembrance is "a milieu filled with religiosity," in which the "Haitian common people [...] are, a bit like the French Middle Ages, a people enslaved by a feudal caste and condemned to take refuge in a naïve faith, to escape into the marvelous."[130] *L'Espace d'un cillement*, as mentioned above, is divided into "mansions," a direct reference to European medieval theater; the epigraph to the novel's final *mansion* is, furthermore, a quotation from medieval Spanish mystic poet Sor Juana de la Cruz. As we will see in this section, the *Romancéro aux étoiles* extends and develops the ongoing analogy in Alexis' oeuvre between the Haitian present and the European Middle Ages.

A few critics familiar with Alexis' writings note this literary medievalism, attributing it—importantly, for our purposes—to Alexis' connection with Louis Aragon. Writer Rassoul Labuchin, Alexis' Parti d'Entente Populaire comrade, explicitly attributes Alexis' medieval motifs to Aragon's influence: "Aragon's poetry hearkens back to the Middle Ages, hearkens back to France's childhood, and Jacques followed this path."[131] Claude Souffrant makes a similar connection between the medievalisms of Aragon and Alexis in his reading of the peasant scenes in *Les arbres musiciens*: Alexis' use of "popular forms, rhythms and symbols" in the novel echo, for Souffrant, Aragon's "nourishing" his writings with

---

128 Alexis' name for the Haitian revolution he envisions is the "Révolution Nationale Anti-Féodale et Anti-Imperialiste." *Le marxisme, seul guide possible de la revolution haïtienne*. Paris: C3 Éditions, 2021, p. 175.
129 *Ier Congrès*, Compte rendu complet, p. 269.
130 Souffrant, *Une Négritude socialiste*, p. 72.
131 Interview with Rassoul Labuchin. YouTube. 2014.

"medieval myths and rhythms."[132] I would suggest that Alexis' project of marvelous realism is more substantially in dialogue with Aragon's socialist realist rewriting of French medieval forms than has previously been considered, and that this is especially evident in the *Romancéro*.

A brief explanation of Aragon's figurations of the Middle Ages will provide a useful point of reference for Alexis' medievalism. Aragon's troping of the French Middle Ages, most evident in his epic Resistance poem *Brocéliande* (1942), was a means of resisting right-wing narratives of France's past. As Jennifer Brown notes, the Middle Ages in France were "a zone of contested meaning" in the interwar and Vichy years—fascists such as Charles Maurras and Henry de Montherlant encouraged nostalgia for medieval chivalry to counter what they saw as France's decadent modern culture, and under Vichy images of Marshal Pétain were associated with Jeanne d'Arc.[133] Aragon, however, "subverted" nostalgic fascist medievalism to his own devices, investing the Middle Ages with a new, progressive meaning in lieu of a reactionary one. This project of reclaiming national symbols and stories for the left (and from the reactionary right) resembles very closely what Alexis is attempting to do by (re)writing the Haitian popular storytelling tradition in the *Romancéro*.

The first reference to the Middle Ages in the *Romancéro aux étoiles* is, of course, the *romancero* tradition that the title announces. The *romancero* refers to a collective corpus of popular narrative poems going back to the Spanish Middle Ages; a sort of popular historical record in song, the *romancero* is a living form, growing as it collects songs from all strata and classes of over the longue durée of Spanish cultural memory.[134] Already, it should not be difficult to see what attracts Alexis to the *romancero* form: collectively created, total in scope, and rooted in popular practice of oral storytelling, the "inexhaustible romancero," for Alexis, is an ideal candidate for the national literary form of Haiti. Thus, the tales included within the *Romancéro* span centuries of Haitian

---

132 Souffrant, *Une Négritude socialiste*, p. 74.
133 See Brown, Jennifer Stafford. "'Au feu de ce qui fut brûle ce qui sera: Louis Aragon and the Subversive Medieval." *Romanic Review*, Vol. 101, No. 3 (May 2010), pp. 325–342.
134 "Romancero." *Encyclopedia Britannica Online*. Communist poet Gabriel Garcia Lorca's *Romancero gitano* (1928) also hearkens back to the medieval *romancero* tradition while blending in modern elements. Anderson, Andrew A. "Federico Garcia Lorca." *The Cambridge History of Spanish Literature*. Cambridge: Cambridge University Press, 2004, p. 597.

history and pre-history across various identifiable discrete periods, from pre-Columbian indigenous legends ("Dit de la Fleur d'Or") to Afro-Haitian folktales ("Tatez o'Flando," "Dit de Bouqui et Malice," and others) to modern analogues ("Le Roi des Songes"). In several tales, the Haitian present, recent past, and deep history are co-present in a more direct way: "Chronique d'un faux amour" deploys the *zombi* figure to tell a tale of a modern bourgeois woman's social alienation, while the eponymous "enchanted" Sub-Lieutenant Wheelbarrow, a racist Southern US marine, betrays the US occupation and disappears into the peasant countryside, his story integrated into local legend. Taken as an ensemble, the tales of the *Romancéro* represent every social class and nearly every historical ethnic group of Haitian society, placing them on an equal footing.

Alexis' *Romancero* finds another architextual model in the anthology form. Here, I refer specifically to the version of "anthology" promoted by Aragon in the 1950s as part of his "national poetry" initiative. Aragon describes the anthology as the contemporary socialist literary form *par excellence*:

> It is the time of anthologies, where not only [the poet's] own ordered poems, but the whole vast French treasure trove, all this experiences which sensibility reillumines, must quickly be gathered together for him, so that this song perceived by him is not lost, this national melody that he has happened upon everywhere, from unknown sources to great public domains.[135]

Aragon invokes this "time of anthologies" to emphasize the aim of his "national poetry" aesthetics to socialize literature and literary culture, to bring about a "return to poetry by all and for all." As we saw in Chapter 2, Aragon envisions not only creating poetry that the great mass of people would understand, but also changing how literature is socially instituted, eliminating the distance between writer and people and promoting collective, transindividual processes of literary production.

Alexis similarly wanted to revolutionize the social institution of Haitian literature by bringing the writers—and the written word—to the Haitian people. In "Du Réalisme Merveilleux des Haïtiens" he asserts that "The gravest problem is that there is no possible communication between the people and those of its children who are valuable

---

135 Aragon, *Journal d'une poésie nationale*, p. 25.

creators, who honor and illustrate its culture."[136] Alexis schematizes an ambitious project for reorganizing Haitian culture in his little-known essay *Le marxisme, seul guide possible de la révolution haïtienne*:

> For us, without denying the professional tradition and universal humanism of our time, writers and artists who come from the ruling classes must put themselves in the school of our living popular oral literature, of our popular art, of our folklore. On the other hand, popular writers and artists (composés, simidors, sambas, etc.) without renouncing the folkloric tradition must familiarize themselves with the Haitian and universal professional achievements in arts and literature. Life has given us this rare chance, to have a working-class people who has never ceased to be creative, therefore for Marxist aesthetics the path is clear in Haiti: formally adopt the popular artistic lens while redressing that within it which walks on its head, in making dynamic what it static, in purifying [*épurant*] popular culture certain defeatist, ambiguous and unhealthy aspects that however must not be mechanically amputated, but positively and dialectically transcended.[137]

In such a cultural revolution, bourgeois writers would go among the people, learn traditional storytelling practices from peasant simidors and sambas, and incorporate these forms into their writings, and peasant creators would, in turn, gain access to the written word and connection to the broader world republic of letters.[138] Alexis thus envisions undoing the current class distribution of cultural forms and practices, performing a *tri* that would sift out what is living and what is dead among them and instituting a Haitian literary canon that would synthesize them all, and that would be shared in common by all within a Haitian book culture. The *Romancéro*, then, can be understood as a prototype model of what such a reformed Haitian literature could possibly look like.

In *Littératures soviétiques* (1954), in which Aragon promotes Soviet literary forms and institutions, we see a similar vision of non-literate cultures transitioning, via socialism, to modern book culture: "written culture (*pismennost*) has been for more than forty peoples an acquisition posterior to the October Revolution, and they have only acceded to it thanks to the new conditions of Soviet life."[139] As an example of this cultural development, Aragon takes the novel *The Last of the Udege*

---

136 Alexis, "Du réalisme merveilleux," p. 110.
137 Alexis, *Le marxisme*, pp. 85–86.
138 Alexis, *Le marxisme*, p. 86.
139 Aragon, *Littératures soviétiques*, p. 79.

by Aleksandr Fadeyev, based on James Fenimore Cooper's *Last of the Mohicans*. The nomadic Udege tribe is able to survive in the novel not by continuing its pre-modern traditions unchanged, but by transitioning to socialism—the Udege tribe were collectivized and resettled in the 1930s. The novel's hero, Djansi Kimonko, existed in real life and became the first published Udege author. "This people," says Aragon, has not disappeared. It has awoken to national consciousness, to art."[140]

Aragon paints an exaggeratedly rosy portrait of the conditions of indigenous peoples in the Soviet Union, and his attitude certainly reflects the "fraternalism" that Césaire diagnosed in PCF ideology regarding the global South, here applied to indigenous nations of the Soviet Union. Nonetheless, Alexis shares some of Aragon's thinking about cultural development: like Aragon, Alexis views cultural development as a process of sublation, or *aufhebung*, the Hegelian concept that means to negate, to put an end to, and to preserve all at once. The French word *dépassement*, an analog of "sublation," is repeated nearly 40 times in *Le Marxisme, le seul guide possible de la Révolution haïtienne*, where an entire section is devoted to the concept.[141] Alexis quotes Hegel directly on sublation: "That which is sublated is not thereby reduced to nothing. Nothing is immediate; what is sublated, on the other hand, is the result of mediation; it is a non-being but as a result which had its origin in a being. It still has, therefore, in itself the determinate from which it originates."[142] This dialectical movement from the immediate to the determinate, from the in-itself to the for-itself, is just how Alexis envisions the future development of Haitian culture and society. In a way that recalls Mallarmé's famous adage that everything exists in order to end up in a book, the *Romancéro* is a crystallization of this *aufgehoben* Haitian culture.

---

140 Aragon, *Littératures soviétiques*, p. 80.
141 For an incisive discussion of "dépassement" in this treatise, see Cadet, Jean-Jacques, "Le marxisme, seul guide possible de la Révolution haïtienne. Préoccupation épistémologique: élargir la théorie." *Revue Legs et Littérature*, No. 18 (2021), pp. 53–64.
142 Hegel, G.W.F. *Science of Logic*, Vol. 1, Book 1, §184. Marxists Internet Archive. Quoted in Alexis, *Le marxisme*, p. 42.

Conclusion

Restoring Alexis' writings to their Cold War context makes visible Alexis' connections to a vast transnational and intertextual network of tropes, conventions, genres, models, types—one stretching across all three Cold War "worlds," from Aragon to Lukács to Mao—in a way that a Francophone or postcolonial or regional approach alone does not. Furthermore, reading Alexis' writings through a Cold War lens complicates some of the assumptions about literary form and aesthetic value that we have inherited from the Cold War and that still linger on. It complicates, in particular, the association of the radical tradition in Francophone Caribbean literature almost entirely with avant-garde poetry, modernism, and surrealism. If the literary works of Alexis' realism read differently from its orthodox Marxist—and indeed, at times, vulgar Marxist—theoretical texts, these texts are nonetheless products of the same aesthetic and political vision.

Finally, treating Alexis'—or Césaire's, or Depestre's—writings as interventions in a global Cold War literary debate allows us to consider Caribbean authors as not simply bystanders or victims of the superpower struggle, but as witnesses and actors with a unique critical purchase upon this world order, writers actively involved in contesting its ideological currents and engaged in working out aesthetic responses to it. Alexisian realism is not simply a European formula foisted upon the Haitian real, nor is it in any way reducible to the formulaic socialist realism that Adorno sums up so aptly as "boy-meets-tractor literature";[143] it is an attempt to harness realism as a literary resource towards the defeudalizing and regeneration of Haitian culture.[144] We need not fully endorse every aspect of Alexis' Cold War political alignments to acknowledge in his socialist realist novels a rigorously disciplined politico-aesthetic project aimed the ultimate and worthy goal of, in his own words, *"donner un sens à la vie haitienne"*—giving both a *meaning* to Haiti's past and current history of struggle and a *direction*, a path toward its future emancipation.

---

143 Adorno, Theodor. "Reconciliation under Duress." *Aesthetics and Politics.* New York: Verso, 2007, pp. 151–176.
144 Joe Cleary notes the perception of Soviet-style realism as either a "defeudalizing literary solvent" or an "alien Western imposition" among Third World writers. Cleary, Joe. "Realism after Modernism and the Literary World System." *Modern Language Quarterly*, Vol. 73, No. 3 (2012), p. 264.

Epilogue

"One can't purely and simply throw everything that has been marked by the experience of the October Revolution in the garbage. There were things that were magnificent because they were lived in authenticity."

(René Depestre[1])

Several years ago, I travelled to the Haitian city of Cap-Haïtien to participate in the Haitian Studies Association conference. The year's theme was "Haitian Eco-Systems," and I was presenting a paper on Jacques Stephen Alexis' socialist realist representations of the Haitian peasantry, material now included in Chapter 4 of this book. At the keynote address, attendees gathered to hear the speaker, environmental biologist and educator Florence Sergile, give a lecture on the ecological challenges facing contemporary Haiti. It was an informative and erudite presentation—rigorous, yet mercifully formulated not to go over the heads of the many humanists in the audience—but it was also a call to action. She asked us to think of the vast piles of refuse lining the beaches outside town that we had seen from our chartered buses en route to the pleasant, well-manicured hotel where the conference was held. Dr Sergile asked us to look closely at this mass of *déchets* on the return drive, and to discern specific items and materials. Finally came our homework assignment: to identify one item and think of a potential social use for it. How, she challenged us to ask, could new and generative uses be made of material that others before us had discarded and forgotten?

---

1 Bonniol, "Entretien avec René Depestre," p. 9.

I realized just before my panel the following day that the project that would become *Cold War Negritude* was, in a sense, analogous to this assignment. The Cold War writings I have analyzed in this book have been either discarded, as in the case of Depestre's exercises in national poetry, or nearly shorn of the ideological context of their production, in the case of Alexis. As Jodi Dean suggests, we need not remain "stuck in the ruins of communism"; instead, "we can scavenge the ruins for past hopes and old lessons and put these remnants to use as we organize and build."[2] Writing in the third decade of the twenty-first century—30 years after the official end of the Cold War but also now well after the end of Francis Fukuyama's "end of history"—what remnants can be potentially salvaged from the 1950s interventions of Depestre, Césaire, and Alexis?

The First Congress, of course, has hardly been relegated to the status of historical *déchet*. To the contrary, it has received a groundswell of renewed critical interest, much of this from innovative scholars in global Cold War literature such as Cedric Tolliver and Duncan Yoon. It is indeed thrilling to read the proceedings of the Congress, to appreciate Diop's masterful stagecraft and statecraft, the simple audacity of the project and its sheer symbolic force, and it is exciting to anticipate a growing corpus of scholarship on this watershed event and its afterlives. The twenty-first-century reader of the First Congress feels acutely the discrepancy between the addled and degraded public sphere of the early twenty-first century and *Présence Africaine*'s spectacle of high liberal civic culture. The greatest contribution of the First Congress—despite Diop's insistence on culture—is perhaps a political one: it exemplifies the powerful gesture that consists in the strategic suspense of ideological antagonisms, when it counts, to build coalitions among ideologically diverse groups opposed to domination.

Depestre's poems of the 1950s still lie mostly dormant. If the Marxist poetic *études* of *Minerai noir* do not achieve the same aesthetic success as Depestre's later works such as *Arc-en-ciel pour l'occident chrétien* or *Hadriana dans tous mes rêves*, they nonetheless represent a rigorously conceived materialist and realist counterpoint to the hegemonic modernist tendencies in the Negritude canon, and ought to be read more widely and in productive tension with more canonical texts. The poems of *Minerai noir* also afford a glimpse into the particular feelings, attitudes, and practices of what was vital in the old comrade relation: its

---

2 Dean, *Comrade*, p. 25.

rigorous egalitarianism, its locus beyond the individual, and its promise of both belonging and discipline.

Of all the works discussed in this book, Césaire's melancholic poetry of *Ferrements*, written from a place of rupture, defeat, disappointment, and uncertainty, is perhaps the text that feels most contemporary. The collection reflects a poetic vision that has been "amputated from its principle of hope," to cite Enzo Traverso.[3] To live in the twenty-first century is to look back upon the ruins of the preceding century's great principle of hope. And yet, the failure of any given alternative does not ratify Margaret Thatcher's capitalist realist axiom that "there is no alternative." The poems of *Ferrements* reward an attentive reading by revealing that despair is not their final word. The future they look forward to is not one that will surge forth like lava from a volcanic eruption, but one that must be felt out and worked through like a path out of the desert.

Alexisian realism is distinct in its syncretism, its audacity and experimentalism, its sheer variety and breadth. It is also remarkable, especially to a contemporary reader, for its unapologetic and steadfast belief in a future. For critic David Scott, the post-Cold War neoliberal order is haunted by the ghosts of foreclosed "revolutionary futures past," a present without an imaginable future.[4] Fredric Jameson, in the same vein, has famously said that it is easier to imagine the end of the world than the end of capitalism. What one encounters at the end of every work by Alexis, however—whatever else one might say of Aragon, he was a perceptive enough reader of Alexis to notice this—is a horizon open to future emancipation, like a door he leaves open, no matter how dim the events of the final chapter. In *Compère Général Soleil*, as Hilarion lays dying, he has a vision of the titular sun, a vision of future redemption that he passes to his wife Claire-Heureuse: "General Sun! You see him, there, just on the border, at the doorstep of our homeland! Never forget it Claire, never. Never."[5] The final thoughts of Eglantina, the disalienated subject born from the former Nina Estrellita, in the closing line of *L'Espace d'un cillement*: "¡Quien sabe!"[6] And, most powerfully, the closing of *Les Arbes Musiciens*: "The musician trees fall

3   Traverso, *Left-Wing Melancholia*, p. 83.
4   Scott, David. *Omens of Adversity: Tragedy, Time, Memory, Justice*. Durham, NC: Duke University Press, 2013, p. 14.
5   Alexis, *Compère*, p. 350.
6   Alexis, *Espace*, p. 346.

down sometimes, but the voice of the forest is still just as powerful. Life begins."[7] This twenty-first-century reader cannot help but hear in this last phrase a distant echo of the 2018 address by Brazilian President Lula da Silva; having been convicted in a corrupt, politically motivated trial, Lula addressed a crowd of Workers' Party supporters before turning himself in, saying: "Do what you want, the powerful can kill one, two or 100 roses. But they'll never manage to stop the arrival of spring."[8] Lula and Alexis—and Césaire, in the leftist odes of *Ferrements*, and Depestre, in his fidelity to a "solar, human us"—make visible the potential of a redemptive progressive victory to come that lies even within the moment of impasse and defeat.

In their writings, the 1956 cohort has left us salvageable political visions, resources that we can and should reuse to help us think through our current situation. They stand with us in "temporal solidarity," to borrow Gary Wilder's apt term. Depestre's comradely poetics, Césaire's Cold War poems, and Alexisian realism are all concrete efforts to imagine and invent precisely the alternative progressive forms of solidaristic relation that the Cold War superpower struggle rendered all but impossible, and that contemporary late neoliberalism leaves scrambled and foreclosed. The writings I have analyzed in this book are not mere relics of a bygone historical moment; they are still intact resources for those seeking, as their authors did, to bring the world into a more just alignment.

---

7 Alexis, *Arbres*, p. 406.
8 Cowie, Sam. "Lula Begins Prison Sentence in Brazil after Turning Himself in to Police." *The Guardian*, 7 Apr. 2018. https://www.theguardian.com/world/2018/apr/07/crowds-in-sao-paulo-block-lula-from-handing-himself-in.

Bibliography

"Ier Congrès international des écrivains et artistes noirs: Paris, Sorbonne, 19–22 septembre 1956: compte-rendu complet." *Présence Africaine*, Nos 8–10 (Jun.–Sep. 1956).
Adorno, Theodor. "Reconciliation under Distress." *Aesthetics and Politics*. New York: Verso, 2007, pp. 151–176.
Alexis, Jacques Stephen. *Compère Général Soleil*. Paris: Gallimard, 1955.
———. "Contribution à la Table Ronde sur le folklore et le nationalisme." *Optique* (Jun. 1956), pp. 25–34.
———. "Du réalisme merveilleux des Haïtiens." *Présence Africaine*, Nos 8–10 (Jun.–Nov. 1956), pp. 245–271.
———. "La Belle Amour Humaine 1957." *Europe*, Vol. 49, No. 501 (1971), pp. 20–22.
———. *Les arbres musiciens*. Paris: Gallimard, 1957.
———. *L'espace d'un cillement*. Paris: Gallimard, 1961.
———. *Le marxisme, seul guide possible de la revolution haïtienne*. Paris: C3 Éditions, 2021.
———. "Où va le roman?" *Présence Africaine*, No. 13 (Apr.–May 1957), pp. 81–101.
———. *Romancéro aux étoiles*. Paris: Gallimard, 1960.
Alliot, David. *Le Communisme est à l'ordre du jour. Aimé Césaire et le PCF*. Paris: Pierre-Guillaume de Roux, 2013.
Anderson, Andrew A. "Federico Garcia Lorca." *The Cambridge History of Spanish Literature*. Cambridge: Cambridge University Press, 2004.
Anderson, Kevin B. *Marx at the Margins: On Nationalism, Ethnicity, and Non-Western Societies*. Chicago, IL: University of Chicago Press, 2010.
Anderson, Perry. *Considerations on Western Marxism*. New York: Verso, 1976.
Anglade, Georges. "Le dernier codicille d'Alexis. Sur le parcours de Jacques Stéphen Alexis dans la théorie littéraire." *Présence Africaine*, Nos 175–176–177 (2008), pp. 546–573.

Apter, Emily. *Unexceptional Politics: On Obstruction, Impasse and the Impolitic*. New York: Verso, 2018.
d'Arboussier, Gabriel. "Une mystification dangereuse: théorie de la négritude." *La Nouvelle Critique* (Jun. 1949), pp. 34–47.
Aragon, Louis. *Journal d'une poésie nationale*. Lyon: Les Ecrivains Réunis, 1954.
———. "Le poète assassiné." *Les lettres françaises*, No. 1110 (Dec. 16–23, 1965), p. 16.
———. *Les Yeux et la mémoire*. Paris: Gallimard, 1954.
———. *Littératures soviétiques*. Paris: Denoël, 1955.
Arendt, Hannah. *The Origins of Totalitarianism*. Boston, MA, Mariner Books, 1973.
Arnold, A. James. *Aimé Césaire. Gènese et transformation d'une poétique*. Würzburg: Könighausen & Neumann, 2020.
———. *Modernism and Negritude: The Poetry and Poetics of Aimé Césaire*. Cambridge, MA: Harvard University Press, 1981.
Aune, M.G. "The Medieval Stage." California University of Pennsylvania. Online.
Bächler, Wolfgang. "Der Schwarzer Tito." *Die Zeit*, Nov. 8, 1956. Zeit Archiv Online.
Badiou, Alain. "The Communist Hypothesis." *New Left Review*, Vol. 49 (Jan.–Feb. 2008), pp. 29–42.
———. *Radar poésie: Essai sur Aragon*. Paris: Gallimard, 2020.
Baldwin, James. "Princes and Powers." *Encounter* (Jan. 1957), pp. 51–60.
Bird, Robert. "Articulations of (Socialist) Realism: Lukács, Platonov, Shklovsky." *e-flux Journal*, Vol. 91 (May 2018). Online.
Bloncourt, Gérald and Löwy, Michael ed. *Messagers de la tempête: André Breton et le Surréalisme en Haiti*. Montreuil: Le Temps des cérises, 2007.
Bongie, Chris. *Friends and Enemies: The Scribal Politics of Post/Colonial Literature*. Liverpool: Liverpool University Press, 2008.
Bonner, Christopher T. "Alioune Diop and the Cultural Politics of Negritude: Reading the First Congress." *Research in African Literatures*, Vol. 50, No. 2 (2019), pp. 1–19.
———. "The 'Ferments' of Poetry: The Geopolitical Vision of Aimé Césaire's Cold War Poems," *International Journal of Francophone Studies*, Vol. 19, Nos 3–4 (Dec. 2016), pp. 275–300.
———. "Islands Between Worlds: Cold War Caribbean Literatures." *Palgrave Handbook of Cold War Literature*. Edited by Andrew Hammond. Cham, Switzerland: Palgrave, 2020, pp. 431–450.
Bonniol, Jean-Luc. "Entretien avec René Depestre." *Gradhiva*, Vol. 1 (2005), pp. 1–21.

Booker, M. Keith and Juraga, Dubravka. "The Reds and the Blacks: The Historical Novel in the Soviet Union and Postcolonial Africa." *Studies in the Novel*, Vol. 29, No. 3 (1997), pp. 274–296.

Bosteels, Bruno. "Post-Maoism: Badiou and Politics." *Positions: East Asia Cultures Critique*, Vol. 13, No. 3 (2005), pp. 575–634.

Boym, Svetlana. *The Future of Nostalgia*. New York: Basic Books, 2001.

Brecht, Bertolt. *The Collected Poems of Bertolt Brecht*. Translated and edited by Tom Kuhn and David Constantine. New York: Liveright, 2018.

Brennan, Timothy. *Wars of Position: The Cultural Politics of Left and Right*. New York: Columbia University Press, 2006.

Breton, André. "Martinique, Charmeuse de serpents: Un grand poète noir," *Tropiques*, No. 11 (May 1944), pp. 119–126.

Brooks, Peter. *The Melodramatic Imagination: Balzac, Henry James, Melodrama, and the Mode of Excess*. New Haven, CT and London: Yale University Press, 1995.

Brown, Jennifer Stafford. "'Au feu de ce qui fut brûle ce qui sera': Louis Aragon and the Subversive Medieval." *Romanic Review*, Vol. 101, No. 3 (May 2010), pp. 325–342.

Buck-Morss, Susan. *Dreamworld and Catastrophe: The Passing of Mass Utopia in East and West*. Cambridge, MA: MIT Press, 2002.

Bush, Ruth. "Performances of the Past at the 1966 World Festival of Negro Arts." In Murphy, D. ed., *The First World Festival of Negro Arts, Dakar 1966*. Liverpool: Liverpool University Press, 2016, pp. 97–112.

Cadet, Jean-Jacques. *Le marxisme haïtien: Marxisme et anticolonialisme en Haïti (1946–1986)*. Paris: Delga, 2020.

———. "Le marxisme, seul guide possible de la Révolution haïtienne. Préoccupation épistémologique: élargir la théorie." *Revue Legs et Littérature*, No. 18 (2021), pp. 53–64.

Casanova, Laurent. *Pourquoi je suis communiste*. Paris: Éditions du Parti Communiste, 1947.

Casanova, Pascale. *The World Republic of Letters*. Translated by Malcolm DeBevoise. Cambridge, MA: Harvard University Press, 2007.

Caute, David. *The Dancer Defects: The Struggle for Cultural Supremacy during the Cold War*. Oxford: Oxford University Press, 2003.

Césaire, Aimé. *Du fond d'un pays de silence. Edition critique de* Ferrements. Edited by Lilyan Kesteloot, René Hénane, and M. Souley Ba. Paris: Orizons, 2012.

———. *Ecrits politiques. Tome 1: Discours à L'Assemblée Nationale*. Edited by René Hénane. Paris: Jean-Michel Place, 2013.

———. "Interview." *L'Express*. May 19, 1960.

———. *Poésie, théâtre, essais, discours*. Edited by A. James Arnold. Paris: CNRS, 2013.

———. "Réponse à Depestre, poète haïtien (Éléments d'un art poétique)." *Présence Africaine*, No. 1 (Apr.–Jun. 1955), p. 114.
Césaire, Suzanne. "1943: Surrealism and Us." *The Great Camouflage: Writings of Dissent (1941–1945)*. Edited by Daniel Maximin. Translated by Keith L. Walker. Middletown, CT: Wesleyan University Press, 2012.
———. *Le Grand camouflage. Ecrits de dissidence (1941–1945)*. Edited by Daniel Maximin. Paris: Seuil, 2009.
———. "Tropiques." *Aimé Césaire: Poésie, théâtre, essais, discours*. Edited by A. James Arnold. Paris: CNRS, Planète Libre, 2013, pp. 1311–1314.
Childers, Kristen Stromberg. *Seeking Imperialism's Embrace: National Identity, Decolonization, and Assimilation in the French Caribbean*. Oxford: Oxford University Press, 2016.
Clark, Katerina. *The Soviet Novel: History as Ritual*. Chicago, IL: University of Chicago Press, 1981.
Cleary, Joe. "Realism after Modernism and the Literary World System." *Modern Language Quarterly*, Vol. 73, No. 3 (2012), pp. 63–87.
Clifford, James. *The Predicament of Culture*. Cambridge, MA: Harvard University Press, 1988.
Combe, Dominique. Preface. Crowley, Patrick and Hiddleston, Jane eds., *Postcolonial Poetics: Genre and Form*. Liverpool: Liverpool University Press, 2011.
"Conclusion." *Présence Africaine*, No. 11 (Dec. 1956–Jan. 1957), pp. 100–102.
Condé, Maryse. "Fous-t'en Depestre; laisse dire Aragon." *Romanic Review*, Vol. 92, Nos 1–2 (Jan.–Mar. 2001), pp. 177–184.
Confédération Générale du Travail de Martinique. "Quelques dates historiques du movement ouvrier." http://www.cgt-martinique.fr/syndicat-cgt-martinique-dates-historiques.asp.
Contributions au Ier Congrès des écrivains et artistes noirs. *Présence Africaine* 14–15 (Jun.–Sept. 1957).
Cowie, Sam. "Lula Begins Prison Sentence in Brazil after Turning Himself in to Police." *The Guardian*, Apr. 7, 2018. Online. https://www.theguardian.com/world/2018/apr/07/crowds-in-sao-paulo-block-lula-from-handing-himself-in.
Curto, Roxanna. *Inter-Tech(s): Colonialism and the Question of Technology in Francophone Literature*. Charlottesville: University of Virginia Press, 2016.
Dadié, Bernard. "Le fond importe plus." *Présence Africaine*, No. 6 (Feb. 1956–Mar. 1956), pp. 116–118.
Dash, J. Michael. "Aimé Césaire: The Bearable Lightness of Becoming." *PMLA*, Vol. 125, No. 3 (2010), pp. 737–742.

———. "Imaginary Insurrections: New Criticism on Caribbean Writers." *Research in African Literatures*, Vol. 43, No. 3 (Fall 2012), pp. 115–125.
———. *Literature and Ideology in Haiti, 1915–1961*. London and Basingstoke: Macmillan, 1981.
———. "Martinique Is (Not) a Polynesian Island: Detours of French West Indian Identity." *International Journal of Francophone Studies*, Vol. 11, Nos 1–2 (2008), pp. 123–136.
———. "Marvelous Realism: The Way Out of Negritude." *Caribbean Studies*, Vol. 13, No. 4 (Jan. 1974), pp. 57–70.
———. *The Other America: Caribbean Literature in a New World Context*. Charlottesville: University of Virginia Press, 1998.
Davis, Gregson. *Aimé Césaire*. Cambridge: Cambridge University Press, 1997.
———. *Non-Vicious Circle: Twenty Poems by Aimé Césaire*. Stanford, CA: Stanford University Press, 1984.
Dayan, Colin (Joan). *Haiti, History, and the Gods*. Berkeley: University of California Press, 1995.
Dean, Jodi. *Comrade: An Essay on Political Belonging*. New York: Verso, 2019.
Depestre, René. "Alioune Diop, l'un des pères de la civilité démocratique mondiale." *Gradhiva*, Vol. 10 (Oct. 2009), pp. 164–169.
———. *Bonjour et adieu à la négritude*. Paris: Laffont, 1980.
———. *Bonsoir tendresse, autobiographie*. Paris: Odile Jacob, 2018. E-Book edition.
———. "Dans les décombres du carnaval." Interview. *Cultures et Conflits*, No. 84 (2011), pp. 133–142.
———. "Lettre à Charles Dobzynski." *Les Lettres françaises* No. 573 (Jun. 16–23, 1955), pp. 1, 5.
———. "Pour que lèvent les blés humains (fragments)." *Les lettres françaises*, No. 573 (Jun. 16–23, 1955), p. 5.
———. *Rage de vivre: œuvres poétiques complètes*. Paris: Seghers, 2007.
———. "Réponse à Aimé Césaire (Introduction à un art poétique haïtien)." *Présence Africaine*, No. 4 (Oct.–Nov. 1955), pp. 42–62.
Desanti, Dominique. *Nous avons choisi la paix*. Paris: Seghers, 1949.
Desportes, Georges. "Points de vue sur la poésie nationale." *Présence Africaine*, No. 11 (Dec. 1956–Jan. 1957), pp. 88–99.
Deuxieme Congrès des écrivains et artistes noirs: Rome, 26 mars–1er avril 1959, tome 1: L'unité des cultures négro-africaines. Présence africaine, 24–25 (numéro spécial), 1959.
Deuxième Congrès des écrivains et artistes noirs: Rome, 26 mars–1er avril 1959, tome 2: Responsabilités des hommes de culture. Présence africaine, 27–28 (numéro spécial), 1959.
Diop, David. "Contributions au débat sur la poésie nationale." *Présence Africaine*, No. 6 (Feb.–Mar. 1956), pp. 113–115.

———. "Notre Nouvelle Formule." *Présence Africaine*, Nos 1–2 (Apr.–Jul. 1955), pp. 5–7.

Diouf, Sylviane. A. *Slavery's Exiles: The Story of the American Maroons*. New York: NYU Press, 2014.

Djagalov, Rossen. "The Zone of Freedom? Differential Censorship in the Post-Stalin-Era People's Republic of Letters." *The Slavonic and East European Review*, Vol. 98, No. 4 (Oct. 2020), pp. 601–631.

Dobrenko, Evgeny. *The Political Economy of Socialist Realism*. New Haven, CT and London: Yale University Press, 2007.

———. "Socialist Realism." *The Cambridge Companion to Twentieth-Century Russian Literature*. Edited by Evgeny Dobrenko and Marina Balina. Cambridge: Cambridge University Press, 2011, pp. 97–114.

Douaire-Banny, Anne. "Sans rimes, toute une saison, loin des mares. Enjeux d'un débat sur la poésie nationale." Mar. 20, 2011. http://pierre.campion2.free.fr/douaire_depestre&cesaire.htm.

Dubois, Laurent. *Avengers of the New World*. Cambridge, MA: Harvard University Press, 2005,

———. *Haiti: The Aftershocks of History*. New York: Picador, 2012.

Dumont, Jacques. *L'amère patrie: Histoire des Antilles françaises au XXe siècle*. Paris: Fayard, 2010.

Dunstan, Sarah C. *Race, Rights, and Reform: Black Activism in the French Empire from World War I to the Cold War*. Cambridge: Cambridge University Press, 2021, pp. 242–246.

Edwards, Brent Hayes. "Césaire in 1956." *Social Text*, Vol. 28, No. 2 (2010), pp. 115–125.

Fanon, Frantz. *Les damnés de la terre*. [1961] Paris: La Découverte, 2002.

———. *Peau noire, masques blancs*. [1952] Paris: Gallimard, 1995.

———. *The Wretched of the Earth*. Translated by Constance Farrington. [1961] New York: Grove Books, 2005.

Fields, Barbara J. "Slavery, Race and Ideology in the United States of America." *New Left Review*, Vol. 181 (May/Jun. 1990), pp. 95–118.

Fields, Barbara J. and Fields, Karen. *Racecraft: The Soul of Inequality in American Life*. New York: Verso, 2012.

Fignolé, Jean-Claude. "Marvelous Realism! Metamorphosis of the Real?" *Journal of Haitian Studies*, Vol. 16, No. 1 (2010), pp. 40–57.

Fonkoua, Romuald. *Aimé Césaire (1913–2008)*. Paris, Perrin, 2010.

Fonkoua, Romuald-Blaise and Claxton, Mervyn. "Liminaire / Introduction." *Présence Africaine*, Nos 175–177 (2007), pp. 11–17.

Garaudy, Roger. *L'itinéraire d'Aragon. Du surréalisme au monde reel*. Paris: Gallimard, 1961.

Garraway, Doris. "What is Mine: Césairean Negritude Between the Particular and the Universal." *Research in African Literatures*, Vol. 41, No. 1 (Spring 2010).

Genette, Gérard. *Figures III*. Paris: Seuil, 1971.
———. *Paratexts: Thresholds of Interpretation*. Translated by Jane E. Lewin. Cambridge: Cambridge University Press, 1997.
Getachew, Adom. *Worldmaking after Empire: The Rise and Fall of Self-Determination*. Princeton, NJ: Princeton University Press, 2019.
Gil, Alex and Glover, Kaiama L. *In the Same Boats*. Online. http://sameboats.org.
Glissant, Edouard. *Le discours antillais*. Paris: Gallimard, 1981.
———. *Soleil de la conscience*. 1956. Paris: Gallimard, 1997.
Glover, Kaiama L. *A Regarded Self: Caribbean Womanhood and the Ethics of Disorderly Being*. Durham, NC: Duke University Press, 2020.
———. "'The Francophone World Was Set Ablaze': Pan-African Intellectuals, European Interlocutors and the Global Cold War." *Postcolonial Studies* (2021), pp. 1–20.
Godineau, Laure. "Le retour d'exil, un nouveau exil? Le cas des communards." *Matériaux pour l'histoire de notre temps*, Vol. 67, No. 7 (2002), pp. 11–16.
Goldmann, Lucien. *The Hidden God: A Study of Tragic Vision in the* Pensées *of Pascal and the Tragedies of Racine*. [1956]. Translated by Philip Thody. London: Verso, 2016.
Gorki, Maxim. "Soviet Literature." 1934. Marxists Internet Archive.
Gratiant, Gilbert. "D'une poésie martiniquaise dite nationale." *Présence Africaine*, No. 5 (Dec. 1955–Jan. 1956), pp. 84–89.
———. "La place du 'créole' dans l'expression antillaise." *Présence Africaine*, Nouvelle série, Nos 14–15, *Contributions au Ier Congrès des Écrivains et Artistes Noirs* (Jun.–Sep. 1957), p. 252–255.
Hale, Thomas A. and Véron, Kora. "Is There Unity in the Writings of Aimé Césaire?" *Research in African Literatures*, Vol. 41, No. 1 (Spring 2010), pp. 46–70.
Halim, Hala. "*Lotus*, the Afro-Asian Nexus, and Global South Comparatism." *Comparative Studies of South Asia, Africa and the Middle East*, Vol. 32, No. 3 (2012), pp. 563–583.
Halliday, Fred. "Cold War in the Caribbean." *New Left Review*, Vol. 141 (Sept.–Oct. 1983), pp. 5–22.
Hallward, Peter. *Absolutely Postcolonial: Writing Between the Singular and the Specific*. New York: Palgrave, 2001.
———. *Badiou: A Subject to Truth*. Minneapolis: University of Minnesota Press, 2003.
Hammond, Andrew ed. *Cold War and Literature: Writing the Global Conflict*. New York: Routledge, 2005.
———. *Global Cold War Literature: Western, Eastern, and Postcolonial Perspectives*. New York: Routledge, 2012.
Hartman, Saidiya. *Scenes of Subjection: Terror, Slavery and Self-Making in Nineteenth-Century America*. Oxford: Oxford University Press, 1997.

Hassan, Salah D. *How to Liberate Marx from His Eurocentrism*. Ostfildern, Germany: DOCUMENTA (13), Hatje Cantz Verlag, 2013.
———. "Inaugural Issues: The Cultural Politics of Early *Présence Africaine*, 1947–1955." *Research in African Literatures*, Vol. 30, No. 2 (Summer 1999), pp. 194–221.
Heady, Margaret. *Marvelous Journeys: Routes of Identity in the Caribbean Novel*. New York: Peter Lang, 2008.
Hegel, G.W.F. *Aesthetics*. Vol. III, Part 3. Marxists Internet Archive.
———. *Science of Logic*, Vol. 1, Book 1. Marxists Internet Archive.
Hénane, René ed. *Aimé Césaire. Ecrits Politiques: Discours à L'Assemblée Nationale, 1945–1983*. Paris: Jean-Michel Place, 2013.
Hollier, Denis. *The Politics of Prose: Essay on Sartre*. Translated by Jeffrey Mehlman. Minneapolis: University of Minnesota Press, 1987.
Howlett, Jacques. "Le Ier congrès des écrivains et artistes noirs et la presse internationale." *Présence Africaine*, No. 20 (1958), pp. 111–117.
Howlett, Marc-Vincent and Fonkoua, Romuald. "La maison *Présence Africaine*." *Gradhiva*, Vol. 10 (2009), pp. 107–130.
Humphrey, Anna Jovic. "Aimé Césaire and 'Another Face of Europe.'" *MLN*, Vol. 129, No. 5 (Dec. 2014), pp. 1117–1148.
"Jacques Stephen Alexis n'a jamais été à Fort Dimanche." *YouTube*, Apr. 22, 2022. Uploaded by AyiboPost. www.youtube.com/watch?v=etNX8oB1Oss&t=741s.
Jaji, Tsitsi. *Africa in Stereo: Modernism, Music, and Pan-Africanism*. Oxford: Oxford University Press, 2014.
Jameson, Fredric. *The Antinomies of Realism*. New York: Verso, 2012.
———. "Cognitive Mapping." In Nelson, Cary and Grossberg, Lawrence eds, *Marxism and the Interpretation of Culture*. Urbana and Chicago, IL: University of Illinois Press, 1988, pp. 347–360.
———. *The Political Unconscious: Narrative as a Socially Symbolic Act*. Ithaca, NY: Cornell University Press, 1981.
Jones, Donna V., *The Racial Discourses of Life Philosophy: Negritude, Vitalism, and Modernity*, New York: Columbia University Press, 2010.
Joseph-Gabriel, Annette K. *Reimagining Liberation: How Black Women Transformed Citizenship in the French Empire*. Champaign, IL: University of Illinois Press, 2019.
Jules-Rosette, Benetta. *Black Paris: The African Writers' Landscape*. Urbana and Chicago, IL: University of Illinois Press, 1998.
Kaisary, Philip. *The Haitian Revolution in the Literary Imagination: Radical Horizons, Conservative Constraints*. Charlottesville: University of Virginia Press, 2014.
Kalliney, Peter. *The Aesthetic Cold War: Decolonization and Global Literature*. Princeton, NJ: Princeton University Press, 2022.

Kaussen, Valerie. *Migrant Revolutions: Haitian Literature, Globalization, and US Imperialism*. Lanham, MD: Lexington Books, 2008.
Kelley, Robin D.G. *Freedom Dreams: The Black Radical Imagination*. Boston, MA: Beacon Press, 2002.
Kesteloot, Lilyan. *Black Writers in French: A Literary History of Negritude*. Washington, DC: Howard University Press, 1991.
Kesteloot, Lilyan, and Kotchy, Barthélemy. *Comprendre Aimé Césaire. L'homme et l'œuvre*. Paris: Présence Africaine, 2000.
Kesteloot, Lilyan, Hénane, René, and Souley Ba, Mamadou ed. *Du fond d'un pays de silence. Édition critique de* Ferrements, *d'Aimé Césaire*. Paris: Orizons, 2012.
King, Richard H. *Race, Culture, and the Intellectuals*. Baltimore, MD: Johns Hopkins University Press, 2004.
Kish, George. *A Source Book in Geography*. Cambridge, MA: Harvard University Press, 1978.
Kojève, Alexandre. *Introduction à la lecture de Hegel*. Paris: Gallimard, 1947.
Kwon, Heonik. *The Other Cold War*. New York: Columbia University Press, 2010.
Landi, E. "Insurrection du Sud de Septembre 1870." Serge Letchimy personal website. Published Sep. 28, 2009. Internet.
Laroche, Maximilien. *Contributions à l'étude du réalisme merveilleux*. Québec: Université Laval, GRELCA, 1987.
———. *Le* Romancéro aux étoiles *et l'œuvre romanesque de Jacques-Stephen Alexis*. Editions Fernand Nathan, 1978.
Lazarus, Neil. *The Postcolonial Unconscious*. Cambridge: Cambridge University Press, 2011.
Le Carré, John. "Interview. John Le Carré at the NFT." *The Guardian*, Oct. 5, 2002. Online.
Legum, Colin. *Pan-Africanism*. New York: Praeger, 1962.
Lukács, Gyorgy. "Critical Realism and Socialist Realism." *The Meaning of Contemporary Realism*. Translated by John and Necke Mander. London: Merlin Press, 1963.
———. *The Historical Novel*. Translated by Hannah and Stanley Mitchell. London: Merlin Press, 1962.
———. "Narrate or Describe?" *Writer and Critic and Other Essays*. Edited and translated by Arthur D. Kahn. New York: Grosset and Dunlap, 1971, pp. 110–148.
———. *Theory of the Novel*. [1915]. Translated by Anna Bostock. Cambridge, MA: MIT Press, 1971.
———. "Tribune or Bureaucrat?" *Essays on Realism*. Edited by Rodney Livingstone. Cambridge, MA: MIT Press, 1981.

Macey, David. *Frantz Fanon: A Life.* New York: Picador, 2001.
Majumdar, Nivedita. *The World in a Grain of Sand: Postcolonial Literature and Radical Universalism.* New York: Verso, 2021.
Mao Zedong. "On Contradiction." 1937. Marxists Internet Archive. Online.
———."Talks at the Yenan Forum on Literature and Art." 1942. Marxists Internet Archive. Online.
Martelli, Roger et al. *Le Parti Rouge: Une histoire du PCF 1920–2020.* Paris: Armand Collin, 2020.
Marx, Karl. *Capital. Volume One.* Translated by Samuel Moore and Edward Aveling. Edited by Friedrich Engels. Marxists Internet Archive.
Massé, Guirdex. "Cold War and Black Transnationalism: Aimé Césaire and Mercer Cook at the First International Congress of Black Writers and Artists." *Palimpsest: A Journal on Women, Gender, and the Black International*, Vol. 4, No. 2 (2015), pp. 115–134.
Mayakovsky, Vladimir. "How Are Verses Made?" 1926. *Volodya: Selected Works.* Edited by Rosy Carrick. London: Enitharmon Press, 2016, pp. 224–266.
Ménil, René. *Antilles déjà jadis, précédé de Tracées.* Paris: Jean Michel Place, 1999.
———. "Une doctrine réactionnaire: la négritude." *Action: Revue théorique et politique du Parti Communiste Martiniquais,* No. 1 (Aug. 1963), pp. 37–50.
———. "The (Revised) Birth of Negritude: Communist Revolution and 'the Immanent Negro' in 1935." *PMLA,* Vol. 125, No. 3 (May 2010), pp. 743–749.
Miller, Paul B. "¿Un Cubano Más? An Interview with René Depestre about his Cuban Experience." *Afro-Hispanic Review,* Vol. 34, No. 2 (Fall 2015), pp. 157–175.
Mouralis, Bernard. *Littérature et développement: essai sur le statut, la fonction et la représentation de la literature africaine d'expression française.* Paris: Agence de cooperation culturelle et technique, Silex, 1984.
Moyn, Samuel. *The Last Utopia: Human Rights in History.* Cambridge, MA: Belknap, 2010.
Mudimbe-Boyi, Elizabeth. *L'Œuvre Romanesque de Jacques-Stephen Alexis: une écriture poétique, un engagement politique.* Kinshasa: Editions du Mont Noir, 1974.
Munro, Martin. *Exile and Post-1946 Haitian Literature: Alexis, Depestre, Ollivier, Laferrière, Danticat.* Liverpool: Liverpool University Press, 2007.
———. *Shaping and Re-Shaping the Caribbean.* London: Modern Humanities Research Association, 2000.

Nekrasov, Viktor. *Both Sides of the Ocean: A Russian Writer's Travels in Italy and the United States.* Translated by Elias Kulukundis. London, Four Square Books, 1964.

Nesbitt, Nick. *Caribbean Critique: Antillean Theory from Toussaint to Glissant.* Liverpool: Liverpool University Press, 2013.

———. *The Price of Slavery: Capitalism and Revolution in the Caribbean.* Charlottesville and London: University of Virginia Press, 2022.

———. *Voicing Memory: History and Subjectivity in French Caribbean Literature.* Charlottesville and London: University of Virginia Press, 2003.

Noland, Carrie. *Voices of Negritude in Modernist Print: Aesthetic Subjectivity, Diaspora, and the Lyric Regime.* New York: Columbia University Press, 2015.

"Notre Nouvelle Formule," *Présence Africaine*, Nos 1–2 (Apr.–Jul. 1955), pp. 5–7.

"Obsèques de Paul Eluard." Online video clip. Institut National de l'Audiovisuel. www.ina.fr.

Padmore, George. *How Russia Transformed Her Colonial Empire: A Challenge to the Imperialist Powers.* London: Denis Dobson, 1946.

Palcy, Euzhan dir. *Aimé Césaire, une voix pour l'histoire.* JMJ Productions. 1994.

"Périple au sens de Voyage." Académie française. Online. https://www.academie-francaise.fr/periple-au-sens-de-voyage.

Pietz, William. "The 'Post-Colonialism' of Cold War Discourse." *Social Text*, Vol. 19/20 (Autumn 1988), pp. 55–75.

Popescu, Monica. *At Penpoint: African Literature, Postcolonial Studies, and the Cold War.* Durham, NC: Duke University Press, 2020.

Prashad, Vijay. *The Darker Nations: A People's History of the Third World.* New York and London: The New Press, 2007.

Price, Richard. *Maroon Societies: Rebel Slave Communities in the Americas.* Baltimore, MD: JHU Press, 1996.

Prieto, Eric. *Literature, Geography, and the Postmodern Poetics of Place.* London/New York: Palgrave Macmillan, 2012.

"Quand les écrivains belges prennent Jacques Stephen Alexis au pied de la lettre – 24/05/12 –CEC." *YouTube*, Apr. 28, 2016. Uploaded by Littafcar. https://www.youtube.com/watch?v=NgiwpOORHNk&t=15s.

"Quelques dates historiques du movement ouvrier." Confédération Générale du Travail de Martinique. http://www.cgt-martinique.fr/syndicat-cgt-martinique-dates-historiques.asp.

Ramazani, Jahan. *Poetry of Mourning: The Modern Elegy from Hardy to Heaney.* Chicago, IL and London: University of Chicago Press, 1994.

Rancière, Jacques. "Who Is the Subject of the Rights of Man?," *The South Atlantic Quarterly*, Vol. 103, No. 2–3 (2004), pp. 297–310.

Rasberry, Vaughan. *Race and the Totalitarian Century: Geopolitics in the Black Literary Imagination.* Cambridge, MA: Harvard University Press, 2016.

Rebérioux, Madeleine. "Le Mur des Fédérés." *Les Lieux de Mémoire*, Vol. 1. Edited by Pierre Nora. Paris: Gallimard, 1984.

Richardson, Michael and Fijalkowski, Krzysztof. *Refusal of the Shadow: Surrealism and the Caribbean.* New York: Verso, 1996, pp. 1–37.

Roberts, Neil. *Freedom as Marronage.* Chicago, IL: University of Chicago Press, 2015.

Robin, Régine. *Socialist Realism: An Impossible Aesthetic.* Stanford, CA: Stanford University Press, 1992.

Rosello, Mireille. "'The Césaire Effect,' or, How to Cultivate One's Nation," *Research in African Literatures*, Vol. 32, No. 4 (2001), pp. 77–91.

Ross, Kristin. *The Emergence of Social Space: Rimbaud and the Paris Commune.* New York: Verso, 1988.

Roumain, Jacques. *Gouverneurs de la rosée.* [1944]. Paris: Zulma, 2013.

Rubin, Andrew. *Archives of Authority: Empire, Culture, and the Cold War.* Princeton, NJ: Princeton University Press, 2012.

Rumeau, Delphine. "Du monument au rituel, les poèmes funéraires d'Aimé Césaire." *Présence Africaine*, No. 189 (2014), pp. 27–38.

Sapiro, Gisèle. *The French Writers' War, 1940–1953.* Translated by Vanessa Doriott Anderson and Dorritt Cohn. Durham, NC: Duke University Press, 2014.

Saunders, Frances Stonor. *The Cultural Cold War: The CIA and the World of Arts and Letters.* New York: The New Press, 2nd edition, 2013.

Sartre, Jean-Paul. "Orphée noir." *Anthologie de la nouvelle poésie nègre et malgache.* Edited by Léopold Sédar Senghor. Paris: PUF, 2011, pp. ix–xliv.

Sauvy, Alfred. "Trois mondes, une planète." *L'Observateur*, Aug. 14, 1952, p. 14.

Scott, David. *Omens of Adversity: Tragedy, Time, Memory, Justice.* Durham, NC: Duke University Press, 2013.

Senghor, Léopold Sédar. *Anthologie de la nouvelle poésie nègre et malgache.* Paris: PUF, 2011.

———. *Qu'est-ce que la littérature?* 1948. Paris: Gallimard, 1985.

———. "Reply to Albert Camus." *Portraits (Situations IV).* Translated by Chris Turner. London: Seagull, 2009.

———. "Réponse." *Présence Africaine*, No. 5 (Dec. 1955–Jan. 1956), pp. 79–83.

Séonnet, Michel. *Jacques Stephen Alexis ou le voyage vers la lune de la belle amour humaine.* Paris: Lamourier, 1983.

Shepperson, George. "Pan-Africanism and 'Pan-Africanism': Some Historical Notes." *Phylon*, Vol. 23, No. 4 (1962), pp. 346–358.

Shringarpure, Bhakti. *Cold War Assemblages: From Decolonization to Digital*. New York: Routledge, 2019.

Slaughter, Joseph. *Human Rights, Inc.: The World Novel, Narrative Form, and International Law*. New York: Fordham University Press, 2007.

Smith, Matthew J. *Red and Black in Haiti: Radicalism, Conflict, and Political Change 1934–1957*. Chapel Hill, NC: University of North Carolina Press, 2009.

Sobanet, Andrew. *Generation Stalin: French Writers, the Fatherland, and the Cult of Personality*. Lincoln: University of Nebraska Press, 2020.

Souffrant, Claude. *Une Négritude socialiste: religion et développement chez Jacques Roumain, Jacques-Stephen Alexis, et Langston Hughes*. Preface by Paul Ricœur. Paris: L'Harmattan, 1978.

Spillers, Hortense. "Mama's Baby, Papa's Maybe: An American Grammar Book." *Diacritics*, Vol. 17, No. 2 (1987), pp. 64–81.

Spivak, Gayatri Chakravorty. *Critique of Postcolonial Reason*. Cambridge, MA: Harvard University Press, 1999.

Stalin, Joseph. "Marxism and the National Question" [1913]. Marxists Internet Archive, https://www.marxists.org/reference/archive/stalin/works/1913/03.htm.

Swaim, Bob dir. *Les Lumieres Noires*. 2006. Film.

Tolliver, Cedric. *Of Vagabonds and Fellow Travelers: Black Diasporic Literary Culture and the Cold War*. Ann Arbor: University of Michigan Press, 2019.

Tolliver, Julie-Françoise. *The Quebec Connection: A Poetics of Solidarity in Global Francophone Literature*. Charlottesville: University of Virginia Press, 2020.

Toumson, Roger and Henry-Vilmore, Simonne. *Aimé Césaire: le nègre inconsolé*. Chateauneuf-le-rouge: Vents d'ailleurs, 2002.

Traverso, Enzo. *Left-Wing Melancholia: Marxism, History, and Memory*. New York: Columbia University Press, 2017.

Von Tunzelman, Alex. *Red Heat: Conspiracy, Murder, and the Cold War in the Caribbean*. New York: Henry Holt, 2011.

Vasilyev, Georgi and Vasilyev, Sergei. *Chapaev*. Lenfilm, 1934.

Verdin, Philippe. *Alioune Diop, le Socrate noir*. Paris: Lethellieux, 2010.

Véron, Kora. *Aimé Césaire*. Paris: Seuil, 2021.

Wade, Amadou Moustapha. "Autour d'une poésie nationale." *Présence Africaine*, No. 11 (Dec. 1956–Jan. 1957), pp. 84–87.

Warwick Research Collective. *Combined and Uneven Development: Towards a New Theory of World-Literature*. Liverpool: Liverpool University Press, 2015.

Watson, Jini Kim. *Cold War Reckonings: Authoritarianism and the Genres of Decolonization*. New York: Fordham University Press, 2021.

Westad, Odd Arne. *The Global Cold War*. New York: Cambridge University Press, 2012.

Wilder, Gary. *Freedom Time: Negritude, Decolonization, and the Future of the World*. Durham, NC: Duke University Press, 2015.
Wilson, Edmund. *Red, Black, Blond, and Olive*. New York: Oxford University Press, 1956.
Wylie, Hal. "Elisabeth Mudimbe-Boyi, *L'Œuvre Romanesque de Jacques Stephen Alexis*." Book review. *World Literature Today*, Vol. 67, No. 2 (Spring 1993), p. 46.
Yoon, Duncan M. "Cold War Creolization: Ousmane Sembène's *Le Dernier de l'empire*." *Research in African Literatures*, Vol. 50, No. 3 (2019), pp. 29–50.
——. "Figuring Africa and China: Congolese Literary Imaginaries of the PRC." *Journal of World Literature*, Vol. 6, No. 2 (2021), pp. 167–196.
Zhdanov, Andrei. "Report on the International Situation to the Cominform." Sep. 22, 1947. *Seventeen Moments in Soviet History*. https://soviethistory.msu.edu.
Žižek, Slavoj. *The Sublime Object of Ideology*. New York: Verso, 1989.
Zubel, Marla. "From Decolonization to Destalinization: Aimé Césaire and the 'Polish Question.'" *Journal of Postcolonial Writing*, Vol. 59, No. 2, pp. 157–171.

Index

Adorno, Theodor 188
Adotevi, Stanislas 70n32
Africa 17–18, 28, 49, 53–54, 57, 83–84, 86, 119, 122
Afro-Asian Writers' Association 13
Alexis, Florence 146n4, 151, 153n31
Alexis, Jacques Stephen 11, 14, 16, 18, 23–25, 110, 145–188, 191
    alignment with communism 20–21, 73n42, 148–149
    death of 7, 146
    at the First Congress 30–31, 35, 41, 44–45, 48–51, 54, 56
    literary aesthetics of 14, 19, 22, 24, 145–88
    relationship with Aragon 15, 146, 148, 153, 183–8, 191
    travels and exile of 4–6, 8, 149
    see also realism: marvelous realism
Algerian War of Independence 10, 44, 141–142
alexandrin verse 67, 89, 94, 95, 96, 101–102
alignment 2–4, 10, 23–24, 63, 68, 81–82, 89–91, 105–106, 111, 126, 139, 147–149, 152, 179, 183, 192
    see also geopolitics, nonalignment
Alliot, David 20, 59n1, 65n14, 126n71
Amado, Jorge 13, 21, 90–91
Anderson, Perry 19n56
Anglade, George 148–151, 182

anticommunism 6, 19, 34n30, 77
antifascism 14, 89
Anti-superstitious campaign in Haiti 159, 162
Apter, Emily 40
Aragon, Louis 14–15, 21, 33n27, 94, 181
    and Alexis 15, 146, 148, 153, 183–188, 191
    Césaire's opposition to 59–61, 64–65, 74, 76, 108
    and Depestre 59–69, 74–77, 89–91, 94, 98–102
    see also national poetry
Arbenz, Jacopo 10
Archimède, Gerty 7
Arendt, Hannah 26
Arnold, A. James 71 112n27, 124–125
atomic weapons 19 60n2, 90

Badiou, Alain 97, 98, 176
Baldwin, James 25, 32, 34, 46
Bandung Conference (1955) 10–11, 23, 29
    as inspiration for First Congress of Black Writers and Artists 29–31, 33, 64
Bildungsroman 45, 163
    First Congress as 51–56
bipolar global order 6–10, 15, 20, 23, 110, 114
Bissol, Léopold 7, 107
Blanchot, Maurice 121–122

Bloch, Ernst 161
Bloncourt, Gérald 4, 18
blood, racial metaphor of 74–76
Bond, Horace Mann 40
Bongie, Chris 17
Bonsoir tendresse (Depestre) 88–89
Brazil 64n11, 75
Brecht, Bertolt 96
Brennan, Timothy 50, 50n71
Breton, André 3n9, 3n12, 4, 68, 83, 169
British Commonwealth 6
Buck-Morss, Susan 11

Cadet, Jean-Jacques 20, 73n42, 151n22, 187n141
Cahier d'un retour au pays natal (Césaire) 43, 46, 51, 53, 66n20, 82–83, 108–112, 118–120
Camus, Albert 76
capitalism 9, 10n25, 18, 28, 33n27, 85–86, 95, 119–120, 141, 162, 171, 178, 191
    and imperialism 84, 149
Casanova, Pascale 21
Castro, Fidel 9, 133, 146
Catholic Church (*also* Catholicism) 29, 34, 75, 138, 159
Césaire, Aimé 1, 4, 7–8, 10–11, 13–16, 18–24, 59–77, 105–144, 177, 187–188, 190–192
    on Aragon 59–61, 64–65, 74, 76, 108
    at the Assemblée Nationale 76, 105–106
    Césaire–Depestre debate 15n44, 19, 23, 59–77, 82
    elegies of 124–136
    at First Congress 25, 32, 43, 51–54
    geographic imaginary of 111–124
    melancholy politics of 118, 124, 128, 136
    membership and split with French Communist Party 7, 10n26, 15, 18, 21–22, 24, 62, 76n52, 82, 105–108, 113, 119–121, 123–124, 138, 140–142
    see also Negritude
Césaire, Suzanne 2, 3n9, 18, 39, 83, 107
Chapaev (film) 174
China (People's Republic of) 8, 10, 20, 120, 148n4, 154
Clark, Katerina 95n100, 161
Cleary, Joe 188n144
Clifford, James 71
Cold War
    in the Caribbean 4, 6–7
    cultural Cold War 12, 63, 64n9, 68n27
    Eastern Bloc 8, 20, 21, 110, 146, 154n37
    end of 103, 151, 191
    in francophone postcolonial studies 16–20
    global Cold War 4–7, 11, 17–19, 23–24, 26, 33, 112n27, 188, 190
    superpowers 9, 10n25, 11n28, 12–13, 29, 32–33, 41, 55, 110–111, 136–137, 139–140, 142, 188, 192
colonialism 5, 26, 29, 49, 57, 100, 106, 119–120, 122, 132, 141, 146
    neocolonialism 8, 113–114
    see also anticolonialism, decolonization, imperialism
Combe, Dominique 61n7
communism 6–7, 10, 14, 22–24, 32, 68, 88–89, 91–92, 102, 110, 123, 125, 147–151, 190
    see also Marxism, socialism, Soviet Union, Stalinism
Compère Général Soleil (Alexis) 24, 154–160, 170, 175, 177–178, 191
comrade relation 91–93, 97n103, 99, 190
    see also Dean, Jodi
Condé, Maryse 61n6, 89
Congress for Cultural Freedom 12, 32
Cook, Mercer 32, 39n39
Cooper, James Fenimore 187

Côte d'Ivoire 137
Creole languages
    Haitian 40, 183
    Martinican 46–47
Crétinoir, Albert 128–129, 133–134, 136
Cuba 91, 155, 157, 180
Cuban Revolution 6, 10
cultural diplomacy 11–12, 106
cultural politics 19, 31, 38–39, 50, 56–58, 62–63, 68n26
Curto, Roxanna 48, 100, 101n116

Dadié, Bernard 66
Damas, Léon Gontran 15, 79
D'Arboussier, Gabriel 15n46, 70n36, 79–80, 81, 87
Dash, J. Michael 3n8, 14n43, 15–16, 61n6, 71, 72, 78, 109n21, 131–132, 176
Davis, Gregson 108n16, 115–116, 120n56
Dean, Jodi 92–93, 96n103, 99, 107, 190
decolonization 5–6, 9, 11n28, 12, 24, 33, 35, 54, 55n84, 57–58, 60, 64, 107, 109
decolonization/Cold War conjuncture, 9, 17–18, 23, 100, 113, 132
    see also colonialism, Third World
Delgrès, Louis 128–129, 132–133
departmentalization (DOMs) 6–7, 119, 131
Depestre, René 4, 6–8, 11, 13–16, 18–24, 50, 59–103, 108, 110, 146–147, 149, 190–192
    on Alexis 146n4, 147
    Cold War exile and travels of 6–8, 64n11, 75, 80n60, 90–91
    critique of Negritude 77–87
    debate with Césaire 15n44, 19, 23, 59–77, 82
    at the First Congress 34–35
Desanti, Dominique 82, 128n77
Desportes, Georges 66
Dessalines, Jean-Jacques 41, 132–133

development 12, 45, 52–55, 65, 69, 81, 86, 99, 101n116, 105–106, 113, 117, 138, 144, 146, 148–150, 165–167, 175–176, 181–182, 186–187
Dien, Raymonde 93
Dien Bien Phu, battle of 10
Diop, Alioune 23, 25–29, 31–32, 34–35, 38–39, 41, 45–46, 51, 54, 54–58, 63–64, 80, 89n84
Diop, Cheikh Anta 34
Diop, Christiane Yandé 39
"Discours à la Maison du sport" (Césaire) 19, 114
Discours sur le colonialisme (Césaire) 52–53, 106
Djagalov, Rossen 21, 154n37
Dobrenko, Evgeny 154
Dobzynski, Charles 59–60, 62, 65, 67, 69, 89, 94
Dominican Republic 157–159
Douaire-Banny, Anne 67, 89
Dover, Cedric 54
Dubois, Laurent 86n75
DuBois, W.E.B. 13, 27, 33, 39
Duvalier, François 6, 7, 167
    dictatorship of 24, 78, 146, 152, 167n80

East Berlin 7, 91n87
East Germany 10, 106
Ehrenbourg, Ilya 153
Éluard, Paul 14, 90, 128–132, 136
Encounter (magazine) 12, 32
Estimé, Dumarsis 6, 40, 90
Europe 53, 55, 72, 83, 85–86, 106, 119–120, 136
European Economic Community 105
existentialism 2, 79

Fadeyev, Aleksandr 153, 187
Fanon, Frantz 8–10, 15n46, 20, 25, 33, 44–45, 56, 110, 114
fascism 5, 14n43, 110, 127

Ferrements (Césaire) 24, 107–112, 114, 118–122, 124–126, 128, 136, 142–144, 191–192
feudal mode of production (*also* feudalism) 95, 162
   semi-feudalism 163, 183, 188
   see also Middle Ages
Fields, Barbara 74, 85
   and Fields, Karen 74
Fignolé, Jean-Claude 152
First Congress of Black Writers and Artists (*also* Premier Congrès) 11, 19, 23, 25–58, 66n20, 67, 68n25, 168, 172, 190
   see also Diop, Alioune
First World Festival of Negro Arts (1966) 36
Fonkoua, Romuald 31n21, 45, 89, 107
fossil fuel 86–87
France 3, 66, 79, 90–91, 106, 119, 131n87, 134, 146, 184
francophone postcolonial studies 16–17, 19, 103
French Communist Party (*also* Parti communiste français, PCF) 7, 14–15, 18, 20–21, 23–24, 33–34, 59, 61–62, 68–69, 76n52, 78–79, 82, 89–90, 105–107, 120–121, 129, 144, 146, 153, 187
French departmentalization law (1946) 7, 119
Freud, Sigmund 2, 135
Fukuyama, Francis 190
fungibility 85

Garaudy, Roger 107, 169
Garraway, Doris 116, 117n43
Genette, Gérard 81, 165
geography 110–112, 132m92, 137
   geographic imaginary of Césaire 111–124
   see also Césaire, Aimé
geopolitics 5, 6n15, 8–9, 18–24, 45, 63, 110–111, 114, 117, 120, 124–125, 132, 139–140, 158–159

Getachew, Adom 11n27
Gide, André 64
Gil, Alex 7
Girard, Rosan 7
Gladkov, Feodor 153
Glissant, Édouard 26, 127, 131, 143, 152
Glover, Kaiama L. 7, 8, 72n36
Goldmann, Lucien 148, 153
Goll, Ivan 81–84
Gomulka, Wladyslaw 10, 121
Gorky, Maxim 153
Gratiant, Gilbert 18, 46–47, 65–66, 107
Griot movement in Haiti 77–78
Guadeloupe 7, 128, 132n94
Guatemala, US intervention in 8, 10, 90, 137
Guillen, Nicolas 13
Guillevic 65
Guinea 10, 142
Guyana 10
Guyane (French Guiana) 7

Habermas, Jürgen 38
Haiti 40, 60, 80, 88, 132n94, 149, 161, 189
   in the Cold War 6–7
   Haitian peasantry 75–76, 155, 157, 159–160, 162–164, 166–167, 170–172, 183, 185–186
   Haitian revolution of 1946 3–4, 6, 14, 77, 146
   ruling class of 156, 160, 165, 169, 186
   US occupation of 6, 90, 158, 182, 185
Halliday, Fred 6n15
Hallward, Peter 56
Hartman, Saidiya 85
Hazoumé, Paul 53
Hegel, G.W.F. 3, 87–88, 122, 137
Hegelian philosophy 30, 80n62, 187–188
Heidegger, Martin 47–48
Hénane, René 108n17, 124

Hikmet, Nazim 21, 93
Ho Chi Minh 149
Hollier, Denis 147n8
Howlett, Jacques 33–34
Howlett, Marc-Vincent 31n21
human rights 26, 36, 40, 43–44, 55–57
Hungarian revolution of 1956 10, 20, 120, 137

imperialism 3, 9, 10n25, 28–29, 31, 41, 84, 111, 149, 151
    cultural imperialism 10n25, 62n8
    US imperialism 90, 158, 164
In the Same Boats (digital humanities project) 7–8
Italian Communist Party 10
Italy 8, 21, 120
Ivy, James 54

Jagan, Cheddi 10
Jameson, Fredric 31, 114, 191
jazz 142, 167
Joachim, Paulin 44, 46
Jones, Donna V. 47n62
Joseph-Gabriel, Annette 16
Journal d'une poésie nationale (Aragon) 59, 73n41, 99

Kaisary, Philip 61n7
Kalliney, Peter 13, 18
Kaussen, Valerie 155n38
Kelley, Robin D.G. 22n62
Kennedy, John F. 9
Kesteloot, Lilyan 108n17, 124, 130
Khrushchev, Nikita 9, 21, 121, 146
    secret speech (1956) 20, 120
Kimonko, Djansim 187
Kojève, Alexandre 30
Korean war 90

L'espace d'un cillement (Alexis) 147, 154, 175–181, 183, 191
L'Humanité journal 33
"L'Internationale" anthem 97
La Ruche journal 4

La vie est à nous (film) 97
Labuchin, Rassoul 149, 183
Lacanian psychoanalysis 99, 123
Lamming, George 54
Laroche, Maximilien 150–151
Lasebikian, E.L. 46
Lazarus, Neil 17
Le Carré, John 90, 105
Le marxisme, seul guide de la revolution haïtienne (Alexis) 19, 183n128, 186–187
Légitime Défense journal 2
Lenin, Vladimir I. 22, 153n32, 175
Les arbres musiciens (Alexis) 49, 154, 159–177, 183
Les armes miraculeuses (Césaire) 118, 122
Les Lettres françaises journal 33, 59, 60n2, 65, 94, 106, 146
Les Yeux et la mémoire (Aragon) 90, 98–101
Lescot, Elie 4, 90, 159, 165, 171
"Lettre à Maurice Thorez" (Césaire) 22, 23, 24, 61, 62n8, 66n20, 106, 107, 113, 120, 121, 124, 141, 149
liberalism (politics) 12, 15, 24, 69, 190
    and the First Congress 33–36, 38–41, 43–45, 50, 55, 57–58
Literaturnaya Gazeta journal 21, 106
lodyans form 151, 182
Lorde, Audre 72
Lotus journal 13
Lukács, Gyorgy 145, 153, 158, 159n49, 161, 165–166, 175, 178, 180–181, 188
Lula da Silva, Luis Ignacio 192
Lumières noires (film, dir. Swaim) 44
Lumumba, Patrice 139–140
Luther, Martin 138

Macey, David 44
macumba religion 74–75
Madagascar 137
Magloire, Paul 6
Mahgoub, Abdel Khadiq 145

Majumdar, Nivedita 17
Mallarmé, Stéphane 73n41, 187
Mao Zedong 21, 49–50, 149, 153, 171, 179, 188
Marcenac, Jean 33n27
marronage (also "marroner") 71–73
Martin, Henri 93
Martinique 2, 3n9, 10n26, 67, 113, 115, 119–120, 127, 131, 144
    1870 insurrection in 133
    communism in 7, 18
    French repression in 7, 133–134
Marx, Karl 2, 83n70, 87, 153n32, 161–162
Marxism 13, 16–17, 20, 22, 31, 32n24, 33–34, 49, 61–62, 73n42, 75, 77–78, 89n81, 94, 103, 119, 121, 125, 144–149, 151–156, 169, 174, 188
    Marxism-Leninism 12, 28, 70n30, 94, 148, 161, 165
    Western Marxism 19, 24, 153–154
Marxist aesthetics 17, 19, 21–23, 182, 186, 190
Mayakovsky, Vladimir 59, 98, 101
Ménil, René 2–3, 15n46, 18, 69n28, 107–109, 136
Mexico 8, 180
Middle Ages 177, 183–184
Milton, John 125
Minerai noir (Depestre) 19, 23, 63, 77, 80, 80–83, 88, 93–94, 97, 100, 102, 190
modernism (literary) 3–5, 12–15, 17, 21, 24, 51, 60, 62, 65–66, 73n41, 77, 84, 150, 167–168, 188, 190
    see also surrealism
modernity 5, 12, 55, 112
Monnerot, Jules-Marcel 19
Montella, Carlo 21
Morocco 10
Moscow 7–8, 21, 101, 106, 138–140, 149
Mounier, Emmanuel 64
Mouralis, Bernard 28n13

Moyn, Samuel 44
Munro, Martin 121–122, 151

Nasser, Gamal Abdel 10, 11n28
national poetry, *see poésie nationale*
NATO 9, 60, 90, 105–106
Nazi Germany 110
Ndengue, Jean-Marie 70n32
Negritude 1–2, 4, 14, 20, 22, 30, 33n27, 39, 47n62, 48, 51, 59, 62–63, 69n28; 70–71, 77–83, 87, 102–103, 116, 167, 190
Nekrasov, Viktor 21
Nehru, Jawaharlal 11n28
neocolonialism *see* colonialism
neoliberalism 144, 191–192
Neruda, Pablo 21, 90–91
Nesbitt, Nick 17, 30n19, 64, 67n22, 69n29, 80n62, 108, 144
New Caledonia 131
Nicol, Davidson 53
Nkrumah, Kwame 28
noirisme 6, 78, 146
Noland, Carrie 60n4
Non-Aligned Movement 141n119
nonalignment 20, 23, 68, 111, 136, 143–144
    see also alignment
nuclear arms *see* atomic weapons

"Orphée noir" (Sartre) 1–2, 15, 43, 68n24, 78, 102, 124, 136, 172
Orwell, George 136

Padmore, George 28, 39
Pan-Africanism 15, 27–28, 34, 39, 64, 68
    Pan-African Congresses 27–29
Paris 2, 4, 7–8, 11, 21, 25, 27–28, 64n11, 68, 75, 80n60, 89–90, 106–107, 146, 160
    see also Paris Commune
Paris Commune 129–131
Parti d'Entente Populaire 146, 149, 183
Parti Progressiste Martiniquais 144

Picasso, Pablo 40, 42
Patterson, Orlando 96
Paul, Emmanuel C. 41
Pietz, William 140
poésie nationale (*also* national poetry) 15, 23, 59–60, 63–67, 69–70, 72, 88–90, 92–94, 98–99, 108, 185, 190
Poland 10, 20n58, 82, 120, 126, 128n77
political belonging 16, 23, 71, 74, 77, 79, 92
Popescu, Monica 13, 18
postcolonial studies 16–17, 19, 56–57, 103, 188
see also francophone postcolonial studies
Poznan worker revolts 10, 121
Prague 7–8, 90–91
Prashad, Vijay 11n28
Présence Africaine journal 10, 14–15, 23, 25, 33–5, 38–41, 43, 46, 60, 63–65, 67–68, 69n28, 80, 89n84, 102, 168
Price-Mars, Jean 38–41
propaganda 11, 34n30, 66, 97
public sphere 29, 36, 38–39, 41, 57, 190

Rabemananjara, Jacques 27, 29–30, 44, 51–53, 102
race 2, 15, 34, 47, 51, 62–63, 70, 72, 74–80, 85, 87, 92, 105n4, 142, 156
critical race theory 85
racecraft 74
racism 1–3, 44, 73, 78, 85, 182, 185
Ramazani, Jahan 127, 135
Rancière, Jacques 57
Rasberry, Vaughn 18
realism (literary) 21, 48, 51, 60, 63, 109n21, 150, 188, 191–192
marvelous realism 24, 54, 150–151, 182–185
and modernism 13–14, 21, 24
socialist realism 12–13, 15–17, 22–24, 60n4, 61n7, 66, 108, 128, 145–146, 149–150, 152–154, 158, 176, 180–181, 188
Renoir, Jean 97
Rimbaud, Arthur 109, 135
Robert, Admiral Henri, 2
Romancéro aux étoiles (Alexis) 24, 154, 181–187
Roosevelt, Eleanor 25
Ross, Kristin 109, 143
Roumain, Jacques 3n8, 152n27, 155–156, 170
Roy, Claude 65
Rubin, Andrew 12
Russian Revolution (*also* "October Revolution") 5, 102, 181, 186, 189

Sanders, Bernie 59
Sapiro, Gisèle 68
Sartre, Jean-Paul 2–4, 64, 147n8, 178
and Camus 76
see also "Orphée noir" (Sartre)
Saunders, Frances Stonor 68
Sauvy, Alfred 136
Scott, David 191
Second Congress of Black Writers and Artists (Rome, 1959) 26, 32n24, 144
Second World War 3–5, 159
Seghers, Anna 21
Seghers, Pierre 65
Senegal 36, 67, 84
Senghor, Léopold Sédar 4, 15–16, 26, 30, 34, 68, 79–80, 83, 89n84, 168, 172
debate with Alexis 35, 47–51
Sergile, Florence 189
SHADA (Société Haitiano-américaine de Développement Agricole) 159, 162–163, 165
Sholokhov, Mikhail 153
Shringarpure, Bhakti 12, 73n41, 153
Slaughter, Joseph 29, 36, 38, 55–56
slavery 79n59, 82, 83n70, 85–86, 95, 124, 132, 141

Smith, Matthew J. 78n53
Sobanet, Andrew 20
socialism 9–10, 95, 106, 113, 114n34, 125, 128n77, 152, 154, 158, 161, 186–187
   see also communism, Marxism, realism: socialist realism
Société africaine de culture 32n24, 57, 69n28
solidarity 10, 16, 20n58, 23, 29, 59, 77–78, 93, 97, 100, 102–103, 130, 144, 156
   anticolonial 13, 29, 31, 68, 110, 151
   class 16–17, 23, 33n27, 80
   racial 23, 68
   temporal solidarity (Wilder) 192
   see also political belonging
sonnet 60n2, 61, 66–67, 72, 88, 94
Sorbonne 25, 28–29, 35
Sorel, Edith 90
Souffrant, Claude 20, 151n22, 183
South Africa 48
Soviet Union (*also* USSR) 5, 10–12, 21, 34, 105–106, 110, 114, 121, 137–138, 140–142, 146, 148–149, 154, 187
Spillers, Hortense 85
Spivak, Gayatri Chakravorty 41
Stalin, Joseph 34, 93, 106, 124, 137
   death and funeral of 106, 110, 138
   on the nation 70n30, 113n34
   personality cult of 10
   on writers 144
Stalinism 10, 20, 22–23, 61–62, 68, 72, 75n48, 91, 95, 99, 121, 151
sublation 117n44, 187
Suez Canal crisis (*also* "Suez") 5, 9–ͤ 23–24, 110, 114
Sukarno 11n28
surrealism 2–4, 14–15, 22, ͪon4, 65, 81, 103, 107–10ͪ ͪ, 167, 169, 182, 188

Tempels, Faͪ ͪlacide 168
Thatcher, Margaret 191

Third World 6, 9, 13, 23, 33, 54, 60, 106, 109–110, 112n27, 113n34, 119, 124, 136–140, 153, 188n144
Thorez, Maurice 93, 105–106
Till, Emmett 128, 129, 134–135
Tito, Josep Broz 10n26, 20, 105, 141n119, 143
Togliatti, Palmiro 10, 121
Tolliver, Cedric 18, 156n41, 158, 162n61, 190
Tolliver, Julie-Françoise 18
Tolstoy, Alexei 153
Tolstoy, Leo 166
Traverso, Enzo 20, 125–126, 144, 191
Triolet, Elsa 21, 89
Tropiques journal 2
Trujillo, Rafael 158
Tunisia 10
Tutuola, Amos 53
Tzara, Tristan 65

Udege people 187
Une Saison au Congo (Césaire) 108, 139–141
Union Française (*also* "French Union") 10, 142
United Nations (UN) 40, 43, 55n84, 137
United States (US, America) 5–7, 10n25, 11–12, 17, 21, 30–33, 60n2, 73, 90, 135, 137–138, ͪͪͪ, ͪͪͪ ͪͪͪ, 175, 178, 182, 185
Universal Declaration of Human Rights (UDHR) 25, 28–29
   see also human rights
universalism 16, 17, 31n21, 33, 40, 43, 44, 50, 82, 103, 141, 147, 152

Véron, Kora 3n9, 106n5, 107, 109
Vichy regime 2, 3, 184

Vienna 7, 8, 80n60, 91n87, 106
Vietnam war 137
vodou religion 72, 74–75, 88, 159, 164–165

Wade, Amadou Mustapha 54, 66
Warsaw 126–127
Watson, Jini Kim 17n53, 18, 146
West Indies Federation 6
Westad, Odd Arne 5, 12, 113–114n34
Western Marxism *see* Marxism
Wilder, Gary 16, 128, 132, 192
Wilson, Edmund 152n27, 153n32

World Congress of Intellectuals in Defense of Peace at Wroclaw (1948) 82, 106, 126, 128n77
Wright, Richard 25, 32, 39, 40, 54

Yoon, Duncan 18, 190
Yoruba poetry 46, 48, 53
Yugoslavia 20, 141n119

Zhdanov, Andrei (*also* Jdanov) 9, 88, 181
Žižek, Slavoj 31n21, 117n44, 123n64
Zola, Emile 48
Zubel, Marla 126n72

www.ingramcontent.com/pod-product-compliance
Lightning Source LLC
Chambersburg PA
CBHW071408300426
44114CB00016B/2231